MAKING IT INTO A
TOP
GRADUATE SCHOOL

ALSO BY HOWARD GREENE AND MATTHEW GREENE

Greenes' Guides to Educational Planning: The Hidden Ivies

Greenes' Guides to Educational Planning: Inside the Top Colleges

Greenes' Guides to Educational Planning:
Making It into a Top College

Greenes' Guides to Educational Planning: The Public Ivies

Greenes' Guides to Educational Planning:
Presenting Yourself Successfully to Colleges

MAKING IT INTO A
TOP
GRADUATE SCHOOL

TEN STEPS TO SUCCESSFUL GRADUATE SCHOOL ADMISSION

Howard R. Greene, M.A., M.Ed.,
and Matthew W. Greene, Ph.D.

HarperResource
An Imprint of HarperCollins*Publishers*

HarperCollins books may be purchased for educational, business, or sales promotional use. For information please write: Special Markets Department, HarperCollins Publishers, Inc., 10 East 53rd Street, New York, NY 10022.

FIRST EDITION

Designed by Stratford Publishing Services, Brattleboro, Vermont

Library of Congress Cataloging-in-Publication Data have been applied for.

ISBN   0060934581

04 05 RRD 10 9 8 7 6 5 4

Contents

Preface

Over the course of our careers in education, we have worked directly with thousands of students considering their future and the role graduate education plays in preparing them for it. We help them sort out the myriad professional opportunities and decide how best to prepare for the right one. As our economy becomes an information-based one in which knowledge and expertise are the coin of the realm, increasing numbers of young and older adults are applying to graduate school. To allay the confusion and anxiety in the graduate school marketplace, we have developed a Ten Steps strategy based on the expertise and experience of the professional staff at Howard Greene and Associates, who have counseled thousands of individuals seeking direction in their lives. One of our earlier books, *Beyond the Ivy Wall: Ten Essential Steps to Graduate School,* enjoyed three reprintings over its lifetime. The Ten Steps approach has been described by a number of professional career advisors at leading universities as an invaluable tool and essential, practical guide to gaining admission to the nation's selective graduate programs for motivated people of all ages and backgrounds.

In *Making It into a Top Graduate School,* we expand our approach with updated information. Our goal is, once again, to help men and women of all ages create a workable personal plan that matches their aspirations and skills with the most appropriate graduate education. Preparing for admission to any graduate program is so different from preparing for admission to college that many prospective applicants (some in midcareer) are unsure how to qualify themselves, get ready for entrance tests, prepare applications, and choose and pay for a graduate education suited to their interests and capabilities. Even current college students or recent college graduates will find in this book the answers to the questions they most frequently ask career counselors and graduate admissions officers, as they discover just how varied are the admissions requirements and procedures of the many, many excellent graduate programs.

We cover all the essential factors: trends in graduate education, determining the candidate's academic qualifications, locating the most appropriate programs, and calculating how to pay for graduate school and how much debt will be incurred. We offer instructive case histories and worksheets, task checklists, sample essays and résumés, and interviewing techniques that have proved useful in our counseling. We also discuss the categories and rankings of various graduate programs.

The spirit is intentionally upbeat, with a can-do orientation to success if you follow the steps we have developed. You are the author of your own history. Our role is to help you outline what that history might be.

MAKING IT INTO A
TOP
GRADUATE SCHOOL

Introduction

Trends in Graduate Studies

The vast majority of students enrolling in undergraduate colleges today are already contemplating further education at the graduate school level, whether or not they have an idea of what they wish to do with their lives. Advanced degrees have always been perceived as the requisite passport into the professions, by our definition any endeavor that requires advanced education and is sustained by mental rather than manual skills. To be a practitioner in a profession conveys a sense of dedication to a field of knowledge. The most popular professions remain law, medicine, business, education, engineering and technology, and, at an increasing rate, information technology and computer sciences. The acceleration of technological change, global competition, medical and scientific discoveries, and the consequent ethical and legal implications call for new ways of learning and continual educational upgrading for the ambitious individual on a professional career track. As we enter the new millennium, with all its promise of exhilarating opportunities and unexplored frontiers of knowledge, many other professions will require advanced training, for example, communications specializations, health care, the visual and performing arts, and management of nonprofit organizations.

Attaining advanced training in an academic discipline or professional program does not mean that you will have acquired all the skills and information needed for the rest of your working life. In fact, you are more likely to spend a good part of your career studying and learning new techniques, laws, rules, business principles, ways to teach, and so on. In graduate school, you will build the knowledge base that becomes your foundation for all future learning. Intellectual and emotional agility and adaptability will become your critical skills in managing your own career.

We learned firsthand from the results of our survey of more than 4,000 undergraduates for *Inside the Top Colleges* that one of the three most important goals of students in selective colleges is to secure their future in a career that has personal meaning to them and potential value to society. They articulated their determination to continue their education in graduate school in order to meet these goals. The growth in the number of graduate school students today is dramatic evidence of the trend in our society. In each of the past four years, 1.8 million students were enrolled in degree-granting graduate programs. Within the next five years, more than 1.9 million ambitious men and women will be enrolled in graduate school. Here are some of the most popular disciplines in which advanced degrees were earned in recent years. The figures are rounded numbers of advanced degrees awarded annually:

Education: 122,000
Business and Marketing: 103,000
Law: 40,000
Health professions: 42,000
Engineering: 32,000
Public administration and services: 25,000
Medicine: 16,000
Social sciences and history: 20,000
Psychology: 18,000
Visual and performing arts: 12,000
Computer and information sciences: 12,000
Divinity and ministry: 6,000

Within the next five years, almost 80,000 professional degrees and 430,000 master's degrees will be awarded annually. These numbers demonstrate the continuing flow to graduate schools not only of immediate or recent college graduates, but also of experienced adults who need specialized training to further their careers or to change directions entirely. The number of potential candidates is measured in the millions. Focused and specialized training will further the opportunities and advancement for anyone who sets his or her sights on a productive, dynamic professional life.

Women and Graduate Education

A particularly significant change during the past decade is that more women are entering and completing graduate degree programs in most disciplines, the exceptions being the physical sciences, engineering, technology, and business. But these fields, too, are appealing to an increasing number of women and minorities as glass doors and ceilings are removed. In fact, since more women than men graduate from college each year, the increasing number of women of all ages seeking advanced degrees has resulted in greater competition for admission to the major graduate school programs. Law school enrollments are a prime example of this pattern. In the past twenty years, the number of men enrolled has remained constant, while the number of women has risen by 14,000.

An Older Population of Students

The other significant trend in graduate school education is the greater maturity of the student population. Today, more than half of all graduate students are over the age of 30. This reflects the value of gaining work experience and exposure to determine one's commitment to a particular profession or the need for more intensive training to advance one's career. Someone with an advanced degree in a specialized field will enjoy greater marketability for the remainder of his or her career. Over time, the percentage of immediate college graduates entering advanced degree programs has dropped dramatically. Fewer and fewer students will receive their diploma in June and enroll in graduate school the following September. This trend is true even for medical students, a training for which many years of study are required. In the past, older students faced a bias against their age in admissions. Today this is not the case. We encourage most students who ask our advice to put off enrolling in graduate school until they have gained greater perspective from internships and work in a relevant career track. Aside from the potential for choosing the wrong field because of limited exposure, the recent college graduate risks the burnout factor. Sixteen straight years of study on a structured academic track can leave people exhausted. Travel, internships, assistantships, volunteerism, and paid employment represent opportunities for an entirely new adventure and the chance to refresh yourself prior to undertaking the intensity of graduate studies. Only a third of individuals who plan to train in the law enter directly from their undergraduate studies. Business schools have shown a steady rise in the age of their enrolled students over the years, the average now being 27 to 28 years. Successful applicants also demonstrate significant work experience in a wide variety of fields prior to beginning their formal management training.

The Financial Rewards of a Graduate Degree

The economy was exceedingly kind to educated workers, young and old, in the 1990s. Job opportunities for college graduates currently exceed the supply. You may want to forego graduate school for now, gaining experience and knowledge on the job, but in the long run, advanced training of a more specialized nature can ensure a career in which you are in the driver's seat. The U.S. Census Bureau provides some convincing statistics regarding the differences in income to be gained from advanced degrees. For example, doctors, lawyers, and business graduates earn twice as much as educated workers with only a bachelor's degree. Those with a professional graduate degree will earn $95,000 on average yearly, with a Ph.D. $77,000, and with a master's degree $51,000, compared to $41,000 for those with no advanced degree. Over a life's career, someone with a Ph.D. will earn more than $3 million in comparison to the $1.6 million than someone with a bachelor's degree will earn.

Rapid Changes in Our Society

A direct correlation exists between the lightning pace of change in all facets of our world today and the shifts in popular jobs and careers. Think about the roller-coaster world of e-commerce and the new economy that led many college graduates into this field. Would many of these adventurers have been better served by determining what their true interests and priorities were before heading into a seemingly upward spiral of big money and opportunities? Would graduate training in a discipline have been a better course of action? Of course, this avenue is still available to any and all comers. Just remember that a variety of boom-and-bust careers are always in play. As you consider your future options, we urge you not to "follow the money." You have only to consider the recent abrupt changes in the world of Internet business to understand that your true purpose is to determine what career suits you best and how to prepare for it. During an average working life of thirty to forty years, you can expect peaks and valleys in all professions, so choose the one you are most likely to enjoy, and you will excel. Many counselors advise being prepared for multiple careers during the course of your life. Advanced education provides you that flexibility.

Graduate Studies: A New Kind of Challenge

Graduate studies of any kind are much more narrowly focused than undergraduate studies, with their survey courses and electives. An undergraduate major, even a senior thesis, does not even approach the kind of commitment that you will be held to in any graduate program. This choice determines the direction of your career in a way no bachelor's program does. Many people, whatever their backgrounds and experiences, find it frightening to make a specific choice of graduate school training. These are some of the issues you need to consider:

- How do I decide if I should pursue graduate studies?
- If I should, when should I begin my studies? Right after college, after working a few years, or in midcareer? Does it make an important difference?
- If I do decide to apply to a graduate program, where should I apply? For which graduate schools am I a reasonable to strong candidate for admission, and which institutions will best serve my interests and capabilities?
- What entrance exams are required, and how do I prepare for them? What is the best way to approach the applications to enhance my chances for acceptance?

Sources of Confusion

Applying to graduate school is significantly different from your earlier experience in applying to college. Finding the right graduate program can be a bewildering and potentially disappointing process, especially because the professionally trained guidance counselors available to most high school students are scarce for potential graduate students. In addition, there is much less need to commit to a specialized field of study at the college level, so the range of choices is wide. We have seen far too many aspiring graduate students take a scattershot approach to applying to graduate programs, sending out reams of applications without careful consideration of the appropriateness of their goals. Many students fall prey to the "halo effect" we described in *Inside the Top Colleges*—that is, "It's either one of the top three grad schools or nothing," or "Even if I don't know what I want to do with my life, a degree from a prestigious graduate school will help me." This is a misconception that can short-circuit a potentially rewarding future. Others, in contrast, fail to recognize or articulate their unique strengths and diminish their chances to gain admittance to a first-rate program.

Here are questions we commonly hear at our offices:

- Is graduate education worth the cost?
- Why does it cost so much, and why are there fewer scholarships for the fields I am considering?
- When do I apply, and what do they want me to tell them on the applications?
- What entrance exams are required, and how do I best prepare for them?
- If I have been out of college for some time, can I compete for admission against the competitive students just coming out of college?
- How do I know whether there will be good career opportunities when I graduate with an advanced degree?
- How highly regarded does a graduate school have to be to make it worth my while to enroll?

- What are the advantages of waiting a few years before applying to graduate school?
- Is it really necessary to get an MBA if I want a career in business?
- Should I study law when there are so many lawyers practicing already?
- What is the best thing I can do while I'm in college to get into law school, business school, medical school, etc.?
- Is it a good idea to get a graduate degree even if I am not certain what I want to do with my life?
- What is the future of a career in education, and can I make a secure living in the field?
- If I am not a good test taker, do I still have a chance to get accepted to a good graduate program?
- Isn't it just about impossible to get into professional schools of medicine or veterinary medicine?
- How do I learn about fellowships to continue my studies?
- Is it worth my while to commit to a doctoral program if I am not considering teaching?
- How can a graduate degree advance a career in politics and public service?
- I understand there are a number of dual-degree programs. What are they exactly, and is there a benefit to such a program?
- What is the hottest field of study right now if my real aim is to make a lot of money?
- I am not really thrilled by the prospect of more academic study. Will it really help me in the future?
- Is there any advantage or disadvantage to doing part-time graduate studies as opposed to enrolling full-time?
- Is it worth taking the risk of leaving a high-paying job for graduate school and going into debt?
- They say the professional media people do not place any value on journalism or communications graduate training. Is this true?
- Is it harder for me as a minority student to get accepted into a good graduate school?
- Now that I have been out of college for a while, I know what career path I want to take, but I need graduate training and did

not take the right courses in college. Does this automatically exclude me from getting in?

- I did not perform well in college. How do I compensate for this in graduate admissions?

Personal Factors to Consider

First and foremost, you must develop and articulate to yourself your personal mission statement. That's correct, a personal mission statement. This includes answers to these questions: What are my highest personal values, and what do I stand for? What accomplishments and goals do I want to fulfill during my lifetime? What kind of environment do I want to be a part of? With what types of people do I want to associate? What kind of activities have mattered the most to me and given me the most satisfaction? Once you have pondered these questions and arrived at answers that give you a sense of yourself, you will discover that the rest is a matter of designing the right strategies and tactics to realize your goals.

We challenge you to separate your personal mission in life from the desires, possibly demands, of persons whose influence and personal support matter to you: your family, close friends, a significant other, or your peer group. The choice of your career and lifestyle is about you, rather than the ambitions or preferences of others. As counselors to hundreds of college graduates who are in search of their future, we urge you to avoid the frequently observed "drift factor." Many individuals, uncertain of their true abilities and disposition, afraid to risk putting a particular talent to the test, or without a vision of what they want to achieve in life, drift into a randomly picked graduate program for lack of a clearer direction. This can, and often does, result in an unsatisfying, costly, stressful, and wasteful experience. The attrition rate is quite high in many programs. Although it can take a year or two of advanced study to determine your interests and aptitude in a field, the well-prepared prospective graduate student can do the research and legwork ahead of enrollment to minimize the potential for a mistake.

HOW TO DETERMINE YOUR CAREER PATH

Take two of the most widely used personality assessment tests to gain insight into your preferences: the Myers-Briggs Type Indicator and the Strong Interest Inventory. Each presents a series of multiple-choice questions regarding your preferences in activities, interests, values, and goals and then matches your response pattern with careers in which people with similar preferences and personality types have been successful.

The Myers-Briggs gives an assessment of your psychological type based on four opposite pairs of attributes: judging/perceiving, thinking/ feeling, extrovert/introvert, and sensing/intuition. Years of research by psychologists and career specialists show that all people can be categorized into one of the sixteen personality types comprised of a combination of four of these characteristics. You can then match your personal type with a long list of appropriate careers and occupations. The Myers-Briggs will match your likes and dislikes with people in careers who possess similar preferences. You can obtain a copy of the assessment from their website, www.mbti.com.

The Strong Interest Inventory relates more directly to jobs and occupations. The test shows how your interests are similar or dissimilar to the interests of people who are successful and satisfied in their work in a wide range of professions. The findings can be helpful in expanding your list of potential career options as well as confirming choices you already are considering.

A third assessment, which we have also found useful as a counseling tool, is the Self-Directed Search tool. This also is a multiple-choice test that measures personality types based on six distinct areas: enterprising, conventional, artistic, social, realistic, and investigative. The results are matched with career choices that are likely to appeal to the individual.

Combined with your own reflection on your goals and aspirations, your discussions with friends, family, and mentors who know you well, and perhaps the advice of a career counselor, these assessments can help you both narrow and expand your field of choices in order to start down the right path.

Do What You Are Best Suited For

Talk with seasoned professionals, and they will tell you what matters in achieving personal and professional success in life. Your work needs to fit your personality as well as your native talents and aptitude. It should be a natural outlet for self-expression, a means to accomplish what you most care about. The ideal goal, one worth struggling to attain, is to be able to do your best at what you are best suited to do. As you consider your future, think about what you would want your life's work to be if it were a calling rather than a job. You cannot separate a career, a discrete activity that fills so great a portion of your life, from your psyche and your soul. You need to act on your own belief system. You will then be able to deal with the complexities and constant conflicts that will confront you throughout your work life. It takes great reservoirs of energy, which must be continuously replenished, to be successful in life. Positive energy flows only as long as you are happy and stimulated by your activities. What words can be sweeter than "I love what I do and find I can give it my fullest attention. I could never have imagined putting in so many hours of concentrated work in school or college and gaining such satisfaction"? Naturally, the opposite also holds true. Frustration and depression, a sense of having lost your direction and optimism, drain the reservoir of energy and spirit, leaving little or none left to flow into the demands of the work at hand. Your relationships, personal and professional, are commonly affected by this loss of spirit.

Your Undergraduate Studies

If you are still in college and contemplating your future direction, realize that whatever your field of concentration during your undergraduate years, you are not likely to remember the greater part of the information you have studied. So what is it that you should take away from the time and effort you have put into the many papers you have had to research and write, and the exams for which you have had to prepare? How will this help you in your adult life? If you have applied purposeful effort to your studies, you will have created a small portable bag, like that carried by the family doctor of an earlier time, filled with special skills and techniques for solving problems. This knowledge bag can accompany you anywhere and any time you need it. The ability to read complex material for meaning and insight, to reduce complicated issues to their simplest terms and bring them to a logical solution, to think facilely in numerical and symbolic language, to research any topic, and to use with ease technological tools to complete tasks more readily prepares you for whatever future you decide to fashion for yourself.

In addition to the critical thinking and writing skills developed with a liberal arts education, students can pursue studies at the undergraduate level that are prerequisites for their graduate work. Such is the case with medicine, engineering, music, or any of the academic disciplines.

Harry Lewis, dean of Harvard College, talks about the goals he sees for the liberal arts undergraduate experience at Harvard. This philosophy applies to all undergraduates in colleges across the country:

> *I hate to see people not performing up to their academic potential because they are not really interested in what they are studying. They are studying a subject for the wrong reason: because they think they are supposed to, because their families want them to, because they're worried about making an adequate living. They have the notion their concentration defines them—that they can major in mathematics only if they are going to be a mathematician, and they don't really think they can be a mathematician as a profession. Almost every instance of academic failure at Harvard has to do with some mismatch between motivation and what people are studying. When people here fail academically, it's always because something has gotten in the way, not because they cannot do the work.*

Harvard Alumni Magazine, Sept./Oct. 1999, p. 77.

Questions to Be Asked

We counsel anyone contemplating graduate training to answer certain questions, whether the goal is to prepare for a professional career in law, medicine, engineering or technical sciences, education, health sciences, architecture, or the arts, or to go into business, government service, politics, university research and teaching, or the ministry. Throughout this book, we tell the stories of 12 individuals who had to consider all of these questions and the issues they raise. Each person arrived at the point at which graduate training became essential to meet his or her eventual goals. How these students worked out their plans and successfully applied to the right graduate programs will provide you with an overview of the process. The questions they asked are being asked today by thousands of well-educated, highly capable people, who contemplate postgraduate training as a means to advance their dream of having a career that matters to them.

HOW TO DECIDE WHETHER YOU SHOULD ENROLL
IN GRADUATE SCHOOL

Ask these hard questions to determine whether graduate school is an appropriate direction for you.

How goal oriented am I?

How strongly do I care about the career I am considering?

How important is an advanced degree to my future career track?

How hard am I willing to work? Can I motivate myself to study intensively at this time?

How do I determine if I should go immediately or wait for a few years?

How confident will I be in competing directly with a cohort of smart, ambitious students who are highly goal oriented?

How willing am I to live with fewer comforts and less financial security than I presently enjoy?

How will I pay for two or more years of education? Am I willing to go into debt to secure the degree?

Is this the most advantageous time for me to leave my present situation, or am I best served by delaying graduate studies?

Do I have the aptitude for and intellectual attraction to the field I am contemplating?

Did I enjoy my undergraduate academic experience?

Am I ready for more focused, intensive academic work?

Do I have a good understanding of various graduate and career options?

Have I done enough exploration to feel confident about the choice I am making?

The Meaning of Graduate Education

Applying for admission to a graduate school will be considerably different from your experience in applying for admission to undergraduate college. You are no longer part of a vast national group of teenagers all preparing for college admission and taking the SAT or ACT under the direction of their school's college counselor. You probably had the support and counsel of your family, who played an active role in your future. There was little or no question about your enrolling in college, and you did not have to concern yourself with your choice of major and career plans. It was enough to know that a college education was an essential step in preparing for whatever the future held in store for you.

There is no automatic progression to graduate school that is called for today. Your classmates, upon graduating, go off in a variety of directions. Some have already applied to medical school, others have landed entry-level jobs in occupations they believe they will like, and others may spend a year or more traveling or perfecting a talent they did not have time for in college.

Sooner or later, though, a majority of college graduates will consider further studies. Times are changing. It used to be said that you did not need a college degree to get on in life. Before World War II, most high school graduates could not afford the cost of college, so only 15 to 20 percent of potential candidates ever attended. Today, almost 70 percent of high school graduates enroll immediately in college. This demographic change has made graduate training ever more significant in getting a leg up in the competitive marketplace. Even alumni of the top colleges across the country recognize that their prestigious diplomas will not guarantee them professional security for life. The graduates of the top private and public colleges and universities have the highest rate of enrollment in professional graduate programs. On average, 75 percent of the most ambitious and talented pool of college graduates will enroll in advanced degree training within a 10-year period.

Anyone can get into a graduate program somewhere, although in many instances the degree may carry little recognition and the education may be no higher than that of an undergraduate curriculum. Although more than 100,000 MBAs are conferred yearly by more than 800 institutions, the American Assembly of Collegiate Schools of Business certifies only 200 of these institutions. Without this accrediting agency's stamp of approval, the value of the degree can be close to useless in the job market, even if the teaching and learning were of some value.

As more and more college graduates take up the graduate school option, more and more graduate school degree programs open up to meet the demand. Some are easy to gain acceptance to and often promise more than they can actually deliver. "Diploma mills" are spreading their message and making themselves more easily accessible by way of the Internet and distance learning. More than ever, *caveat emptor*—the buyer beware—is sound advice. You can waste precious time and money if you fail to get the opinions of professional educators and people in the professions you are considering about (a) the academic quality of a graduate school and particular program and (b) the respect it is accorded by the profession. Even top institutions have mediocre to poor departments in some graduate fields. A graduate education requires a major commitment on your part. In choosing to apply to one or more schools, you owe it to yourself to be skeptical about their claims of what they can do for you. On the other hand, don't fall into the commonly held belief that you will attain a first-class education only at one of the most prestigious universities.

The Many Paths to Graduate School

We know from our many years of experience that if you follow our Ten Steps, you are likely to find the answers to these and other questions about graduate education. Obviously, we cannot answer all of everyone's questions, so you must be prepared to do much of your own research. We do suggest a number of sources that will help you launch your investigation. We believe our Ten Steps can bring some order and rationality into the confusion you will likely experience as you try to make sound judgments about applying to graduate school and undertaking a program of intensive study.

Such decisions are often reached only after hesitation, soul-searching, consultation, and, occasionally, false starts. With the whole universe of career options open to you, the process bears little resemblance to college admissions, and you are faced with a new set of considerations. The stories we present here of people who found their respective paths after much self-reflection, research, and planning should give you confidence that you, too, will reach your ultimate purpose. These students were at first unsure of what graduate program might suit their talents, personality, and experience.

We counsel thousands of college seniors, recent college graduates who have made their initial forays into the workplace, and men and women who are in midcareer and want to start an entirely new career. A number of our clients already have earned an advanced degree and want to consider going to a higher level of training or changing their field of interest. By following the Ten Steps, such individuals overcame their doubts and quickly found new possibilities in further education. We assure you that you can and will do the same.

Four Basic Reasons to Go to Graduate School

The first question that we put to all who come to our office is, "Why are you contemplating graduate work?" Responses vary. Some people want to advance their careers, others wish to make more money, and some covet the added prestige another degree may bring. There are also those who say they just love to study and enrich their minds, but they need advice on how to get back into the academic environment after spending time in "the real world." The majority of people we meet are confident that they possess the aptitude or capacity for advanced studies, but some need bolstering. We do find that few prospective graduate students understand the nature of advanced studies. They commonly view graduate school as a continuation of undergraduate studies, just narrower in scope and more practical. This is definitely not the case.

As one professor at Harvard University's graduate school put it to us, "Many who talk to me about undertaking a graduate program have no idea what this means. They have an expectation that graduate work is going to be simply a continuation of their college education. Believe me, there is very little relation between college and graduate school. Graduate work is significantly more intense, individualistic, and demanding."

Those who hope eventually to get a graduate degree need to discover first just why they want to go to graduate school. This is a question you must answer for yourself, although a professional advisor can help you sort out your issues. We have found four basic, legitimate reasons for attending graduate school:

1. A graduate degree is essential for going into certain professions: law, health care (medicine, dentistry, veterinary medicine, public health, mental health, hospital administration), teaching at the college level, school administration and guidance, social work, engineering, and scientific research, to name some of the most obvious.

2. A graduate degree can help you improve your professional position economically or in terms of responsibility. MBAs on the whole earn more money than do non-MBAs; engineers with advanced degrees usually end up with bigger responsibilities and more income; teachers with master's or doctoral degrees are better paid and have greater opportunities for administrative leadership positions; business people with specialized training and knowledge are better suited for top management and consulting positions. Note that we say only that another degree is *likely* to help you, not that it will automatically. As with all

undertakings in life, what you make of your further education will determine your success.

3. Advanced training in a discipline or profession will give you greater flexibility in the marketplace. You will find that you can move to different jobs within your field more readily or change your career entirely, taking with you the intellectual and strategic skills you have acquired.

4. A graduate degree can give you the personal satisfaction and confidence derived from advanced learning. Some individuals work for years on a master's or doctoral degree because they are on a learning adventure and need the guidance and structure such university-based study offers. Many earn a law degree with no intention of practicing law, but because what they learn will have so many applications in business, politics and public affairs, education, and the health professions.

WHY ACCOUNTANTS NEED A GRADUATE DEGREE

The American Institute of Certified Public Accountants (AICPA) points out that a bachelor's degree is no longer considered adequate training for becoming a certified public accountant. Among the reasons cited are the dramatic expansion in the body of accounting and financial knowledge in the last several decades, the increasing complexity of business methods, the significant role financial auditing plays in the business world, expanding oversight of multinational corporations, conglomerates, franchising, and greater scrutiny by the public and governmental agencies. A review of corporate leaders in recent years shows that many were trained in accounting in their early careers. "Accounting firms need better educated and more committed graduates who can advance to the higher ranks rapidly," says the AICPA.

The pass rate among candidates taking the CPA examination, one of the toughest of all the tests for entrance into the professional ranks, is substantially higher for those holding advanced degrees. Accountants

(continued)

with a master's degree also have more job opportunities, starting salaries 10 to 20 percent higher than the salaries of accountants with only a bachelor's degree, and increased prospects for promotions in accounting firms and corporations. More states now require that a candidate have an accredited graduate degree before sitting for the CPA examination. The AICPA is in full support of this requirement.

Choosing the Right Program Is Critical

Choosing the right postgraduate training program is critical. Today there are so many professional career opportunities that there are more chances for making the wrong choice. Some of the reasons you might go astray:

- The number of graduate degree options is growing. Merely sorting out the opportunities at hundreds of institutions is a major task. Finding the right direction for your talents and interests, even within a defined professional field, may require considerable time and effort. Many graduate schools have an economic need to meet their enrollment goals with strong students. You could be enticed to enroll in a program for which you are not suited or that may not be of value to you.
- If you do not do enough research on opportunities in the fields that interest you, you may overlook an exciting program of much greater interest and eventual value than traditional programs.
- Some students go to a particular graduate school because it is a family tradition, only to find they are not suited for the program.
- There are those who start law school expecting it to be a continuation of their liberal arts studies of government or political science and not a set of courses consisting largely of technical training.
- The halo effect of a prestigious institution can blind you to opportunities at other institutions. It is immature or superficial

to think, "If I can't get into one of the top ten MBA schools, I won't go at all. I'll do something else." Not to go to graduate school when it fits well with your long-range plans is irrational, detrimental, and limiting.

- There is a tendency to overlook the many excellent graduate programs offered by the great state universities at reasonable costs, and consequently to decide against advanced education, because it seems too expensive.
- The optional nature of a graduate degree leads some to consider such training unnecessary.
- Misunderstanding about the financial costs and benefits can lead to a faulty decision. For example, passing up an opportunity to attend a prestigious institution that offers the best program in order to save money may be penny-wise and pound-foolish. Going into debt for the short term may well convert into greater rewards in the long run.
- Many candidates apply only to graduate schools in the state or region in which they plan to work professionally. They should know that it is more advantageous to train in the most highly regarded program, regardless of its location.

THE SEARCH FOR VALUES: ONE CHAPLAIN'S ENCOUNTER WITH YOUNG AMERICANS

A profound shift has taken place in the value systems of young Americans in our time. Gone is the drive of people who grew up in the Depression to find a job at an early age and stay with it for life, to live in a single town for most of their lives.

The young people I see move from job to job with frequency and have unparalleled access to communications media, travel, exposure to foreign countries, often through community service projects or international business. Family affections and ties may remain strong, but the need to live close to family less so.

(continued)

Large institutions—corporations, law firms, educational institutions, and even our religious centers—have frequently failed this generation. Many sensitive young people are treated like cattle, their deepest interests not spoken to, their true values and aspirations left unexplored. What is most regrettable is that the fierce energy of this generation could find fulfillment in any one of these settings.

The failure of our primary institutions to understand and challenge this generation has resulted in an outpouring of spiritual literature, "how to" books in popular psychology, known as self-help. An entire section of the neighborhood Barnes and Noble or Borders bookstores is full of motivational-spiritual titles pitched to educated and caring young adults. Of course, the next section of the bookstore contains hundreds of guides to getting ahead in the business world, starting your own company to make millions, and so on. How do you know what really matters?

What is important is to cut beneath the fluff. Those called upon to counsel young men and women seeking direction in their personal and professional lives would do well to ask these questions:

- What is most important in your life?
- As you were growing up, what sorts of occupations had the deepest attraction for you?
- What really do you want out of life, beyond meeting your basic material and security needs?
- How do you find enjoyment in life?
- Do you have impulses to serve or help others? To make the world a better place?
- Where do you see your life heading at this point? Is this the direction you want it to take?

These questions are not exhaustive. Not all need to be answered at one time, but some are useful to suggest a wider world than the immediate one and its problems and opportunities.

Note. These comments were shared with us by the Reverend Dr. Frederick Quinn, who is a chaplain at Washington National Cathedral, a former senior career officer in the Foreign Service, and the author of numerous books and articles on law, government, religion, and history.

Graduate School Is So Different from College

In a very real sense, a four-year undergraduate college is a continuation of high school, a place where students are nurtured, guided, encouraged, and shaped by teachers, administrators, student personnel officers, and one or more of the large number of student organizations to which they can belong. Graduate school, in contrast, is closer to the world beyond the ivied walls, in which intense competition demands a high level of achievement and productivity for success. In any quality graduate program, the workload is often unbelievably heavy, the competition to excel is fierce, and the days unrelieved by organized extracurricular activity or sports are many. There is much less institutional concern for the personal life of the graduate student. The practical side of living is, except in a handful of heavily endowed institutions, the student's responsibility. For example, it is up to the student, married or single, to find affordable housing and transportation to classes. This represents a huge challenge for most students in such pricey communities as New York, Palo Alto, Cambridge, Berkeley, or Princeton.

On the whole, a graduate student's existence is spartan, with time for a movie or bull session over a six-pack of beer limited to Saturday nights. Graduate school is definitely not "the time of your life." To succeed, you must be highly organized, hugely focused on your studies and faculty expectations, full of stamina, and more flexible than demanding, since the curriculum is more rigid and the emphasis on grades in the top schools extreme.

The Law School Admission Council/Law School Admission Service, as one good example, advises students, "If you are not willing to work—and work hard—don't go to law school. You can expect to spend sixty, seventy, eighty hours a week reading cases and law review articles." We can add another caveat: it is not enough to complete all of the required work well. To gain recognition and have a shot at a position in a major law firm, you need to be better than the majority of your classmates.

Another difference from undergraduate college is that the length of time required to complete a graduate degree can vary greatly. There is no guarantee in many programs of graduating in a fixed period. Graduate schools are filled with people on a variety of time schedules. Some are taking a lighter course load while they work part-time or attend to their family; some meet with different requirements from their advisor or the department as a whole. On average, the professional schools in medicine, law, business, engineering, health fields, architecture, and journalism hold to a standard schedule for graduation for full-time students.

When you were an undergraduate, almost all of your classmates were in your age bracket, 18 to 22 years old. In contrast, graduate schools are filled with people in their late 20s, 30s, and even 40s. Younger graduate students benefit from association with older classmates, but there is also the potential for some tension and distance. The younger students may have an edge academically, because graduate school follows closely on the heels of their undergraduate work, while the older students are likely to be rusty in their academic skills but more able to handle the stress and demands, owing to their years of practical experience in the competitive world. One professor in a leading business school put it this way, "The older students come up with solutions to management problems more quickly than those who recently got their bachelor's degree, but they struggle to absorb the reading. I like the mixture of older and younger students in my classes. There is a symbiotic relationship that forms. One group stimulates the other in a mysterious way."

The Ten Steps to Graduate School

We have distilled these Ten Steps in applying to graduate school from our success in helping qualified students discover the programs that suit them and to which they will be admitted.

1. Identify yourself as a potential lawyer, doctor, entrepreneur, teacher, or other professional. Make sure you are suited by temperament and aptitude for a particular graduate program.
2. Gain an understanding of the nature of graduate education and admissions procedures to determine your preparedness for entrance.

3. Explore graduate program opportunities and the enormous variety of degree offerings to determine whether particular graduate training can put you in a stronger career position.

4. Assess your academic qualifications for major graduate schools. Decide if you need additional credits in subjects related to the field in which you plan to study.

5. Learn what particular tests are required for admission and then prepare to the best of your ability, because the results are crucial to your chances for acceptance.

6. Strengthen your writing skills in order to be able to submit strong personal statements or essays, since these are essential elements in admissions consideration.

7. Get "real world" experience in a job or internship to prove to yourself and admissions committees that you have the capacity for service in society, particularly in the field you have chosen.

8. Market your strengths to admissions committees. They appreciate candidates who present themselves fully and honestly, and do not display false modesty.

9. Examine the many ways to finance your graduate education. Be sure you are willing to undertake debt, if necessary, and will be able to manage it.

10. Prepare your applications carefully, limiting essays to the required length. Keep a file of dates of transcript submissions and of correspondence with faculty or employers who are sending references to the admissions committees.

At first glance, the Ten Steps may seem burdensome. Why not just apply to a certain number of programs and take what comes your way? That is what many people do, in fact. The competition for the top programs is intense, but simply to get into a random graduate program is senseless. If you make the effort, you may be admitted to a highly respected and worthwhile program that could make all the difference for your future.

The Successful Student Case Studies We Discuss in This Book

The Ten Steps can maximize your understanding of graduate educational possibilities and ensure a career for you that is consonant with your capabilities and desires. This is a big claim, but we know from our many years of experience that the Ten Steps have worked for many others. The case studies of recent seekers that are interspersed throughout this book are profiles of the young people in search of their futures and the fields they decided to pursue. They demonstrate that the Ten Steps work and will inspire a feeling of confidence that the method will work for you.

SVEN: *a candidate for business school*

Sven majored in art history at Princeton University and worked for several years in fundraising and promotion, first for the National Gallery in Washington and then for the Whitney Museum of American Art in New York. His concern was how to move into the upper echelons of management in the nonprofit sector, since he had focused all his undergraduate studies in the humanities. Because traditional MBA training did not seem to fit well with his goal, he felt stuck in his young career.

DOUG: *a candidate for medical school*

Doug had not considered medicine as his career choice until he was well into his undergraduate studies at the University of Rochester. Though he worked hard to catch up on the requisite science courses, he was ill prepared to excel in them. He applied to a number of medical schools in his senior year, but was rejected by all of them. This led Doug to reconsider his ambition to become a doctor since he felt it was a futile pursuit. As he was about to graduate, his questions centered on what he should do. Should he take more science courses as a postbaccalaureate student and reapply to medical schools? Should he fulfill another ambition, which was to live in Spain and perfect his Spanish language skills? Should he enter the teaching profession, since he enjoyed being with children and thought he would make a good science teacher?

SUZANNE: *a candidate for a doctoral degree*

Suzanne spent her undergraduate years at Dartmouth College enjoying her major in art history and comparative languages. She took full advantage of the study abroad programs Dartmouth sponsored, relishing the experiences of traveling and living in different and varied cultures. Her heavy involvement in community service projects, combined with her interest in other cultures, led her to consider a career in international public health. Showing great initiative, she applied for an internship at a hospital in Australia. She also had an interest in law as another avenue for helping indigent people. After several internship experiences, Suzanne did an intensive self-assessment that led her to recognize her true passion was art history and languages. The issues then became how to create a career to combine these areas and what graduate studies she should undertake.

ANDY: *a candidate for medical school*

From high school on, Andy was certain that he wanted to work with children. Eventually he found pediatrics. This field would combine his love for children and his talent in the sciences. At Yale University, Andy concentrated in econometrics, while also taking courses in sciences, psychology, and human development. He applied to medical schools in his senior year at Yale and was accepted to several outstanding programs. At some point in his second year of medical studies, Andy began to question whether he was meant to be a doctor. He was doing well in his studies, but his heart did not seem to be in them. He wondered if he belonged in some other career that would give him more immediate access to children in a way in which he could affect their social and intellectual development.

CARL: *a candidate for business school*

Carl found himself in a bind not uncommon among college graduates, including those who come from another country to study in the United States. He had gone to Tufts University, and now that he had several years of work in the international financial industry under his belt, he thought he needed more specialized training if he was to advance in his career. Because his undergraduate academic performance had been below average, he doubted his ability to convince admissions committees that he had the competency and drive to complete intensive studies at the graduate level. He also doubted whether he could compete in a stringent MBA program. His questions centered on when he should apply, what type of program suited his needs and interests, and how to explain the reasons for his poor showing in his undergraduate studies.

KAREN: *a candidate for law school*

Karen had enjoyed an exceptionally satisfying and successful intellectual experience in college. Majoring in both classics and government at Dartmouth, she initially thought a career in television news would meet her love of languages and current political issues. The opportunity to work for a major television network right after college persuaded her otherwise. The first issue Karen had to resolve was the true nature of her interests: Did she not care any longer about public affairs, or was it the particular working environment that was inappropriate? Her search became one of finding the right outlet to express her combination of concerns and natural abilities.

AMANDA: *a candidate for a doctoral degree*

Amanda changed her field of concentration as an undergraduate at Boston University from communications to anthropology after she took several introductory courses that sparked her interest in the field. This threw her off the track on which she had been comfortably moving. To test how committed she was to an academic discipline, she undertook several field internships. This further confirmed her desire to immerse herself in research in several aspects of cultural studies, and she began a search for the right graduate program.

EDWARD: *a candidate for business school*

Edward underwent a painful experience familiar to countless undergraduates. Because he had a natural aptitude for math and liked science, he was convinced that he wanted to pursue an engineering career at Cornell University. After his first year of studies in an intensive engineering program, he recognized that he did not enjoy the subject matter at all and without concentrated effort would not be successful. With some soul-searching and counsel, he moved into a business management program for the remainder of his undergraduate years to prepare for the airline industry, a field he knew a fair amount about through members of his family. Once he had this focus comfortably in mind, the question became when and where to apply to graduate school. You can profit from learning about Edward's efforts to reset his sights on the right academic training and from his lesson that timing is a key factor in successfully reaching one's goal.

SALLY: *a candidate for business school*

Sally knew from an early age that what she was best at and most enjoyed was the use of words to express her ideas. An inveterate reader and writer, she excelled in her studies at Stanford University, where she took full advantage of the English Department's offerings. After college, she headed into advertising, thinking this was a natural venue for her language skills. Sally reached a point at which she had to decide if she needed professional school training and, if so, what kind and when.

SAMUEL: *a candidate for law school*

Samuel had an especially outstanding academic and student leadership career at Emory University. Torn between his intellectual commitments to religion and philosophy and to political science and government, he considered a number of conflicting directions for his future. A good deal of discussion and research into various career tracks ultimately helped him to decide which way to go. His presentation to graduate schools reflects the nature of his thinking and how he arrived at a resolution that would incorporate all of his major interests.

MATTHEW: *a candidate for business school*

Matthew had a mediocre GPA but a high GMAT score. In his strong personal statements, he was able to account for his academic neglect while showcasing his extensive experience in his family business. His confidence and growth came across clearly, as did the logic of pursuing the MBA.

Other Successful Students Whose Stories Appear in This Book

In addition to these case studies, we include the stories of five other remarkable young men and women who succeeded in fulfilling their graduate school ambitions:

- Alex, who earned his degree in social work;
- Robert, who parlayed his telecommunications experience into an MBA degree;
- Frank, a hospital volunteer who found his niche in industrial psychology;
- Stefan, a lover of words and writing who achieved a master's degree in communications for corporate work;
- Barbara, an English major who joined the ministry;
- Maureen, who took the extra steps to enter a law school;
- Amy, who wrote about her disability with sensitivity in her medical college applications;
- Lucille, who decided that a law degree would enable her to take legal action on behalf of disadvantaged children;
- Richard, a talented entrepreneur who successfully targeted Columbia University's new real estate management program.

These narratives will help you reflect on the issues and priorities that matter to you as you explore your own graduate school and career options. You will recognize some of your own issues as you follow these students' journeys through the Ten Steps. Even better, you will take courage from the successful resolution of their concerns.

STEP ONE

Identify Yourself

The First Consideration: What Is Your Field of Interest?

As you contemplate graduate studies, your first consideration should be your field of interest.

Oh, you already know the field you want to study? You want to be a lawyer, or a business executive, or a foreign service officer? How did you come to such a conclusion? Is it justified by substantial analysis of your experience, record, capacities, aptitudes, tastes, financial capabilities, and energies? Perhaps not? If these questions arouse uncertainty, don't be surprised. Even the most brilliant hesitate, wondering if they have made the right decision, measuring themselves against the stars of their proposed occupation or profession.

Some graduate students do find themselves in the wrong programs and then must change course. Picking an unsuitable graduate program is not always avoidable, and it certainly is not fatal, but it is a false start, a waste of time and money. The first step in identifying the right graduate training for you is identifying yourself. This will help you avoid making impulsive or irrational decisions, such as simply following in the footsteps of a parent, a friend, or someone you admire, without recognizing how different you may be from that person and how uncongenial you may find such a graduate experience.

After you read this chapter, we suggest you carefully complete the Graduate School Questionnaire developed by the counselors of Howard Greene and Associates to help identify yourself. What does it mean to identify yourself? It does not mean "finding" yourself. This is not a psychological test or a proposal for self-therapy. One aspect of

GRADUATE SCHOOL QUESTIONNAIRE

Candidate's full name: _____

_____

College(s) attended or presently attending: _____

_____

Year graduated or expect to graduate: _____

_____

Undergraduate major: _____

Minor: _____

_____

Faculty advisor: _____

_____

Overall grade point average: _____ In major: _____

Academic awards or scholarships: _____

_____

Graduate test(s) taken: _____

Date(s) taken: _____

Score(s): _____

Work, internship, and volunteer experience (during summers or since graduation): _____

_____

_____

1. Why are you considering graduate school, and what are your eventual goals? _____

   _____

   _____

   _____

2. What are the key characteristics you hope to find in a graduate school? _____

   _____

_____

_____

3. What degree or program are you considering? Are there any schools or programs you have an interest in at this time? _____

_____

_____

_____

4. How important to you are the location and size of an institution?

_____

_____

_____

5. Will you need financial aid? _____

_____

_____

_____

6. Do you wish to study full- or part-time? _____

_____

_____

_____

7. Please list your most important extracurricular pursuits in and out of your college community. Indicate the depth of your involvement and any positions of leadership. _____

_____

_____

_____

8. How would you assess yourself as a student? What do you consider to be your areas of academic strength and weakness? Do you think your transcript and advisor/faculty reports are a fair evaluation of your academic abilities? _____

_____

_____

_____

9. Tell us anything about yourself that would help us to understand you better—your personality, values, background, interests, and aspirations; the influence of certain people in your life; and any obstacles or handicaps you have overcome. _____

_____

_____

_____

10. Please attach your résumé to the questionnaire for our review. If you do not have one, this is a good time to create one.

_____

qualification to do graduate work is that you are not seriously lost or troubled, for graduate studies call for tremendous effort and concentration. Identifying yourself means becoming more thoroughly acquainted with aspects of your personality that may have a bearing on your graduate experience. These include your capacity and enthusiasm for academic work, special talents or limitations, values, lifestyle preferences—in short, an inventory of those elements of your personality that are relevant to your expectations for advanced specialized studies.

In the following sections, we provide examples of how others have responded to the Graduate School Questionnaire. We suggest that you spend as much time as necessary thinking about the questions and your responses. More recent college graduates, being used to answering questionnaires, will probably move through this one rapidly, and so to you we say: Slow down. This is not a quiz. There is no time limit. You should provide a portrait, rather than a snapshot, of yourself. The more seriously you take each question, the better your start toward your coveted graduate degree and career.

Going through the questionnaire, older graduate school applicants will first notice requests for information about college attendance, grade point average, and a faculty advisor's telephone number or e-mail address, all of which may have to be sent for. You should have this information available for any admissions officer or graduate school faculty member seeking an in-depth impression of you. Some of you may not have taken any graduate tests yet; you can indicate when you plan to take them. We discuss these tests in Step Five. They play a significant role in admissions consideration.

Work or internship experience is so important that we give it a full discussion in Step Seven. You should fill in this line honestly. If you have not had much work or internship experience, make note of it. In Step Seven we discuss whether you might be well advised to postpone applying to a graduate school until you have spent more time working or interning. You will learn from several of the case studies how additional work experience made the difference in acceptance into a top graduate program. More and more graduate schools, particularly professional degree programs such as business and law, prefer applicants to have as much as two to six years of work experience after college before starting their programs. Instructors have come to appreciate the maturity and insights that develop from working or interning.

Note the quality of your work as you fill in this section of the questionnaire. Bagging groceries in a supermarket or working in a fast food restaurant is not going to impress graduate admissions committees, even though this may be how you helped finance your college education. You will very likely be competing with applicants who have had serious responsibilities and accomplishments, such as running a summer camp program, tutoring children or adults, learning a craft and working at it, managing a business or starting one of their own, helping a legislator write laws, writing computer programs for a company or institution, helping direct a community service organization, or interning in a vital enterprise of some sort. Older applicants may already be well-paid managers or specialists in relevant fields seeking further training.

Why Are You Considering Graduate School?

As we suggested in the Introduction and repeat in the questionnaire, the first question you must answer is, Why are you considering graduate school at this time and what are your eventual goals? Here are possible answers to stimulate your thinking, however sure you may feel about your initial response.

Why Law School?

- To become a trial lawyer, a corporate attorney, a litigator, a criminal defense lawyer, a mergers and acquisitions attorney, a judge, a district attorney, a legislator, or a politician.
- To become acquainted with the law in preparation for a business career.
- To become a lawyer working for the government, a libel expert, or a member of your family's law firm.
- To become a specialist in taxes, law enforcement, estate law, entertainment law, legal ethics, constitutional law, marine law, military law, international law, or intellectual property law.
- To become a law professor.
- To become a journalist specializing in legal stories.

Why Medical School?

To become:
- a pediatrician
- a primary care doctor
- an orthopedic surgeon
- an obstetrician/gynecologist
- an endocrinologist
- a neurologist
- a psychiatrist
- a surgeon
- an allergist
- a bioengineer

- a cardiologist
- a dermatologist
- an internist
- an ophthalmologist
- a medical researcher
- a hospital executive
- an editor of a medical journal
- a pathologist
- a public health officer
- an athletic team physician
- a medical writer
- an executive in research for a drug company
- a medical professor
- a medical school dean
- a medical journalist

Why an MBA?

To become:
- a financier
- an entrepreneur
- an accountant
- a chief executive officer
- a chief financial officer
- a marketing executive or consultant
- a life insurance executive
- a technology company leader
- a securities analyst
- the head of a governmental agency
- an auditor
- an investment banker
- a management consultant
- a college professor
- the head of a nonprofit agency or institution
- a media executive
- the head of a family business

Why an M.A., an M.S., an M.S.W., a Ph.D., or an MFA?

To become:
- a teacher in a particular discipline
- a doctoral candidate in a specialized discipline
- a social worker
- a librarian
- a museum curator
- a journalist
- a writer
- an architect
- an engineer
- a newscaster
- an artist
- a musician
- a counselor
- a school administrator

What Are Your Eventual Goals?

What we just demonstrated is the necessity to pinpoint your career, which will direct your graduate school objectives. If you want a Ph.D. in economics, for example, what do you expect it to lead to? Some people are shy about stating their objectives, for fear they will appear too ambitious. Don't be shy. Be goal directed, and be open about it.

Of course, it is not always possible to be certain about your course through graduate school, or life for that matter. A medical student starts out in pediatrics and switches to psychiatry, a corporate lawyer becomes a merchant banker, a college professor goes to Washington, D.C., to be a political advisor and never returns to teaching. Nevertheless, making a projection of your future can help you make the right choice of graduate training.

If you find it difficult to focus on a single goal, write down a number of relevant options. Keep in mind the advantages of having taken one or more of the personal inventory surveys that can help you focus on a somewhat narrower field of careers. There are so many opportunities in our system of higher education and in our burgeoning domestic and global economy that making choices is sometimes difficult. As you consider various programs, you will find that some institutions stimulate a stronger response than others, and you will begin to see more clearly what the right direction is for you. Informational interviewing—talking with various people in different professions and graduate fields—may further help you understand your many options.

What Are the Key Characteristics You Hope to Find in a Graduate School?

Many people have difficulty imagining graduate education. The term "graduate school" doesn't automatically conjure up images of ivy walls, athletic traditions, dorm parties, Greek organizations, many new friends, and lots of extracurricular activities. This is because it is a wholly different experience from your undergraduate life, both academically and otherwise. You may be studying on the same campus where all the undergraduate action is, but you will not be part of that. It will appear to be kid's stuff. You will be studying harder and learning a great deal from contact with your fellow graduate students and professors.

To know what characteristics you would like in a graduate program, you need to know the range of possibilities. Perhaps the most important characteristic is the general academic quality.

SELECTING AN ACADEMIC GRADUATE SCHOOL

1. Is the institution oriented toward research or course work?
2. Does the department have many faculty in a variety of research groups, or does the strength rest in one or two members?
3. Do the research interests of the faculty represent many specialties within the discipline? Does the department's strength lie in a particular area or are many of the subspecialties equally strong? What

(continued)

articles or books or research findings of note have come out of the department recently?

4. What is the relationship between students and faculty? Are faculty members accessible to students? Do the faculty create opportunities for students to research and write with them?

5. What do present graduate students say about their experiences in the program? How good are potential faculty advisors? What is the quality of life like? Is the location a positive or negative factor in the experience?

6. Is there much financial aid available in the form of scholarships, teaching assistantships, or research assistantships? How many students receive funding, and what criteria are used to grant funding?

7. How many Ph.D.s are granted annually? What is the average length of time required to complete doctoral work? How many students drop out of the program?

8. If you enroll in a master's program, will you be able to change to a Ph.D. program easily if your performance is satisfactory? Must you obtain an M.A. or M.S. before you enroll in the Ph.D. program?

9. What are the employment opportunities when you complete the graduate program? Does the department chair or the placement office assist graduates in securing a job? What is the placement record in tenure-track or other career opportunities?

10. How closely do graduate students work together and discuss their work with each other?

11. How well do the faculty get along with one another? Is there any ideological conflict or other departmental strife?

12. Is there a particular faculty member whose work you admire and with whom you would gladly apprentice?

13. How has the department you are considering been evaluated by the university and by external auditors from their academic discipline?

14. If you are expected to teach, what training opportunities are available to you?

15. Is the faculty open to publishing articles with the names of their research assistants, namely, you, in the bylines?

Evaluating a Program's Academic Quality

You can assume that prestigious institutions such as the University of California, Berkeley, Stanford University, Harvard University, Yale University, Cornell University, Columbia University, the University of California, Los Angeles, and Princeton University, to name a few of the top universities, have some of the strongest academic programs. Of course, the listing of top graduate programs varies greatly according to the field you have in mind. If you are qualified and motivated to study at this level, you ought to indicate such academic prestige as a desired characteristic. Remember that enrollments are limited in all of the prestige programs, so you will need to apply for admission to some strong universities with less competition. By what academic criteria should you evaluate institutions?

- One criterion, of course, is accreditation, which at least guarantees that the program does not fall below a level acceptable to qualified members of the profession or the particular discipline.
- Another desirable attribute is a relatively low faculty-to-student ratio; less than 15 to 1 is a good benchmark.
- A third consideration is the number of permanent faculty. A school or department with a large number of adjunct or visiting instructors may be of uneven quality. It also can mean less available time for advising and instruction from such teachers. Too many part-time instructors can reflect an underfunded department with fewer resources for grants and fellowships and research opportunities, since instructors are paid less and do not normally qualify for the benefits that full-time professors receive.

Assess the full-time faculty by examining their credentials as listed in the university's catalogue and on its website. What degrees do they have, and where did they earn them? The dictum "publish or perish" still holds sway within the university world, and the teachers and scholars who rise to the top of the academic ladder are those who have written one or more definitive works in their field. You can easily check out the publications of the people in the programs you are considering. You should ask how many faculty at a certain school garner fellowships from foundations or the government for their research and writing.

Usually institutions boast of the presence on their campus of star professors, but a key question always is, Will Professor So-and-So be on campus while I am there, and will he or she be available to me? Regarding rankings of academic graduate programs, you may find the prominent guides less than helpful. A better measure of a particular department within a university is provided by the professional organization that governs the discipline, for example, the American Psychological Association, the American Political Science Association, or the Modern Language Association.

THE MAJOR PROFESSIONAL DEGREE PROGRAMS

Architecture and design	Law
Business management	Library science
Clinical counseling	Medicine
Dentistry	Nursing
Divinity	Optometry
Education	Pharmacy
Engineering	Psychiatry
Computer science and	Public administration
technology	Public health
Environmental science	Public policy
Forestry	Social work
Journalism and communications	Veterinary medicine

Note. Within each of these fields there are numerous specialties that lead to many different careers.

The Role of the Internship

Some graduate programs mix academic work with internships. Most professional graduate programs require their students to serve an internship as part of their training. This is especially true in the fields of education, social work, psychology, medicine, health care, and applied fields of business management. The graduate student can experience the day-to-day nature of the career he or she is considering and better determine what specific direction he or she wishes to pursue within the field. Many students appreciate the opportunity to mix the theory they are studying with the practical internship experience. Business schools like Babson College, for example, offer students the chance to spend a semester in Europe, Latin America, or Asia working in a multinational corporation.

Program Content

In addition to demanding general academic quality of any program, you ought to identify your interests in terms of more specific academic considerations, particularly the program content. For example, if you are interested in attending law school, do you want to attend one using the case method of study, as most do, or are you of a more academic bent, preferring assigned readings in law strictly from textbooks, which deal with theory and legal history? This same question can be addressed to MBA candidates, who have a similar option. Some programs are heavily weighted toward the study of cases that present genuine management problems to be solved, while others ask you to master the principles of specific subjects, such as portfolio management, systems analysis, information technology, and accounting and finance. Some graduate programs combine these two approaches.

Facilities

Facilities are an important component of any graduate school program. The important factors for learning include the library, the laboratories, the computer center, a hospital affiliation, journal affiliations, the bookstores, lecture halls, classrooms, and the audiovisual center. If you are concerned about access for people with disabilities, check with the dean's office to be certain the school meets all requirements. If you have or are planning a family, you will want to know about less expensive family housing on campus, day care and school choices, and possibly study or work opportunities for your partner. You must think about and list what you will need or desire for your graduate work to be successful, and make sure it is available at the schools to which you apply.

Endowment, Endowment, Endowment

The better graduate schools are well endowed or well supported by state and federal funding. Endowment is the engine that drives the top programs, since it takes substantial financial funding to support first-class faculty, facilities, financial aid, and research. You have a right to expect that any program you might consider is not a shoe-string operation. It is no coincidence that the most prestigious graduate schools have the largest endowments and funding from public sources. This means that capital is available for all purposes and for any talented students who can qualify for admission. Some of the richest institutions are Harvard, with an endowment over $15 billion; the University of Texas system, with over $9 billion; Yale, with more than $8 billion; Princeton, with over $7 billion; Stanford University, with over $7 billion; and Emory University, the University of California, and the Massachusetts Institute of Technology, each of which has more than $5 billion.

Many universities with fewer resources have opted to focus on building and maintaining outstanding graduate programs in a limited number of fields. You need to ascertain which departments have special standing within the university's structure. Billions of dollars for research and faculty support are allocated annually by the federal government. If you are considering a specific discipline that is dependent for its excellence on research and facilities, as is the case in the sciences, technology, and medicine, learn which institutions receive significant amounts of this funding. For example, Johns Hopkins University garnered $754 million in federal support last year; Stanford, $343 million; the University of Washington, $338 million; the University of Michigan $312 million; MIT, $311 million; the University of California, San Diego, $263 million; and Harvard, $253 million.

Living or Working Conditions

If you plan to live on campus, you need to know what the living arrangements are and where you will take your meals, so you should list now what you consider desirable. If you plan not to live in university housing, you must decide how long a commute you are willing to make. Married candidates may have another set of requirements that can be better met at some institutions than others; or certain locations may afford better and more affordable housing than others. Do you hope to use the athletic and recreational facilities? What kind of social life appeals to you? Most institutions have cultural activities, but they vary from campus to campus. How active a role, if any, does the administration play in supporting social activities for its graduate students?

Will you need to earn money while studying for your degree? If so, you will need to find out what opportunities for employment are available and what the rates of pay are. Bear in mind that graduate school demands so much of your time that you probably will not be able to carry a very heavy workload.

Placement and Counseling Services

Programs compete for applicants on the grounds of their record for attracting job interviewers and placing their graduates in high-paying positions. The availability of professional counseling staff can make a difference in the success of your studies and in helping you establish a career direction. By providing access to internships, paid summer positions, and contacts with people in your field, a graduate school can act as pre-employment agency. You should ask the admissions office at any school under consideration for a listing of the companies that recruit on campus and the positions graduates have acquired.

Other Important Characteristics

There are also intangibles some applicants hope to find in a good program, such as the inspiration of good teachers or the thrill of participating in original research in an exciting new field. Some seek to study with a particular professor, who specializes in a field they want to pursue professionally. Others say they hope to escape the paper chase after grades and just enjoy doing quality graduate work. There are those who are concerned about the average age of the students in the school or department, because they are on either the lower end or the upper end of the range. Few wish to be the youngest or the oldest in a close learning and social community.

Every potential candidate for advanced studies we have ever counseled has had quite individual hopes for a graduate experience. You need to examine yours and see if they can be realized in light of what you learn about graduate schools and your qualifications for studying in them.

WHAT ARE THE KEY CHARACTERISTICS
YOU HOPE TO FIND IN A GRADUATE SCHOOL?

Two answers from our files:

I am looking first for a strong MBA program that will give me the training I need for a career in business where I can be independent and earn a good income. At 25, with two years of unique experience in the Peace Corps, I am prepared to enroll anywhere in the country that has a low faculty-student ratio, professors who have lots of business experience themselves, and a school with a solid placement record based on interviews by top banks and consulting firms. I have a strong computer background and expect sophisticated information technology courses as well as accounting.

This young man was directed toward a number of business schools that met his requirements. He finally chose the University of Michigan for a combination of these factors. His training for the Peace Corps made him an appealing candidate because of his proven ability to contend successfully with the challenges and stresses of his assignment in an underdeveloped country where English was not spoken.

I want a master's degree in education from a university that has an extensive curriculum in special education. I have taught in a private school that caters to students with learning disabilities

for three years, and realize that I need and want broader profes-
sional training. The graduate program should have sufficient
depth in its courses to qualify me eventually to run a school for
the disabled or a state department of education in this field. I
expect the program to offer internships and to allow me to take
one or two courses in psychotherapy in its medical school.

This young woman enrolled in the Graduate School of Education at Harvard for a two-year master's degree. Her research led her there because of the opportunity to study with several specialists in learning disabilities, intern at a nearby elementary school that worked with special needs youngsters, and to take classes in the graduate psychology department.

Questions 3–7 of the Graduate School Questionnaire

Questions 3–7 require less comment, but nevertheless are of great importance to you. Question 3 asks you to identify graduate programs in which you have an interest. As you learn more and read on, you should evaluate these choices for their appropriateness. Can you get accepted? Are the programs right for your objectives and your personal tastes? Discussion with a counselor or graduate school admissions representative will help you reach detailed answers to these questions.

Question 4 is a practical question about the graduate school size and location you prefer. Yale Law School is small and intimate, and so are many programs in academic subjects. Those who spent their undergraduate years in large universities often like to do their graduate studies in smaller, more personalized departments. Harvard's and Berkeley's law schools are very big, and many students like the stimulation of a large university, with its many departments and the opportunity to meet many diverse people.

As for the most desirable location, this depends on your personal situation or tastes. A part-time MBA or law or master's program must be located near the student's job. A doctor who plans to practice in the

South might prefer to study at Vanderbilt, Duke, or Emory rather than at a West Coast or midwestern university. Such a choice could have the advantage of getting the graduate an internship and residency training in the region where he or she hopes to set up practice eventually.

Question 5 concerns financial aid, to which we devote the ninth step in this book.

Question 6 is related to Question 5. Do you want to work or study full- or part-time? Many of the top professional schools do not accept or encourage working students. If this is the only way you can afford to attend graduate school or if you have a good position you do not want to leave, you need to seek out schools that will allow you to work toward a degree on a part-time basis.

Question 7 asks you to chart your extracurricular activities during college and afterwards. You will use this record of your talents, energies, and interests later when you are completing applications. The importance of each aspect of this record will vary according to the nature of your intended graduate work. A professional graduate school in law, business, education, or medicine will give greater attention and weight in the decision process to a successful athlete, campus politician, newspaper editor, debater, or community service organizer than will a doctorate program where many of these skills and interests play much less of a role in a successful career.

You will find that most graduate schools give special attention to candidates who have taken time from their studies or their job to volunteer in their community. This is seen as a strong indicator of a future professional who becomes a leader in service organizations on a regional or national level. More graduate programs than ever ask applicants to describe any volunteer work they have been engaged in and what their work contributed to helping others.

Many admissions deans look for the "persistence factor" in a candidate's extracurricular record, for what is often referred to as stick-to-itiveness. Being on the college newspaper or debate team or an athletic team for four years is in itself impressive evidence that you are not a quitter or floater and will most likely follow through on your commitment to graduate work. The same principle holds true for the college graduate who has held a job in one company or field for three or more years. Too many people flit from one position to another with little or no semblance of a rational game plan in mind. This is a category of applicants that usually worries admissions committees.

Assessing Yourself: Questions 8 and 9

Your Academic Record

In assessing their own academic records, many people tend to underestimate or overestimate their capabilities. Just being aware of your own tendency in this regard can be helpful in guarding against boastfulness or false modesty. The record is there. Since it represents four or more years of your performance, it tells a story—if you are prepared to listen to it. It is hard to argue against it with a graduate admissions committee, but there are a few recognized extenuating circumstances, including illness or distress over a family problem or a difficult transition to college studies.

CARL: *an international student seeking an opportunity to prove himself*

Carl was determined to get an MBA from a good university, but first he had to take responsibility for his poor undergraduate performance.

Carl was faced with the challenge of applying to business schools as an international student who had fared poorly in his undergraduate years at Tufts University. The combination of adjusting to a new culture and language, an entirely different style and structure of education, and the personal freedom he was suddenly handed had proved difficult for him. Though these circumstances can be understood, he needed to convince graduate school admissions committees that he could hold his own in a competitive program.

At Tufts, Carl had majored in economics, a discipline he enjoyed greatly. A review of his transcript indicated that he had done poorly in several of the introductory courses and failed introductory calculus his first year. He had received mostly C grades in the majority of his other courses. His GPA to this point in his academic career was a lowly 2.45. Not until his senior year did Carl wake up to the reality of his situation. Realigning his focus and priorities, he achieved all B and B+ grades for his final year.

When Carl contacted us in the late fall of his senior year, we counseled him to begin an intensive job search in the financial field, which was his eventual professional goal, and not to apply to any graduate programs. Our reasoning was this: He needed to finish his last year with a stronger performance, and he had to gain job experience to prove he was mature enough to meet the rigors of an MBA program. Further, he would be best served by preparing for the Graduate Management Aptitude Test (GMAT) after he graduated and had more time to study. The priorities for his senior year were to work hard to improve his grades and to initiate the job search.

His transcript revealed a pattern of strong performance in 10 elective courses in international relations and history. Carl's international background had created his strong interest and knowledge in this field. We suggested that he focus on business schools that had a strong emphasis in international business and economics, and highlight his multinational and language background. Another recommendation was to consider business schools on the West Coast. There he would experience another region of the United States and the Pacific Rim economy, which was a major interest for his professional future.

By concentrating on his studies, Carl did meet his objective of a 3.4 average for his final year at Tufts. He also took advantage of the recruiting season and used all the connections he had to secure his first professional employment. Once working in New York City, he studied assiduously for the GMAT and scored 620. On the basis of his three years of work experience; his improved academic record; positive employer recommendations; and his excellent personal statements regarding his background, what he hoped to achieve in his career, and what he could add to the school community, Carl was accepted to his top two choices, the University of Southern California and Pepperdine University.

Here is how Carl presented himself to the admissions committees in two statements:

The question: How will your work and extracurricular background contribute to your own learning in the program and to the learning experiences of your classmates? What do you feel you would contribute to the small-group emphasis and interactive learning environment of this program? What distinguishing characteristics differentiate you from other applicants to this program?

The answer: My family comes from very different parts of the world with very distinct cultural views and ideologies. My father was born in Peru and mother in Germany. When she was 15 years of age, my mother's family moved from Germany to Chile. My father became a successful businessman, creating his own shipping company. My parents met during the World Cup soccer competition that was being held in Chile at the time and were married two years later.

In 1970 my family had to leave Lima, Peru, where they were living and working, because of the serious political upheaval taking place. They settled in Paris where my father had friends and business associates. There they would live for the next nine years, during which time my older sister and I were born. Four years later we moved to Madrid permanently.

After growing up for the first four years of my life in France, I spent the next ten formative years in Madrid. At the age of fourteen I enrolled in boarding school in Switzerland for two academic years. I then returned to Madrid to complete my high school studies to understand my adopted home country more fully and to prepare to study in the United States. After much investigation of strong studies in economics and international topics, I applied and was accepted into Tufts University.

At both my Swiss International school and Spanish school, I prepared for the International Baccalaureate. In this curriculum I concentrated on languages, history, and mathematics and economics. My language studies were in French, Spanish, and English. I was also encouraged, fortunately, by my parents to travel as widely as possible while growing up. I have been to eighteen countries, for extended periods of time, all over Europe, Latin America, and southeastern Asia.

My experience at work has been internationally oriented in that I am a salesman of financial products to Latin American and Spanish clients. On average, I speak in Spanish to clients 70% of my working time. Quite a few of the products that I purchase and sell for my clients are based in foreign markets, making it a necessity to be current on the political as well as economic situation in these markets. It is for these reasons that I am aware of and affected by international events on a daily basis.

Working in teams of ten people, I have an intimate understanding of small group dynamics and requirements. I believe I can provide both leadership and support to any venture started by a group I work with. I can provide my insights and my ability to understand people's behavior and motives, which is the result both of my work experience and life amongst a number of cultures. The investment management business follows continuously the changing economic environments, and I have learned to maintain an open mind to understand and utilize these changes advantageously.

Having lived, studied, and worked in so many different countries of contrasting cultures, I wish to continue to have contact with multiple nationalities with all their similarities and differences to one another. I believe I will be able to use my skills to the utmost advantage in the global world that now determines success or failure in all kinds of business enterprises.

I would like to work for an international company in the US for a few years after receiving my MBA training. My ultimate goal is to follow in my father's footsteps by becoming an entrepreneur in a field where I can use my knowledge of financial markets and languages. I hope to create a successful international company in countries such as Peru or Spain or other emerging nations that will provide stability and wealth for the local population. The nature of this enterprise will likely be in international finance, manufacturing, or import-export activity.

The question: What do you consider your greatest achievement to date and how does it indicate your promise as a student in our program?

The answer: I consider my success at Bear, Stearns & Company to be one of my most important achievements. Because I had performed poorly in college for the first three years of my studies, I found it hard to get a position in business that would interest me. I was turned down by the companies I interviewed with because of my lack of work experience during college and my grades. I realized then that to get to any of the major companies I wanted to work in I would have to begin on a different course of action. I therefore chose a job in a small, privately held money management firm. The responsibilities would not include direct contact with clients or the securities markets as a trader, but I believed it was a beginning for me to prove myself.

This gamble paid off, because I gained valuable experience with studying the many different financial instruments in play and increased my ability and confidence to perform under very pressured circumstances. I used the tools and knowledge I had learned during this time to find a position that better matched my interests. I learned of an opening at Bear, Stearns and applied immediately.

Achieving this goal proved to be a personal redemption for my mistakes during my early college years, a time of considerable adjustment from Spain and its more restrictive environment to the wide-open world of an American university. I learned a major lesson from this experience, which is if I wanted something that seemed to be out of my reach, with the vision to adjust my sights and take another path and work very hard to prove myself, I could attain my original goal. I also learned that it is all right to make mistakes if I took responsibility for them and figured out what my new course of action had to be. At Bear, Stearns I have learned how to excel in an extremely competitive environment and to perform with the determination and exhilaration that comes with working at my best.

My plan is to continue to work in a leading financial company like Bear, Stearns after graduate training. Once I have gained experience at a high-level management position for five to ten years, I would like to start my own venture in the international arena. Here I will use in the most positive way the advantages I have been given all my life, and not look back on what I failed to accomplish in the beginning of my undergraduate education.

An Honest Self-Portrait

Question 9 asks you to be autobiographical. We cannot tell you what to write, except to recommend that you produce an honest self-portrait, in an effort to see yourself, and then analyze how a committee of strangers, standing in judgment, is likely to react to this portrait. This is what one graduate of UCLA wrote before applying for a master's degree in economics in order to become an economist in the banking field:

> Because my father is an executive with an international oil company, I have lived in Bolivia and in the Middle East. I am very aware of the importance of an international perspective in today's business world. The need among the poor countries for management and fiscal expertise is crucial if they are to develop self-sufficiency. I would like to obtain the expertise in international banking and econometrics necessary for working as a consultant in either the private or public sector to second and third world countries.

This straightforward, factual statement, later developed for use on graduate applications, quickly told an admissions committee that this is someone with an unusual background that has shaped his desire to go into international banking. He has picked a goal that is realistic, given his personal experience. His undergraduate major in history and minor in international studies would serve him well in his intended studies and career. His sensitivity to the social problems of poor countries is reassuring because it is unsentimental and linked to the training he hopes to attain in graduate school.

This candidate was accepted into the master's programs in international economics at Stanford University and the University of Chicago.

The last question of the Graduate School Questionnaire asks for your résumé, which will provide an outline of your background, education, interests, work experience, and goals for your future. Pulling all this information together is an important and time-consuming process, so start early.

Pitfalls in Identifying Yourself

Knowing yourself is the first step toward a graduate degree. But, as we are often asked, how do we know ourselves? How do we develop honest self-scrutiny? There are three factors that reduce the accuracy of self-vision: revealing too much, overvaluing yourself, and being too modest.

Revealing Too Much: Don't dwell too much on the negative aspects of your life—problems with your parents, siblings, teachers, girl- or boyfriend, authorities, roommates, or even your health. Identifying yourself is not an exercise in self-analysis, which could imply that you would be unable to function in a demanding environment. In graduate school, you are going to be the same person you are now. Dwelling on the dark side puts you in a handicapped position, because educators do not welcome a student who may be dysfunctional in a highly intense environment.

Let's say your father wants you to be an engineer or business entrepreneur, but you want to teach English. How will it help you get accepted into a Ph.D. program if you talk with the faculty or admissions officers about this family conflict, which has nothing to do with how well you are going to grasp the subtleties of nineteenth-century literature? Common sense should tell you that your identity as a student is really unrelated to your father's overbearing desire. The attitude you have to assume internally is, "My passion is literature and writing, not science and math. I would make a terrible engineer, so I am just going to move forward and hope my father will support my wishes."

One young woman who returned to us for graduate school counseling unknowingly revealed in her questionnaire her internal conflict. Since we had advised her during her undergraduate search for the right college, we had a strong sense of her personality and her intellectual strengths. She was a superb writer and a voracious reader. Her facility with words and creative expression had much to do with her undergraduate acceptance to Harvard University. Now she expressed a desire to enroll in an MBA program, but her self-assessment and reasons for wanting to move in this direction did not ring true. A long conference in our office helped her see the contradiction in what she was saying and what she was feeling. Behind the desire to get an MBA degree lay the wish to please her parents, who were highly successful business entrepreneurs. Once it became clear to her that she did not have to take this direction, she focused on graduate education in communications and journalism, fields in which her innate talents and personality would thrive.

Overestimating Your Abilities: Being overly generous with yourself or kidding yourself can be another danger. In particular areas you may have good skills but not necessarily the very best. Overconfidence can lead you down stray alleys where you will not attain your goal. Be realistic and understand what excellence is and how you measure up. You can then proceed to work on your skills and consider the appropriate graduate training.

Watch out for the tendency to try to get something for nothing—in this case an unearned esteem. This problem can appear in particular among the offspring of highly successful people who are well known in the world. Their thought processes sometimes go like this: "My mother is one of the top officials in the state; I must have her potential, therefore I am a natural politician, and she can help me get ahead."

So why did this young woman lose the election to a class office in college? In contrast to the young man who is fighting his father's desire that he study in a field that does not suit him, this self-designated "born politician" is blindly pursuing an objective that may be wrong for her in an effort to gain the same stature as her mother. Too often we hear aspiring graduate students state that their parents or close relatives are well connected to certain universities and this will ensure their acceptance. We can tell you from experience that it is rare for an unqualified candidate to be accepted into a top graduate school as a result of a connection.

It really is not difficult to adjust to a more constructive self-image when you reject an inflated one. Just say once to yourself, "What am I really? What are my virtues?" You will find it unnecessary to imagine applause. This realization comes to all those considering a graduate education—at any age. They learn that with graduate work, there is no way to fool professors. Accepting yourself is one appropriate means of identifying yourself.

Underestimating Your Abilities: The obverse of being overly generous with yourself is hiding your light under a bushel. Undue modesty may not necessarily keep you out of a graduate program you want, but it can cause you to aim too low or to fail to catch the attention of the admissions committees in a large and competitive applicant pool. You may run the risk of underestimating your capabilities and not realize your potential. The "Aw shucks, I'm not bad at math" attitude, when expressed by the person who has always had straight As, is not the winning statement he or she thinks it is. In fact, it is annoying and often perceived as manipulative. We have read too many initial drafts of graduate applications in which the undervaluation of skills or success in employment would lead to rejection from an admissions committee. Failure to put your best foot forward reduces the possibility of competing at your own level.

WHEN MODESTY IS NO VIRTUE

A local newspaper report about a brilliant boy, who won a science prize in a suburban high school for experiments on air quality in the city, caught the attention of a Princeton alumnus, who interviewed candidates each year for the admissions committee. He contacted the student and asked him where he was planning to go to college. The young man named a local institution with an adequate environmental studies program. He had never thought of attending Princeton or any other selective college. His family being of modest means, he thought he could not afford such institutions, and thus his plan was to live at home and commute to school to save money.

Persuaded by the alumnus to apply to Princeton and to complete the financial aid application, he was admitted, won a full scholarship, and after a highly successful academic performance, was admitted to MIT for graduate studies in environmental sciences. It is highly unlikely that

(continued)

he could have gone on to MIT from the institution he had originally planned to attend, because of its limited curriculum and less distinguished faculty.

The moral to this story, directed especially to high school students, their parents, and their counselors, is: Aim as high as you can if you have a gift for science or engineering. Underestimating your potential and opportunities early on can be embittering in the long run, as you may find yourself limited in your career because of your educational background. Modesty in such cases amounts to selling yourself and your future short.

In other words, go for the gold!

Having honestly identified yourself, knowing what you are capable of and interested in, you are in a good position to explore the choices for graduate school and recognize those places where you will fit well. You have avoided the three pitfalls of revealing too much, overvaluing yourself, and underestimating yourself. In this process, you should discover what really interests you about graduate study. Your honest appraisal can reveal a self different from the one you thought you knew, which will benefit you greatly in finding the right graduate education. You will prepare better personal statements on the applications and interview in a much more genuine and helpful manner, increasing your odds for being admitted.

Step One Checklist

- Identify yourself as a potential graduate student by filling out the questionnaire.

- Do not think of identifying yourself as "finding yourself"; the graduate school application process is not therapy. View the process as one of self-disclosure and awareness.

- Be sure to think through your goals and how they relate to your experience and capabilities.

- Describe the characteristics you would like to find in a graduate program. Consider academic quality, program content, internships, endowment, facilities, living and working conditions, placement and counseling services, location, costs, and financial aid.

- Assess your academic record as honestly as you can. Beware of overestimating or underestimating yourself.

- Accent the positive and eliminate the negative side of your character as you identify yourself, and carry this spirit into your applications and interviews.

STEP TWO

Understand Graduate Education and Admissions

The Character of Graduate Education

Graduate education is a substantially different experience from undergraduate training. College does not necessarily prepare the average qualified candidate for graduate school. You undoubtedly understand that the work will be tougher, and this is true, but there is more to the difference. You may be startled by the psychological atmosphere of advanced study, a charged excitement aroused by the intensity of your fellow students and top-flight faculty who mean business.

In college, the professors must share their students with the larger campus community, and all the exciting offerings of athletics, extracurricular activities, fraternities, homecoming, community service, socializing, and off-campus studies. Professors understand the positive influence these activities play in the development of young men and women, many of whom are away from the comforts of home. In graduate school, though there may be some intramural sports, publications, and the family concerns of married students, your chief activity will be your studies, pure and simple. College faculty encourage most undergraduates to explore a wide range of intellectual subjects to gain a broad understanding of the human condition and the physical world we live in. In contrast, your graduate faculty will take it for granted that you have reached a point at which you are ready to dedicate your learning to a specific field of study in preparation for a professional career.

Graduate students who have some doubts about their chosen field of study have a difficult time maintaining focus and effort, and may drop out early. Many students complete their work and get their degree without enthusiasm and true commitment, and therefore do not benefit sufficiently from their education. Graduate faculties almost always notice a less than full effort, which does not inspire them to endorse the student for a job in their field. Teachers and graduate programs want to enhance their own reputation and ensure the quality of their field by introducing to it highly motivated, enthusiastic, well-educated graduates.

The amount of time you are expected to spend on your studies may make you reel at first. Sometimes a warning from a teacher is necessary to jolt a student into realizing the effort required to complete a top graduate program. A highly successful journalist and author tells the story of his own experience at the Graduate School of Journalism at Columbia University. The faculty expect their students to put in an 8- to 10-hour day, five days a week, on their school work, just as they would if they were employees of a newspaper, a magazine, or television station. This aspiring journalist once showed up late for a class at about noon. When asked for an excuse, he replied honestly, "Hangover. I was in Greenwich Village until four this morning." He was told that he could get away with that reply just once at Columbia and probably never could do so at a job in the media. An experienced journalist-turned-professor told him, "There are many capable people lined up waiting to take your job, and every editor or producer knows whom he could hire to replace you tomorrow." With that reality check, the myth of the successful, free-living journalist evaporated swiftly.

Graduate students are expected to be more self-directed in their learning. Whatever the required curricula set by the faculty, it is assumed that students will delve further into the topic at hand with extensive reading and research. Students are expected to do their own critical analysis of a topic, as opposed to relying on the instructor to provide the issues and answers. There is usually a closer, often collegial relationship between the teacher and the student, especially in advanced studies in academic disciplines. For a graduate professor, one of the major rewards of teaching students the subject that has occupied his or her life is working with people who are as passionately devoted to the subject as the professor is. Acting as a mentor for committed, hardworking, and intelligent students helps a professor as well. The hope is that new ways of looking at old problems and original research will eventually lead to new discoveries.

Another major difference in a graduate school environment is that you will spend significantly more time alone in your studies, because of the amount of reading, research, and writing required. While you narrow the focus of your studies to one discipline, you must develop a deeper understanding and comprehensive grasp of the work. At the same time, the faculty encourages collaborative learning. Sharing ideas and working together to find solutions to a particular problem is a natural part of graduate studies. In the classroom, do not expect to sit in the back and let other students or the instructor manage the discussion. Whether you are answering Socratic questions in a law school lecture hall or sitting around an English literature seminar table, you, the graduate student, are expected to be a well-prepared contributor.

The Differences between Academic Graduate Programs and Professional Graduate Programs

The goal for learning differs between the traditional academic graduate program and professional school training. The ultimate purpose of an academic graduate program is the discovery of new knowledge and ways of thinking about issues. There is little concern for a final goal or destination. A professional school has a more focused goal of preparing future professionals to excel in their careers by exposing them to theoretical models and applied knowledge and skills. The faculty's attitude is that they know what you need to learn and how best to learn it. The curriculum is more performance based, dedicated to meeting certain objectives. It is also more structured, and the case study method is used in a majority of business and law schools. Team projects and collaboration in preparing class assignments are encouraged more in the professional programs, since this reflects the way professionals operate in their jobs. In counseling potential graduate students over the years, we have emphasized the difference in the personality and learning style between those who will enjoy and prosper in either of the two models of graduate education. You must determine through intensive exploration which type of studies will be a better match for you.

STUDENT TO STUDENT

An important part of your exploration to find the right graduate education for yourself is talking with students who are presently studying in a field you are considering. These are some questions to ask them:

1. If you were back in college, what would you now know to do to prepare for graduate school?
2. How did you decide on the type of graduate program you are enrolled in?
3. What resources did you use to find your program?
4. Would you opt for the same program now? If not, why not?
5. What aspects of your graduate studies have turned out to be most different from your expectations?
6. What was the most difficult thing about the admissions process?
7. What factors in your acceptance were the most influential for you?
8. How would you advise someone considering graduate school to determine the right program?
9. Would you encourage anyone to consider your graduate school? If yes, why? If not, why?
10. Did you have an interview as part of your application process? Is this a good idea? Did it help your chances?
11. Will you share your GPA and test scores to help me get a reality check on the credentials necessary for acceptance?
12. How did you prepare for the admissions tests? What would you advise me on this count?
13. Who does well in your discipline and in your particular program?
14. Where do people go who graduate from your program?
15. Were you sufficiently counseled on job opportunities in your department or school?

Don't Fight the System

When applying to graduate school, play within the rules established by the institutions. Sometimes applicants ask us how they can skirt the required entrance tests or prerequisite foundation courses or letters of recommendation. In every instance, this is the sign of a candidate not prepared or positioned to apply effectively. We advise you to present your case for admission in the best possible way by carefully doing what an institution asks of you. After you have done everything by the book, think of enhancements to your application that will make you stand out above the competitors with roughly similar profiles.

Graduate admissions procedures are more sophisticated and complicated than undergraduate admissions. The professional school admissions committees are full-time professionals, trained to identify top candidates who show the strongest evidence of succeeding in their school's academic program and eventually in the professional world. They have established criteria in mind as they review applications. This is where the benefits of internships, paid work, volunteer activities, and an impressive résumé and personal essays come into play. The admissions professionals know what they are looking for and how to separate an honest and focused presentation from a phony one.

Admission into master's and doctoral academic programs is handled differently. Typically, an assistant or associate dean is responsible for recruiting qualified candidates and overseeing the application process. The individual departments have the most say in who should be admitted based on criteria they set for their discipline. The faculty is looking for students with the intellectual interest and aptitude for advanced study in their field. They weigh heavily the undergraduate academic performance of the candidate in their subject and scores on the Graduate Record Exam and the GRE Subject Tests. They also give a good deal of importance to undergraduate faculty recommendations that address the candidate's abilities and commitment to the discipline, and they factor in the reputation of their department. The graduate faculties also consider the personality match between the candidate and the departmental personnel. Is this a student who will mix well with the small faculty and the present students we are training? Will the student respond to our direction as we prepare him or her for advanced levels of research and writing? Will he or she make a good instructor for undergraduates in introductory courses or be effective in a laboratory setting? Has he or she identified a particular professor to work with on research projects, and is this professor interested? You may be a qualified candidate for an individual graduate program but be denied admission because of one or more of these factors.

You can work within the admissions system successfully by letting it work for you. Remember that graduate admissions committees

- Are more merit based than undergraduate admissions committees are.
- Scrutinize what you say about your hopes, passions, desires, and style of life and assess how these fit your choice of graduate work.
- Look for strong recommendations from your undergraduate faculty since graduate programs sometimes admit applicants largely on the basis of enthusiastic faculty opinion about your work and intelligence.
- Pore over your college transcript to determine how rigorous and appropriate your academic courses were as a preparation for graduate study.
- Read your applications, personal statements, essays, and résumé very closely, and evaluate your interview performance to establish your talent for and commitment to graduate studies.
- Pay great attention to intern and work experience as indicators of commitment to their program and eventual professional success.
- Allocate limited research and teaching assistantships and funding to a very small number of highly focused and talented individuals.

Whither the Doctoral Student

Several trends in recent years have created a confusing and challenging career track for graduates with doctorates in the academic disciplines today. With no ceiling on retirement age now, many tenured professors continue to teach and carry on research into their seventies. Virtually all universities have ceased to enlarge their traditional faculties in order to keep the faculty budget from growing. This results in fewer openings for young faculty to land a job, let alone be offered a tenure-track position. Yet 300,000 people sat for the GRE in the academic year 2000–01, which is an indicator of the high level of interest in pursuing graduate work in an academic discipline.

As an excess of newly minted Ph.D.s attempt to enter the marketplace each year, universities are barely hiring full-time teachers or are taking advantage of part-time or adjunct instructors who are not paid as well and usually do not qualify for the generous benefits given to the regular faculty. Recent studies have shown that two-thirds of the students working for an average six to seven years to attain their Ph.D. want to become full-time, tenure-track faculty members, despite the fact that fewer than half of them will ever reach their goal. There are many tales of frustrated young scholars who have to accept teaching positions at colleges and universities of average or worse repute where the students can be described at best as reluctant learners.

Such organizations as the Woodrow Wilson National Fellowship Foundation have developed programs to assist new Ph.D.s in learning of career opportunities outside academe. Graduate school administrators and teachers at virtually all the leading universities acknowledge that they do not provide counseling on opportunities in other professions in which new Ph.D.s can make use of their knowledge and intellectual skills. We advise prospective doctoral students to be aware of the academic job prospects in your discipline to determine if you are still willing to make such a major commitment. We also encourage you to explore alternative professional outlets that will enable you to use your training. There are many successful transitions from the academic world to the business and nonprofit spheres.

THE NATURE OF A GRADUATE BUSINESS SCHOOL

The MBA is a relatively versatile degree. Some students have a strong focus on finance and are ambitious to work in investment banking; others aspire to work in consulting or general management. Most students work for an MBA because they believe it will enhance their career

(continued)

prospects. In this sense, it is quite different from an undergraduate degree, which is more typically intended to be life broadening.

Most MBA programs, at least those of the first rank, are quite intense in terms of education, social interactions, and career counseling. Since most programs do at least some version of cold calling in the classroom and presentations are common, the program is not for the shy and retiring. Strong analytical skills are also required. Although students come to the MBA from a range of majors, a background in economics and math training is also important.

There are substantial differences across the large spectrum of business schools, but among the top twenty or so, this is more a matter of style and focus than of quality. Rankings vary quite a bit from year to year, and the difference between number one and number fifteen is a matter of a few percentage points on subjective scales. More important differences derive from where the students end up going for jobs: the midwestern schools, for example, send more of their grads to manufacturing than any of the schools on the two coasts (though fewer grads from any of the programs go into manufacturing anymore). West Coast schools still have an edge for technology, while the East Coast dominates finance. Whenever possible, prospective students should visit the classrooms, because style differences are hard to capture without a visit.

Note. These comments were shared with us by Sharon Oster, professor of management and entrepreneurship at Yale School of Management.

How Prestigious Graduate Programs Can Shape Your Future

The prestige of well-respected institutions of higher learning derives from the success of their graduates over succeeding generations. For this reason, corporate recruiters tend to do most of their interviews at the top graduate business schools, law firms and judicial agencies at the top law schools, hospitals seeking residents and interns at the top medical schools, universities to fill teaching and research positions at the top graduate departments, technical companies at the top engineering and science schools, and so on. In order not to overlook excellent students, they turn to the very best regional schools in their area, with which they tend to have long-term relationships and a record of success with those graduates they have hired. Those responsible for recruiting future employees and partners in their work recognize the wisdom of hiring an outstanding performer from a strong, but not necessarily top twenty graduate school, over an average performer at a more prestigious institution.

If you have the luxury of choosing among graduate schools of more or less prestige, enroll in the more prestigious for the sake of your career. Do not make such excuses as "I don't want to be so far from home," "I couldn't live in the city/small town/cold climate/etc. where the better school is located," "I don't want to change my lifestyle and give up my friends," "I don't want the additional debt burden." On the other hand, if after serious consideration you are uncomfortable facing the high pressure of strong peer competitors or there are significant mitigating factors, you should obey your instincts or responsibilities and choose a good alternative that meets your needs and holds promise for your future.

UNDERSTAND THAT NO TWO PROGRAMS ARE ALIKE

There is considerable naiveté among prospective applicants about the nature of particular graduate school programs. Admissions committees often reject applicants who have not studied the catalogues of several or more institutions to compare them. Such applicants literally may not know why they are applying to each of the programs. Two top law or business schools can be equally prestigious but distinctly different in their methods of training and their fields of expertise and emphasis. Some MBA programs in the top ranks use the case study method of teaching, while others do not. Some offer training in manufacturing management or international business or entrepreneuership, while others concentrate in finance and accounting or marketing or nonprofit

(continued)

management. The same distinctions will be found among graduate schools in all fields. It is the responsibility of the applicant to discover these differences or emphases and articulate them in his or her presentations to admissions committees. Expressing precisely what appeals to you about a particular graduate program makes your application more persuasive.

Finding Yourself at Any Stage or Age

A wonderful thing about higher education in the United States is its openness. Graduate programs are one of those last frontiers in which anyone at any stage in his or her life can stake out a claim and take up a new life. Too many individuals are hesitant to consider changing their plans for their future or leaving established jobs or careers, because they are not certain they can make a transition that requires further education. Whatever your age and experience, there are unlimited opportunities to return to school to prepare for that transition. Though it will take thought, research, and preparation on your part, further education is eminently possible. Hundreds of universities advertise their graduate programs for prospective students of all ages and backgrounds today. Graduate studies can be carried on either full- or part-time at most institutions, giving anyone with the desire to change careers the opportunity to do so. With many students in their thirties and forties enrolled in academic graduate programs, and 27 the average age of those enrolled in MBA programs, potential applicants of any age should not hesitate to consider an advanced degree if it corresponds with their career interests and ultimate goal.

SUZANNE: *searching for the right future*

Suzanne came to our office at the end of her junior year at Dartmouth College to begin her search for her future career and the type of graduate school training this would entail. A major in art history, a subject she enjoyed immensely, Suzanne had an overall GPA of 3.4

and a 3.6 in her major. She was an inveterate traveler and explorer, and thanks to Dartmouth's flexible off-campus studies plan, she was able to spend one term studying while traveling around the world on the Semester at Sea program. She also spent one term in Florence through Dartmouth's art history program. Though happy with her studies in art history and languages, Suzanne thought that she should develop a career that would enable her to help others in need. She was considering law, international relations, and public health. Over the course of her senior year, we helped her compile lists of major graduate programs in these fields. Suzanne was then to investigate all three fields to determine which was the most appealing to her. We recommended that she talk with professionals in these areas for deeper insight into the nature of the work and what gave them the most satisfaction.

Suzanne made the decision in the middle of her senior year to "feed two birds with one seed" by combining her love of travel with an internship at a hospital in Australia. This would enable her to test her primary interest at this point, the field of public health and medicine. She, like a majority of today's graduating seniors, wanted to take a break from formal studies and have the opportunity to explore new vistas.

Several months into her internship, Suzanne sent us the following note:

> Greetings from Down Under. I am having a wonderful time in Melbourne and have settled in quite nicely. I absolutely love Australia and have met some fantastic people.
>
> I am writing, as promised, in regards to our last meeting to discuss my career plans. I have enjoyed working at the large, private hospital where I have been placed. It has been a very informative and directional experience for me. However, I knew almost from the beginning that the fields of medicine and public health are not for me. Although I was excited about pursuing a career in this field and intended to complete a Master's program in Public Health, I now know that I need to go back to the proverbial drawing board and rethink my future. I am still enjoying working with the people in the hospital and am learning as much as possible.

I do not intend to act upon my newfound thoughts immediately, which I wish to discuss with you on my return. I am simply going to have fun, take from the internship all that I can, and sort it out when I return home at Christmas. It has become clearer to me that I need to be engaged in a more creative and artistically oriented career.

When she returned home, Suzanne met with us to discuss her love of art history and the possible careers available to her. She listed her favorite experiences throughout college: travel with its emphasis on looking at art and architecture, the summer internship in her sophomore year at Christie's in the Old Masters Drawing Department, and assisting one of her art professors. The thread of continuity in what she most enjoyed made it clear in which professional field she belonged. After some research and interviews, Suzanne took a job with a small computer software company that helped museums catalogue and manage their collections. This proved to be an invaluable exposure to the world of professional art and served to confirm her passion for this field. While working, she studied for the GRE so that she would be positioned to apply to a master's or doctoral program in art history a year later.

Although Suzanne had performed at a high level in her studies at Dartmouth, she had not followed the traditional approach of the future doctoral candidate. She had not done any major research with a professor in art history, although she had worked one term as an assistant to a history of art instructor. She had not made early contact with faculty in the top graduate programs. Nevertheless, her GRE results were very strong, a factor that, combined with her academic performance in art history, would certainly help her to convince a graduate admissions committee that she was qualified to cope with the demands of advanced study and research. The issue was whether she could convince a committee of scholars that she was, indeed, committed to an intellectual immersion in the field and would make a contribution to some area of the arts in time.

With some guidance from us, Suzanne refocused her personal résumé to emphasize her long-standing involvement and training in the arts. Many of her experiences that were not related to her goals were eliminated so that the emphasis on art would come into clear focus. Her employment in the software company provided her with unique training in an area of arts administration that would prove invaluable in her future as a collections manager. The unusual breadth of her travels had provided her with exposure to a wide variety of art and architecture styles and traditions that would inform her studies.

The next step was to determine which graduate programs would meet her special interest in architectural art history and, in turn, be interested in her particular strengths. New York University's doctoral program in their Institute of Fine Arts emerged as the most appealing curriculum and environment. Suzanne submitted her application after crafting the following personal statement, which addresses the issues New York University asks an applicant to consider:

The Todaiji Temple and the Golden Pavilion, Japan; the jade Buddha Temple, China; the Hong Kong Pavilion skyline seen from Victoria's Peak; the Caodai Temple, Vietnam; the Imperial Palace and the Taj Mahal, India; the Pyramids, Egypt; the Church of the Nativity, Israel; the Winter Palace and the Church of Spilt Blood, Russia; the Topkapi Palace and the Hagia Sophia, Turkey; the Hassan II Mosque, Morocco; Brunelleschi's Dome, Italy. These are some of the wonders of architecture that have inspired me to pursue graduate studies in architectural art history.

I was afforded the unique opportunity to circumnavigate the globe on the Semester at Sea program. Throughout my travels I consistently found myself awestruck by the dominant architecture in our ports of call. Shortly after spending six months marveling at the structures and edifices of these distinct regions of the world, I began my Dartmouth Foreign Study in Florence, Italy. It was in this magnificent setting of early art treasures I realized my commitment to and my passion for the study of the history of architectural art. The culmination of the architectural achievement is, in my opinion, embodied in Italian Renaissance creations. In its symmetry and its proportions, this work represents an ideal perfection and grandiosity, which I find entrancing and miraculous. It is in this field that I intend to focus my intellectual energies, with the ultimate goal of achieving Doctor of Philosophy training. I would like to develop a thematic study of Italian Renaissance architecture. Since most of the discipline focuses on a single architect or building, I believe there is great potential for a fresh study of the subject.

As an undergraduate at Dartmouth, I earned a Bachelor of Arts degree with an art history concentration. Since declaring my major in my sophomore year, I have pursued a well-rounded education and related experiences in the arts. As an intern in the Old Masters Drawings Department at Christie's Auction House in New York, I gained an intimate view both of the workings of a major auction house and many of the great art treasures of the world. I came to understand in a more refined way the different classifications of major and minor artistic creations and the importance to our civilization of preserving these gifts. As a teacher's assistant in the art history department at Dartmouth, I was able to understand the nature of research and its importance to first class teaching. I discovered that I enjoyed and grew from the work of researching particular topics in great detail, in thinking about the larger themes of art and culture by studying the works of great and lesser artists over the recorded history of mankind.

I am employed currently by a collections management software company where I am able to participate actively in the intersection of art and technology, and therefore use this knowledge as a basis for art historical and academic endeavors. My reason for taking this position was intentional as I understood that information technology would play an increasingly important role in the study and management of all art enterprises, be they collections, curating, research, writing, or teaching.

My undergraduate education and varied experiences to date have driven home to me how deep my love of art and its cultural and aesthetic significance is. I am eager to begin the next phase of my training that will lead me eventually to teaching at the university level and undertaking scholarly research and writing.

The Institute of Fine Arts is the ideal place to study Italian Renaissance Architecture. Professor Smith, with whom I have met recently, has studied and written on topics which are of great interest to me. His work has been influential in my decision to pursue a career in academia, and I would consider it a great privilege to have the opportunity to study with him. The faculty and the resources of the Institute of Fine Arts are invaluable and unparalleled. Moreover, having lived in New York City for over a year now, I recognize the research and study opportunities the great museums and libraries will provide. New York City and the Institute of Fine Arts are, in combination, a superb setting for advancing scholarship and teaching in the field of my dreams.

There are a number of important lessons to be learned from Suzanne's experience. First, she majored in college in the discipline she loved; second, she did well in her studies despite not knowing where she was headed after college; third, she took advantage of unique learning experiences away from her home campus that helped her to define her ultimate goal; fourth, she investigated other careers that appealed to her; fifth, she sought out internships that gave her important learning opportunities and helped her commit to her first love; and last, she did not give up on herself but persevered in seeking the best choice for her future career.

Take Time to Understand What Graduate Education Is All About

Your success in being admitted to a good graduate school that supports your goals and meets your needs will depend on your willingness to take time to learn a good deal about graduate programs, admissions requirements, and procedures. Many intelligent people start a graduate program without having given sufficient thought to the substance of the courses offered and the value of the curriculum and degree to their career goals.

Bright people have little difficulty in gaining admission to good graduate schools. They often apply without much thought, other than that it would be a good idea to have a law degree or an MBA or an

M.S. At the start of graduate studies, it can be pleasant to be back in the academic harness. In time, the candidate comes to realize that though the graduate school is good, it is not an appropriate place to achieve his or her goals.

Trial and error of this sort is expensive—and avoidable, if you ask yourself a few questions:

1. Do I really understand the nature of the program to which I am applying? Have I any real idea of the course content I must master? If so, does it interest me? Will I enjoy it? Will I be willing to give the work my all?
2. Why am I about to undertake graduate work? How does this particular program help me to fulfill my goals? Is this additional education truly necessary?

Finally, there is the admissions problem. You may investigate a program and apply, only to be turned down. Often the rejection occurs because you have not communicated your commitment to the admissions committee or you have chosen the wrong graduate school. This happens to thousands of applicants each year who are admitted to other schools and go on to get their graduate degrees. Getting into the right program for you calls for scrutiny of a number of options, and for sending applications to several, among which there should be at least one that will respond favorably. Remember, it is always possible to make up your deficiencies and build a stronger foundation for new applications by pursuing further study on a selected basis, for example, part-time graduate study.

We wish to assure you that if you are a good student and take the time to learn what graduate education demands of you and which programs will meet your personal goals, you will surely find one that will accept you, and what is more, you will do well there.

AMANDA: *finding a way to doctoral study by travel and internships*

Amanda's journey from college to the right graduate program is a good example of the need to explore, experience, and ask yourself at each step what you enjoy studying and want to accomplish with your life.

Amanda attended Boston University, where she majored in anthropology, a discipline far afield from her original concentration in the School of Communications. In one of those serendipitous experiences common with liberal arts students, Amanda took a cultural anthropology course and a sociology course to fulfill distribution requirements in the fall of her sophomore year. This was the beginning of her passion for the study of other cultures from a sociological and psychological perspective. We encourage all undergraduates to pursue the studies that pique their interest and arouse their intellectual curiosity. Amanda acted on this nascent interest by transferring from the School of Communications into the College of Arts and Sciences at Boston University.

Amanda investigated available opportunities to study on site in India during her junior year, since this part of the world and its immensely diverse populations had become the focus of her interests. With our encouragement, Amanda applied to the School for International Training for a semester-long program in Rajasthan, India. Here she immersed herself in the dynamics of tribal village life. This experience confirmed her commitment to long-term study of certain anthropological issues as a scholar and teacher.

Amanda had an overall GPA of 3.3 because of a solid but not stellar performance in her first two years. In contrast, her average in her anthropology major was 3.8, a clear indication of her commitment to and talent in her chosen field. Like many intellectual students, Amanda had a history of scoring in the average range on standardized testing. Her SAT scores forecast a challenge for her to achieve impressive results on the GRE. How, Amanda asked, could she possibly gain admission to a preeminent doctoral program in anthropology with her credentials?

Amanda met with us again in the fall of her senior year to discuss her options for graduate programs and strategies for applying successfully. The plan we developed included taking advantage of a fellowship for a term of study at the University of India's psychology and sociology department, which had been offered her upon graduation from Boston University. On her return she would study for the GRE and work on her applications to appropriate graduate schools. Her exposure to Indian cultural life and her specific sphere of interest would have to be presented in a critical and analytical fashion to graduate committees in anthropology. Further, a strong showing on the GRE subject test in anthropology would underscore her knowledge of the field.

By the time she formally submitted her applications to graduate programs in anthropology, Amanda's profile included the following elements: She had scored in the 65 percent range in the general parts of the GRE and in the 90 percent range in the anthropology section. She had completed a fascinating educational experience in India, which served to define the particular area of inquiry she was committed to studying. She also now had two additional recommendations from the University of India that reinforced her own belief that she could undertake scholarly studies successfully and contribute original scholarship to the field in time.

Amanda applied to eight research universities scattered throughout the country and was admitted to four of them. The heads of the anthropology departments at several others sent personalized letters expressing their favorable impression but their lack of spaces in such a limited field to accept her. With great delight, Amanda accepted the offer of admission from the University of Chicago.

There are several critical themes, which transcend all fields of study, that the aspiring doctoral student should emphasize:

- First, you must have a deep, abiding love of a particular subject, a desire that borders on obsession to master the principles of the field and then to move on to your own topic of inquiry.
- Second, you must show indications of this passion for the field through course work, level of performance, and hands-on exposure through fieldwork or research projects.
- Third, you must have at least several strong professional supporters in the discipline to confirm your capability to undertake scholarly pursuits and contribute original work.
- Fourth, you must be willing to apply to a broad range of graduate school programs, since the number of places is limited and acceptance is determined by the individual departments.

- Last, you need to focus on the vital role that a thoughtfully crafted personal statement plays in influencing a department's interest by laying out in detail the rationale for and depth of your commitment to the field and the role this training will play in your future.

Here is a portion of Amanda's written presentation in her applications:

The ongoing dialogues concerning cultural theory and transmission, constructions of the self, and cognitive realism versus cognitive universalism, provide us with crucial perspectives from which to pursue and study any social phenomenon. It is within the realm of these discussions that we must struggle to understand what it is that makes us human and, ultimately, how and why we come to find such a variety of behaviors, practices, and ideas, all being expressed under the name of one species.

My interests in the study of anthropology stem from these fundamental issues. In contemplating what I wish to study in the years ahead I have set before me a series of more specific and related questions and a possible approach from which to address them. I am concerned first with why and how people come to feel alienated or at odds with their own culture and what happens when particular cultural propositions are no longer compelling for them. How do they seek to cope with such discontent or rectify the psychological gap between their own outlook on the world and that which defines their particular culture?

I disagree with social theorists who take the power of culture so far that personality no longer becomes an issue in evaluating the relationship between the individual and his culture. I argue that it is possible for human beings to be mismatched with their cultures and the result is not just the obscure case of the psychopathic deviant. Rather, in a more subtle sense, it may be the unfulfilled person who goes through life believing in, and searching for, a different reality in a world filled with other possibilities.

The question then becomes whether this notion of cultural discontent or psychological disparity is universally experienced or if it is an outgrowth of Western society itself. In what types of societies should we expect to find this trend and in which ones is it more likely to be suppressed.

The second critical issue I plan to address is whether or not it is possible for individuals who view themselves as antithetic to their inherited culture to "shop around" for a new one that reflects their beliefs and actions more appropriately. Is it possible for them to internalize the tenets of another culture that is distinctly different and have them become psychologically compelling? What kinds of processes does this involve and which types of cultural propositions are more likely to become realities?

Finally, what can we hope to learn from these experiences of cultural disenchantment? To what extent does the rapid globalization of access to multi-cultural information and opinion play a role in challenging our steadfast, unconscious acceptance of our own culture and sense of reality? Has or will the ever-expanding window on the larger world contribute to an increased feeling of cultural dissatisfaction?

I would like to address these crucial questions by studying First World immigrant communities in India. I spent a semester in my junior year in India studying tribal village life in Rajasthan. When my project was completed, I traveled throughout the northern part of the country and along sections of the western border. I encountered periodically small communities of Europeans and Americans who had left their respective countries permanently to begin new lives in the subcontinent, in a place they believed would be a better world. Some of these immigrants had been in India for twenty years, while others were very new arrivals. In both cases I found their presence surprising and curious. These were not like the hordes of travelers who pass through India on waves of spiritual tourism; rather they were there to stay permanently.

Having given this unique population much thought since my encounters with them, I have realized that their experiences can provide valuable insights into the theoretical questions that I have chosen to pursue. In Victor Turner's terminology, do they represent more than an enduring "communitas" or are they forever to linger in a "liminal stage?" How has their presence affected their host environment and through what types of cultural channels have they had their greatest impact?

The course work I have completed in anthropology at Boston University has provided me with a solid foundation from which to undertake professional studies in a doctoral curriculum. My experiences in India have created a passion in me for the field and a readiness to commit myself to a life of discourse, research, teaching, and writing in the field, with a focus on the issues and questions I have raised here. The verdicts in anthropology are never really in, thus the need for research and discussion is constant. It is my deepest hope that in the years ahead my research will result in important contributions to the fields of cultural and psychological anthropology, that I might help to bring meaning and understanding to the mystery we call mankind.

It should be clear that prior to her graduate education, Amanda had already developed a depth of knowledge and a passion for the real issues of concern to anthropologists. She integrated her academic and fieldwork experiences to lay out for the admissions committees how her Ph.D. would serve as an extension of her ongoing education. As we discuss later, it should be the goal of all applicants to communicate these aspects of their background so directly.

Step Two Checklist

- Be sure you understand the character of graduate education and how it differs from the undergraduate experience.

- Don't fight the system. Follow to the letter the procedures and requirements for admission.

- Study programs carefully, compare them, and apply only to those that are compatible with your interests and capabilities.

Remember that top graduate schools are open to all applicants, no matter what their background and what college they attended.

Think of your career advancement in educational terms and keep your mind open to further academic work that will fulfill your intellectual and emotional needs.

Give yourself every opportunity to experience work, internships, or travel that will help you to confirm your direction in life.

STEP THREE
Explore the Many Program and Career Options

The Graduate Program Universe

Though most applicants do not have time to examine every graduate program offered in their field of interest, anyone, in today's world of guidebooks and the Internet, can easily draw up a short list of graduate schools that will fit his or her needs. In the Appendix, we provide a selected list of the guidebooks and websites that make the search for specific programs and financial aid feasible.

You may be tempted, if you are qualified, to limit your initial search to the more prestigious institutions, but a more prudent policy is to extend your research sufficiently to include a number of other good universities. The caliber of the programs at these schools may warrant serious consideration, and you will give yourself insurance in case you are rejected at the most selective schools. A number of faculty experts contend that there is not an extraordinary difference in the quality of academic training among the top 20 to 25 professional schools in such fields as business, medicine, law, and engineering. Though the business schools at Harvard and Stanford may have superior reputations in general, they may not have the best faculty and curriculum in your special field. Possibly there is a better education to be had in international finance or entrepreneurship at other strong programs that specialize in these fields. As for master's and doctoral programs, the most important factors for your future are the reputation and availability of the acknowledged experts in a particular discipline. Many of these top faculty hold tenured positions at the great public research universities.

Nonprofessional graduate programs, or academic disciplines, are offered in the academic departments of large, research-oriented universities. These are the higher levels of the school of arts and sciences in most universities and in some smaller institutions committed to advanced degrees in a few disciplines. Dartmouth College, for example, can provide you with excellent doctoral training in physics, math, or computer science, but not in dozens of other specialties. Many colleges of high repute offer master's degrees in many subjects, but not necessarily doctorates. Of the more than 3,500 colleges and universities in America, only 125 fall into the category of doctoral and research universities. That represents a mere 3 percent of all institutions of higher education. These are mostly the very large institutions that devote their resources of faculty and facilities to advanced research and training in many disciplines. They are very important to the advancement of teaching and research, granting more than 50 percent of the doctoral degrees in science and engineering alone each year. Any serious candidate for advanced studies in specialized fields is most likely to consider this category for his or her training.

There is considerable overlap in the uses to which professional and nonprofessional degrees are put. The distinction between traditional academic and professional education has become blurred. Lawyers may be teachers of law; doctors are often medical researchers; economic Ph.D.s have professional careers in banking, business, government, journalism, and think tanks; psychology Ph.D.s increasingly are turning to the private sector for careers in consulting, market research, human resources, and counseling; philosophers are working in hospitals or government as experts on ethical issues and policy planning. Occupational lines are often hard to draw as more well-educated people move in and out of the academy or different professional career sectors. As you explore graduate opportunities, you will discover the variety of combined degree programs universities now offer. You could decide to combine management studies with international relations, medicine or law with engineering, journalism with law, biology with technology, psychology with educational administration or industrial consulting, and so on. If you discover in your personal assessment that you have a strong interest in several related fields, you should investigate dual-degree programs.

It is a good idea to keep these factors in mind as you ponder which kind of graduate training to pursue. You will not be pigeonholed into a single field, a concern we hear expressed by many aspiring graduate students. You may later do studies in a different field as your experience leads you to new interests, or you may enter one of the multitude of combined-degree programs discussed later.

In this part, we describe various graduate programs in some detail. First we look at the "big three" programs of professional graduate study: law, health sciences, and business management. Then we turn to traditional academic graduate study options.

Law School

The Starting Point: Why Law School?

Many people are drawn to the study of law by the glamorous and exciting media images of lawyers as superstar fighters for justice, or members of the president's cabinet, or leading politicians or pundits on national events of great import, or intellectuals who establish the basis for legal decisions in the courts. The prospect of earning a big salary right out of law school is another major reason stated for preparing for a law career. On the other hand, there are a number of college graduates who plan to devote a lifetime to legal good works, aiding the indigent and underrepresented populations in America.

To inject a note of reality, the majority of trained lawyers will work intensive hours at the nuts and bolts of legal transactions in a large legal firm, with a small group, or in individual practice. Most legal work is done for paying clients and can be unexciting by its inherent nature. It is usually very hard work requiring long hours five or more days a week, especially for young associate members of large firms and independent attorneys. The bread-and-butter areas of legal practice are writing contracts, deeds, wills, and closings, directing litigation, filing malpractice suits, and representing clients in divorce proceedings, but the profession continues to develop new specialties that reflect our changing economy and culture. For example, there are lawyers who handle legal issues dealing only with computer technology, virtual intellectual property, international business transactions, environmental protection issues, or

child and family protection. For this, you may be decently, if not exceptionally, rewarded, and you are likely to be highly respected in your
community. Dismissing all fantastic images of yourself as public hero or
millionaire, you must consider why you want a law degree.

Here are some salient points to know about legal education as you
weigh your future. Law is the most generic of the professional graduate programs. Keep in mind that the quality law schools have similar
curricula. A basic review of the first-year program in particular will
indicate the core courses all students are asked to take. In the second
year, but especially the third, comes the opportunity to emphasize
special topics within the law that appeal to you. A legal education
teaches an exacting style of rigorous thinking, clear and concise writing, objective reasoning, and disputation of conflicting interpretations
of the issue at hand. It is not surprising that only one-half of law
school graduates actually practice law over a lifetime; the other half
take advantage of many other opportunities in the public and private
sectors. Of all the professional graduate schools, with the exception
of education, law school now attracts the largest number of women,
about 45 percent of enrolled students. According to the American Bar
Association (ABA), for the first time, more women than men were
expected to enter law school in 2001. One reason for this is the variety
of career tracks in the for-profit and nonprofit fields. As undergraduates, women are more likely to major in the humanities and social sciences, which are excellent foundations for studying law.

SKILLS FOR LAW SCHOOL

The Official Guide to U.S. Law Schools, published by the Law School
Admission Council (LSAC) begins its invaluable guide to the 182
accredited law schools in America with this statement:

> *Law practice is so diverse that it is not possible to describe the
> so-called typical lawyer. Each lawyer works with different clients*

*and different legal problems. Ordinarily, certain basic legal skills
are required of all lawyers. They must know:*

1. How to **analyze** legal issues in light of the existing state of the law,
   the direction in which the law is headed, and relevant policy considerations;
2. How to **synthesize** material in light of the fact that many issues are
   multifaceted and require the combination of diverse elements into a
   coherent whole;
3. How to **advocate** the views of groups and individuals within the context of the legal system;
4. How to give intelligent **counsel** on the law's requirements;
5. How to **write** and **speak** clearly; and
6. How to **negotiate** effectively.

Supposedly those who are admitted to accredited law schools have a
satisfactory capacity for reading and reasoning, yet it is disquieting to
observe that many of those who enter law school fail to complete their
education. In 1998–99, there were 125,627 students enrolled in ABA-
approved law schools, 42,804 of whom were in their first year. Some
3,500 of them failed to complete their J.D. or LL.B. degree. In other
years, as many as 8,000 entering law students left before completing
the degree. Getting into law school, then, is only the beginning. Staying
the course is, for a variety of reasons, beyond the capacity or will of
many aspiring lawyers. Even some well-prepared law students fail to
complete the three years to a degree, for the study of law may prove
boring or incompatible with their interests.

The Top 25 Law Schools

This is our alphabetical list, based on a review of law programs and the
experience of law students and law firms. We have avoided individual
ranking for two important reasons. First, we want to deemphasize the
prestige syndrome that afflicts so many applicants, adversely in many
cases, because it leads to a nonconstructive attitude, i.e., "If I can't get

into A, B, or C top law school, I won't go." Second, there is no scientific basis for ranking law schools in a precise and quantitative way. The majority of deans of the law schools listed below have issued a public statement decrying the notion that any group or publication can quantify the relative merits of individual schools and compare them one against the others. There is a set of factors that qualify a law school for a level of excellence that is universally recognized. Of course, there are many other law schools that provide a first-rate education for aspiring lawyers.

College of William and Mary
Columbia University
Cornell University
Duke University
Emory University
George Washington
   University
Georgetown University
Harvard University
New York University
Northwestern University
Stanford University
University of California,
   Berkeley
University of California,
   Los Angeles

University of Chicago
University of Illinois
University of Michigan
University of North Carolina,
   Chapel Hill
University of Notre Dame
University of Pennsylvania
University of Southern
   California
University of Texas, Austin
University of Virginia
Vanderbilt University
Washington University
Yale University

The following are other regionally acclaimed law schools:

American University
Boston College
Boston University
Fordham University
Tulane University
University of Iowa

University of Minnesota
University of Washington
Wake Forest University
Washington and Lee
   University

Here is what a group of law school deans have to say on the subject of rankings and choosing a law school:

Dear Law School Applicant:

Choosing the best law school for you is critically important to your short-term and long-term future. Getting quality information about the schools that interest you will require some time and effort, but expending that time and effort now will reward you. Several commercial enterprises promote "ranking" systems that purport to reduce a wide array of information about law schools to one simple number that compares all 183 ABA-approved law schools with each other. These ranking systems are inherently flawed because none of them can take your special needs and circumstances into account when comparing law schools. According to students, the factors listed below are among the most important in influencing their choices of law school. These factors are excluded entirely or severely undervalued by all of the numerical ranking systems.

Breadth and support of alumni network
Breadth of curriculum
Clinical programs
Collaborative research opportunities with faculty
Commitment to innovative technology
Cost
Externship options
Faculty accessibility
Intensity of writing instruction
Interdisciplinary programs
International programming
Law library strengths and services
Loan repayment assistance for low-income lawyers
Location
Part-time enrollment option

(continued)

Public interest programs

Quality of teaching

Racial and gender diversity within the faculty and student body

Religious affiliation

Size of first-year classes

Skills instruction

Specialized areas of faculty expertise

Trends in Legal Education

Like all professions, law has had its cycles of boom and bust. In the 1990s, the number of applicants to all law schools declined by 15 percent. Even the top-rated schools experienced a decline, although the quality of applicants remained as competitive as ever. The less selective law schools faced serious enrollment losses, which led them to reduce the size of their entering classes. The primary reason for this change from the previous decade was the opportunities for college graduates in the lucrative fields of technology, investment banking, finance, international trade, and start-up companies in an expanding economy. Business school graduates appeared to be earning considerably greater incomes in the world of finance and banking. Many graduates asked themselves why they should defer enticing job offers to spend three years in law school and incur a good deal of debt. If they were to choose graduate school, why not an MBA program?

As we have now witnessed, the cyclical effect of a complex, globally intertwined economy has taken hold. Now more college graduates are considering attaining a law degree for its value as a specialized field of knowledge, to a large extent a guarantee of meaningful employment, or as training for many other kinds of work. The large law firms are paying previously unheard-of starting salaries and bonuses to attract and retain top performers from the major law schools as legal work expands. The firms are also recognizing the need to balance the intensity of legal work with more flexible time for new lawyers. This is a relative change, since the demands of the job can be exhausting and frustrating, often translating into no real time for a personal life.

Understandably, pay scales in public and nonprofit agencies are significantly lower. Starting lawyers in district attorney offices or the Legal Aid Society and clerks to circuit and federal judges earn one-third to one-quarter the salary of lawyers in the big law firms across the country. Nevertheless, many law school graduates are choosing public interest law and have a vision of becoming a judge someday or directing a major organization charged with protecting the rights of individuals, the community, or the environment.

Many law school deans believe that they must make changes in their programs and emphases to keep up with the changes taking place in our society and its impact on the dynamics of our legal process, and by definition, the practice of law. John Sexton, the dean of New York University's Law School, has stated he foresees major changes in legal education. The curriculum will emphasize international issues. Technology will change how students study and carry out research. Given the high costs of graduate education, Dean Sexton also forecasts a backlash over high tuition. With a law degree now costing between $150,000 and $250,000, most students are going into heavy debt. This has the unfortunate effect of ruling out careers in public service or teaching, to which many students might otherwise commit. He and other deans argue for a system that forgives educational loans for those who enter public service and other low-paying legal careers. Medical schools have had this practice in place for the last decade.

Remember, admission to a selective law school does not come easily. The top schools have always been highly competitive and are becoming more so. We also counsel you to avoid the "nondecision decision" dynamic. Since anyone with a strong liberal arts education can qualify for admission to law school, you may be tempted to apply and enroll because in your senior year of college you have no other plan for your future. Unless you are emotionally committed to the study of law, you will not do well and will not find yourself in a successful career track. There are too many trained lawyers already in practice to make it easy to gain and hold a lucrative and enjoyable situation. You should consider just how difficult law school studies will be. Ask yourself if you are prepared to spend as many as 80 hours a week studying. Are your health and stamina up to the grind? Especially if you have not worked that hard in your undergraduate years, can you assure yourself that you are now prepared to make the necessary sacrifices any law school must ask of you? Finally, can you maintain the pace of intensive reading and research that is required in law studies? The key point is to understand why you want to enroll in law school and what you want to accomplish with your life. Lastly, you should know that only a third of enrolled students began their studies immediately upon graduation from college. This should reassure you that taking time to explore the profession by interning or working after college will only make you a stronger candidate when and if you decide to apply.

CHOOSING YOUR LAW SCHOOL

A word of caution in choosing which law school you hope to attend: It is too easy to pick from the 183 approved schools the most famous and prestigious, with no thought for your own interests and needs. Note that all schools offer the same core curriculum that is essential for building a foundation in the American legal system. Where they vary is in the teaching of specialized fields, the methodology of teaching, the accessibility of the faculty, and the environment of the classroom and community.

On the face of it, who wouldn't jump at the chance to enroll in Harvard School of Law, to pick an obvious example, given its reputation and prestige? A closer look will reveal a number of shortcomings, which the school itself has acknowledged. Invited to study the school's academic and social environment, the consulting firm McKinsey and Company found that student dissatisfaction was very high. Their findings confirmed long-standing criticisms voiced by the student body: classes that are too large, severe grading, faculty disinterest in teaching as compared to their research projects, too much competitive pressure generated among students, too few enrolled women and minorities, and too few minority and female faculty. The administration and faculty are addressing these issues, particularly the complaint of large classes and attention from professors. At present, the ratio of students to faculty is 22 to 1, compared with Stanford's 18 to 1 and Yale's 11 to 1. Look beyond the "halo effect" of particular graduate institutions to be certain you have chosen the most appropriate program that will help you to meet your particular career goals.

Who Gets in Where?

The answer to the double question of who gets into what law school is straightforward. Admission to any law school is based largely on two sets of numbers: your GPA in college and your Law School Admissions Test (LSAT) score. You must be prepared to put these two numbers up against the profiles of recent entering classes of the schools to which you plan to apply. With these numbers in hand, you can divide law schools into three categories: long shot, even chance, and certain. We avoid calling the third category safety or fallback schools, because this is insulting to any accredited school and potentially misleading. The selection of candidates to the majority of law schools today is competitive across the board.

The ABA officially approves 183 law schools, and in principle any of these will prepare you for a successful legal career. In reviewing the status of its member schools, the ABA considers the following data: admissions criteria and selectivity, student finances, faculty credentials, graduation rate, and the percentage of graduates who pass the bar exam in the state where the largest number take the exam. The ABA accrediting committee also asks the law schools to provide the 25th and 75th percentiles of the admitted class's undergraduate GPA, and their score on the LSAT. In addition to the individual law school's own published profile, you should consult the ABA's annual directory in preparing to apply to law school.

What about such admissions factors as your extracurricular record, your essay or application statement, and recommendations? These are helpful in admissions decisions involving many candidates with similar LSAT scores and GPAs, and we discuss their importance in Steps Six through Eight, but there is no getting around the fundamental importance of the numbers.

PROFILE OF A SELECTIVE LAW SCHOOL:
COLUMBIA UNIVERSITY SCHOOL OF LAW

- 6,000 applicants vie for an entering class of 350 places.
- 19% of applicants are offered admission.
- Median GPA is 3.6.
- Median LSAT score is 169.
- Two-thirds of the entering class have worked or completed other studies.
- 200 undergraduate colleges are represented in the entering class.
- 44% of enrolled students are women.
- 36% of enrolled students are a racial or ethnic minority.
- The most popular undergraduate majors, in descending order, are political science, history, economics, literature, science and engineering, and philosophy.
- The LSAT and LSDAS (Law School Data Assembly Service) are required for admission.
- Combined-degree programs include J.D. and M.A., J.D. and MBA, J.D. and MPAd, J.D. and M.S., and J.D. and Ph.D.

Columbia's statement on selection criteria:

Evaluation of an applicant for admission to Columbia Law School includes a determination of the candidate's intellectual and academic qualifications, aptitude for legal study as measured by the Law School Admissions Test (LSAT), and an assessment of whether or not the candidate has demonstrated personal qualities considered requisite to scholastic success, professional dis-

tinction, and public service. In addition to evaluating a candidate's overall academic history and performance on the LSAT,
the Committee examines the applicant's personal essay or statement and letters of recommendation, as well as the following
pertinent information elicited in the application: course selection, special honors and awards, fellowship opportunities,
publications, extracurricular involvement, community service,
political activity, professional contributions, and other work
experience. Regrettably, because of the large number of applicants from all over this country and the world, it is not logisti-
cally possible for personal interviews to be included as part of
the selection process. As a substitute, the Admissions Committee depends upon the insights provided by letters of recommendation and the applicant's personal essay. In addition to
providing the Committee with a more personal sense of the individual qualities of the applicant, this statement affords the candidate an opportunity to present any special information or
factors that may prove useful to the Committee's deliberations.

Study That School Profile

It is critical that you know just where you stand in relationship to the
competition. To apply to one of the top 25 law schools with an LSAT
score below 60 percent and a 2.7 GPA makes no sense. This is not what
we would consider even a long-shot choice; it is a waste of time and
money on your part, your recommenders' part, and for the admissions
committee. Remember, too, that rejections are never pleasant, so the
fewer you have the better. Most important, you need to focus your
efforts on the schools at which you have reasonable to good odds for
admission. To have five acceptances and one rejection is reassuring. To
have several rejections and only one acceptance is discouraging and
unnerving, and the ultimate disaster is having no choices when you are
convinced you want to get a law degree. Be sensible and acknowledge
the reality of your profile and choose where to apply accordingly.

Before applying to any law school, obtain its profile by asking the school directly for statistical information, checking for this information on their website, or consulting the directories of the ABA and Law School Admissions Service. We realize that some readers may not yet have graduated from college and others have yet to take the LSAT. We discuss the question of qualifying for law school academically and taking the LSAT in Steps Four and Six. This initial step is simply exploratory. You can make a preliminary judgment of your probable competitive level based on your performance in college and your results on the SAT while in high school or any additional multiple-choice aptitude tests you have taken.

You may, after a pitiless consideration of your chances, decide that law school is not for you, at least at your present level of accomplishment. Better, then, not to apply at all, or at least to postpone the decision until you have acquired the credentials law schools are looking for. Taking yourself out of the competition does not mean you acknowledge your weaknesses so much as it means you recognize where you stand today and what you might do to change your profile. The wiser course may be to strengthen your GPA before applying by taking advanced courses in a part-time program at a nearby university that will impress admissions committees with your efforts and ability to perform well at this time. You may also need to consider retaking the LSAT, preceded by intensive study preparation, if your original scores were unsatisfactory.

If none of this pays off, you can move on to another professional field, train for paralegal work and join a known law firm for a few years, or begin your studies at a less competitive and intense law school with the goal of transferring after the first year. One of the best-kept secrets is that many top law schools consider transfer candidates who have excelled in their first-year studies in another program. Not that they intentionally raid the best students, but they are fully aware that they may have missed many a promising legal professional in their initial attempt at admissions to their school. We have counseled a number of law students who were successful in transferring to a higher quality law school. We have recommended to potential law school applicants, frustrated by their low GPA or LSAT scores, that they go to work as a paralegal for at least two years. They have then applied and been admitted to highly regarded schools. In some instances their law firm has paid all or part of the costs.

Of Minorities and Women

Law schools, in general, constantly seek to increase the numbers of minorities and women they accept and enroll, but this does not mean that if you fall into either category you are a cinch to be accepted somewhere. Law schools take into consideration any educational disadvantages you may have had, but one reason there are fewer minorities enrolled presently is that the number of candidates is fewer. As noted earlier, more women than men actually apply to law school today, but there is still a small percentage of female professors teaching law. The hope is that some outstanding female graduates will eventually enter the teaching ranks in law schools. The effort to reach out to more students of color and nontraditional backgrounds is the goal of every top law school in the nation. If you consider yourself a minority, you will never be rejected for that reason. We are well beyond the practice of quotas of any sort on candidates who qualify for acceptance. Today, law schools are particularly sensitive to the need to train more minority lawyers so they can play a role in the public and private branches of our society. Government agencies, social concern organizations, and private law firms are eager to hire well-trained lawyers of minority backgrounds.

LAW SCHOOL RECRUITMENT FORUMS

The Law School Admissions Council (LSAC) sponsors information sessions on careers in law and the necessary training each year at sites across the country. Forums took place in Atlanta, Boston, Chicago, Dallas, Los Angeles, New York, Oakland, and Washington, D.C. The LSAC describes their value this way:

People of all ages and backgrounds are discovering that a legal education can open the door to a variety of opportunities, not

(continued)

only in traditional law practice, but in other areas as well. If you have joined the thousands of men and women who are considering law school, the Law School Forums will be an excellent resource for you.

Regardless of your age, background, and goals, the Forums can help you answer these questions:

- *What law schools are best for you?*
- *How does the admissions process work?*
- *What is the best way to prepare for the LSAT?*
- *How can you finance your legal education?*
- *What law school opportunities are available for members of minority groups?*

Forums can also provide you with information that will help answer more personal questions: Do you have the ability and educational background that will help you handle the law school curriculum? What will a legal education train you to do? Will law be a satisfying career for you?

Law school forums are designed to be helpful and informative to all prospective law school students; they have proven to be particularly helpful to people who have been out of undergraduate college for a year or more.

You can gather a good deal of information by perusing the LSAC website: www.lsac.org.

KAREN: *building legal training on a classics foundation*

Karen had a highly successful academic experience at Dartmouth, where she double-majored in classics and government. She had chosen these two fields purely for their interest to her, not because she had a predetermined career goal in mind. After she graduated from college, her interests in current issues and world events led her to accept a position at ABC News as a desk assistant. Karen described her responsibilities as developing story ideas, researching and writing

story synopses, monitoring breaking news stories, and providing cor-
respondents in the field with research materials. Though this position
might sound ideal for anyone with a dream of working in the national
media, Karen found that the work did not provide the opportunity to
think and create ideas in depth, or investigate and report on a discrete
area of national or international concerns. She quit her position after
seven months, having determined that she really wanted to enroll in
law school to become a legal expert in the field of international law.

When she came to our office, Karen was clear about her goal, but
she was concerned that the major law schools would not see her as
focused and realistic in her goal of becoming a lawyer. Would her classics background and work in the news media be obstacles to admission to a top law school? she wondered. There was no question that
her academic credentials and LSAT scores would qualify her for the
top law schools. She had graduated with honors in the classics from
Dartmouth and scored in the 99th percentile on her LSAT. The challenge was for her to present herself as a legitimate law candidate.

We recommended that she accept the position she had been offered
at one of the most prestigious law firms in New York as a project coordinator. This would give her the opportunity to test her interest in the law
and gain significant experience in one or several specialized areas of
legal activity. Karen worked at the law firm Davis Polk and Wardwell for
a full year in a position she defined as follows: "I coordinate a practice
group which is split between the corporate and litigation departments
and deals with cross-border secured transactions and international
bankruptcy law. I conduct legal research, train new members of the
project, manage a large team of attorneys, and support personnel, and
work with information systems specialists on new technology."

Since many law schools encourage candidates to supply additional
information that can cast a light on their personal or intellectual qualifications, Karen wrote the following in her application. This made the
case for the relevancy of her undergraduate major in classical languages and studies to professional training in the law:

> When I stood before the classics department to deliver my honors
> presentation, I saw in front of me excited and hopeful faces. That
> afternoon was not a test in what I had retained or memorized over

four years of intensive studies; rather I had the opportunity for the departmental faculty to discover what I had learned under my own direction. These professors had guided me over my four years by suggesting appropriate readings, questioning me on what I understood and took from these studies. Now they had given me full rein to seek both the questions and the answers on my own.

To complete my Honors program, I had spent my senior year in one-on-one translation and discussions sessions with both a Greek and a Latin professor. During these sessions, the burden of theorizing from the texts, following themes and discussing their import was on my shoulders. My mentors would ask a question, and I would search for the answer through immediate reasoning and analysis. As an example of the interchange I experienced, one question posed by my Latin instructor, "Does Sallust think this man is evil?" led to two months of reflection, research, and writing on my part. My work culminated in a paper in which I argued that Sallust considered himself the model of the virtuous statesman.

While this teaching methodology can be extremely challenging and, at times, frustrating, as questions lead to more questions as well as to the ultimate discovery that there is no one and absolute answer, I found its rewards lay in the process of intellectual inquiry. My honors project, which was conducted throughout in the classical Socratic method of question and response, trained me to think analytically and sequentially. I learned the importance of persistence if I were to resolve a complex issue or question. My embracing of this method of problem solving will, I believe, stand me in good stead in legal studies, something I look forward to with great enthusiasm.

We include excerpts from Karen's personal statement, which she presented to all the law schools to which she applied. Her sense of purpose and direction makes it clear that she has carefully considered enrolling in law school as an essential step to her future career. The details of her work are important for the impact they deliver regarding the importance of her position within a large law firm:

The future of law is unknown and cannot be fully discovered in a law school education. However, a legal education provides the skills with which creative and dynamic individuals are able to shape the future of the American legal structure. With every entry of a "dot com" into the marketplace or the opening of a new branch of an American company in such different societies as Kuala Lumpur, for example, lawyers are being called upon to navigate areas of law which, until quite recently, did not exist. As a member of the Global Risk Management project at Davis Polk and Wardwell, I have seen how new areas of international law are developing to correspond with modern business practices. The lawyers on our team are able to define these new areas because they have the skills that are acquired through rigorous legal training.

The Global Credit Risk Management project is defining a particular section of international law. For investment bank clients we analyze the risks involved in taking securities as collateral when extending credit to customers throughout the world. Since there is little case law or precedent for the work we are doing, we work closely with counsel around the globe to determine which jurisdiction's law would govern a transaction and anticipate how each jurisdiction would evaluate our clients' actions. When we ask a similar set of questions to lawyers in numerous countries, I am fascinated by how differently their respective legal codes have developed over time and thus the challenge of working together to form a common understanding of these complicated contractual issues.

Since the need for this field of law has been growing dramatically as a reflection of expanding global economy, our project has grown in kind. I have been able, as a result, to take on a variety of roles in support of our team. After months of reading and listening, I now participate in conferences, write and edit analyses, and work with counsel in jurisdictions throughout the world. I traveled to Japan recently to meet with Japanese lawyers in an effort to resolve a number of ambiguous issues in our analysis of Japanese law. This fall I have been preparing some of the analysis to safeguard our clients' status as secured creditors in the event of credit failures due to possible Y2K disruptions this January.

In my time as member of the Global Credit Risk Management team, I have increased my responsibilities so much that the firm has hired five people full-time to support my work. I have the creativity, communications skills, and leadership capability to help shape the future of international cooperation and a common legal standard in this field. I have confirmed for myself the need for a formal legal education if I am to understand individual legal practices and laws of diverse nations and place them within a broad theoretical construct.

Through my many years of studying Ancient Greek and Latin, I know that rigorous academic and analytical training provides the essential foundation for advanced study and intellectual discourse. Over the past ten years, my classical studies have grown to include classical art, archaeology and societies which have given me a sensitivity to differing cultures that help to define a number of nationalities to this day. Among other wonderful benefits of my studies, I was able to develop the context with which to understand modern democratic societies and the significance language plays in communicating ideas and ideals. My intensive work in translating Greek and Latin, reading and comprehending the great philosophers and historians of classical times, has created in me a strong work ethic, an appreciation for the inquiring mind, the subtleties of language, and the importance of critical reading skills.

A legal education will provide me with the skills needed to practice law as it exists presently and to understand the evolving nature of the law as it transcends any one nation. As technology has enabled businesses to exist outside the realm of traditional legal constructs, lawyers must be able to create innovative, workable legal solutions. In my future practice of law, I want to shape American law as our companies interact in the global marketplace. I also hope to reform international law so that the laws of individual nations support and secure the international activity of global business. While I am interested in international business, I want to function as an attorney within this special field because it is where legal practitioners will face the most exciting challenges in the future. A demanding legal education will prepare me with the knowledge base to face these challenges successfully.

Karen was determined to do everything she could to ensure herself acceptance to a major law school. With our guidance, she concentrated on 12 of the 25 top schools, and she was accepted at 10: Chicago, Columbia, Duke, Georgetown, George Washington, Michigan, New York, Northwestern, Vanderbilt, and Virginia. Only Stanford and Yale turned her down. Because of the career area she knew she would pursue, Karen chose to enroll in New York University. Here she could concentrate on international law and keep active her relationship with Davis Polk and Wardwell.

Summing Up

Why law school? You should be able to answer this question without summoning unrealistic fantasies about what it means to be a lawyer. Be certain that you are not considering this step as an easy way to avoid making a hard decision about your future.

- Be prepared for long, hard hours of work in law school and thereafter.
- You cannot get into a good law school without the numbers: a good LSAT score and a high GPA.
- Be sure to get the profiles of entering classes at the law schools you are considering and apply only to those with class profiles that more or less match your own performance.
- Law schools are eager to enroll minorities, women, and unique individuals who will add to the diversity of the enrolling class.

Business School

A Word of Caution

Among professionals who have prospered significantly in the past decade are holders of the master of business administration degree. The rush to attain an MBA has led to an unhealthy expansion in the number of programs from 480 in the early 1980s to more than

700 by 2000. The majority of these programs lack accreditation as a result of poor resources, facilities, and faculties. We consider them a serious waste of time and a poor use of financial resources. Unlike a law degree, which qualifies you to take any state's bar exam and, if you pass, to practice law and be an accepted member of an ancient profession, the MBA carries with it no automatic or official professional status.

The outstanding graduate business programs at leading universities such as Harvard, Pennsylvania, Stanford, Chicago, Columbia, and the other MBA schools we list in the top 25 do confer a cachet that leads their graduates to be eagerly sought by businesses, government organizations, foundations, and nonprofit institutions. What a good, sound MBA program does is train you in the art of management and decision making, for management seems to be more art than science, depending as much on judgment, the ability to lead and inspire others, and a capacity for evaluating the character and performance of others as it does on a facility for crunching numbers or inventing business plans on paper.

The carefully constructed case histories that MBA students must read and discuss are themselves often stories of serious management mistakes caused by lack of foresight, the misinterpretation of key information, the failure to heed the advice of senior executives, or the failure to understand the mood of the marketplace. From the creation of the Edsel by Ford Motor Company to the change in Coca-Cola's products, examples abound of hugely bad business decisions. As a professor at Harvard Business School commented to us, "How do you teach judgment?"

Yet the necessity for better and better management leadership makes the bright holder of an MBA valuable to an organization. This is why graduates of the top business schools are recruited heavily. It also explains why so many organizations turn to management consultants, most of whom hold MBA degrees, for solutions to management and organizational problems that seem intractable to the executives who have either created them or inherited them after the last management team has been fired.

The Top 25 Business Schools

Our list of the top MBA programs is based on our research, experience with hundreds of outstanding candidates and graduates, and conversations with professional leaders in a wide array of business professions. As we did with the law schools, we list them alphabetically because we do not believe there is significant statistical differentiation among them. Here, too, we urge you to consider many of the best schools rather than insist on enrolling only if you get into one of the reputed top three or four. Remember, there are at least another 25 MBA programs beyond the first group that can prepare you well for the world of business.

Carnegie Mellon University
Columbia University
Cornell University
Dartmouth College
Duke University
Harvard University
Indiana University
Massachusetts Institute of
    Technology
New York University
Northwestern University
Purdue University
Stanford University
University of California,
    Berkeley
University of California,
    Los Angeles
University of Chicago
University of Michigan
University of North Carolina
University of Pennsylvania
University of Rochester
University of Southern
    California
University of Texas
University of Virginia
Vanderbilt University
Washington University
Yale University

Other outstanding MBA programs are offered at the following institutions:

Babson College
Emory University
Georgetown University
Georgia Institute
    of Technology
Michigan State University
Rice University
Southern Methodist
    University
Thunderbird Graduate School

University of Illinois, Urbana-
   Champaign
University of Maryland
University of Minnesota

University of Notre Dame
University of Wisconsin
Wake Forest University

THE HEUBLEIN STORY—AN MBA CASE STUDY

If you are considering applying for admission to a strong MBA school—and we insist that you apply only to those that are accredited—you must acquaint yourself with some management problems and think about how you would solve them, because this is how you will spend a considerable amount of time in the top schools. The case study method of teaching is not universal, but it is widespread, presumably because it has proved to be successful in developing the habits of sound analysis, reasoned decision making, and judgment. How would you, as an executive at Heublein, have reacted to the question in the following case study: Should Heublein buy the Hamm Brewing Company?

The Heublein Company, a successful maker and marketer of mixed alcoholic drinks sold largely through package stores, hired a new marketing team with no experience in the competitive liquor business. It was made up of people who had been marketers of toothpaste. Their proposal, eagerly taken up by Heublein and with enormous success, was to get into the vodka business. Adopting the easily remembered Slavic name of Smirnoff, Heublein piled up profits by selling a new generation on the idea of learning to drink relatively tasteless and odorless vodka mixed with their products and soft drinks.

When competition from other distillers cut into the profitability of their vodka sales, Heublein decided to use some of the cash accumulated from the early success of this liquor. The Hamm Brewing Company was for sale, and beer seemed like a sensible product to add to the Heublein line of alcoholic beverages and mixes.

The question MBA candidates were asked was: Can you justify a decision to make this acquisition, and if not, why not? You might think about this and then turn to page 123 to find out what actually happened at Heublein.

Note. This case study was provided by the Babson College Graduate School of Business.

What Good Is an MBA?

The management and business training that MBA programs provide is being sought not just by prospective corporate executives, consultants, investment bankers, stockbrokers, and entrepreneurs, but also by health professionals, museum directors, foundations executives, educators, editors, engineers, librarians, city planners, book publishers, media producers and directors, journalists, and labor leaders, among others. Accountants, marketers, human resource managers, systems analysts, financial planners, sales and marketing executives, and production supervisors can all benefit from the advanced level of knowledge MBA work provides.

Much publicity is devoted to the high earnings of top MBA holders, and if you are in their league, more power to you. However, what we said about a law degree applies as well to the MBA: Do not fantasize about the fortune you may make as a consultant, an investment banker, or a Wall Street financier. The best of the MBAs earn as much as $90,000 to $100,000 right out of business school, but not all graduates approach this mark. The median starting salaries vary by $10,000 to $20,000 less for graduates of the very good but not top MBA programs. Keep in mind that the typical cost of gaining your MBA will be $125,000 to $150,000, when you add the tuition and living expenses for a two-year program. Loans to help cover these costs can total as much as $30,000.

You should base your decision to make the commitment to MBA training on your eventual goals. This is why we earlier posed the set of questions on whether to go on to graduate school. For a majority of

MBA candidates, the most important factors are to advance your responsibilities in your present employment or to change careers. If the only purpose you have in mind is to become very rich, you may be making a mistake in studying advanced business management, for there are no guarantees this will happen in your life. Business schools will require you to write in detail about your future goals and how business training will prepare you to meet them. If the answer is just to make a pile of money, you will not stand up well in the selection process.

An MBA education gives you the opportunity to change careers, exposure to talented and ambitious peers, contact with major companies and developing enterprises, high starting salaries and compensation packages, future networking with alumni, in-depth knowledge of the most important business principles and practices, training in working under pressure and meeting goals, intellectual self-confidence, and a credential you carry throughout your professional career.

COUNSEL FROM THE DEAN
OF A TOP BUSINESS SCHOOL

Robert Swieringa, dean of the Johnson School of Business at Cornell University, responded to a set of questions we put to him. There is a great deal of advice here on why to seek an MBA, how to choose the right program, and how to prepare for acceptance.

What skills are necessary to become a successful business and/or corporate leader today and tomorrow?

I believe that successful leaders today need to be able to size up fast-changing situations and to mobilize resources to get results in a dynamic world. The business world is rapidly changing, and the rate, complexity, and magnitude of change will continue to increase dramatically. We are living in Internet time.

To size up fast-changing situations, leaders need information, knowledge, skills, and perspective. They need alternative lenses to quickly and effectively understand the challenges they face. To mobilize resources, leaders need self-awareness about their abilities—their strengths and weaknesses—as well as the abilities that others bring to a given situation. Leaders seldom fail because they lack technical skills; rather, they fail because they lack the ability to work with and lead others—to mobilize for action. And to get results in a dynamic world, leaders need to be able to hit the ground running and to pick up the pace from there. The business world demands "anytime, anyplace," but most importantly, it demands "now."

What function does the MBA or related graduate training serve in preparing for a career in one or more of the many business fields and roles?

The decision to pursue an MBA is a very important investment decision. Investing in human capital is one of the most important things you can do. You come to this decision with high expectations and high aspirations. You want to "fast forward" your career. You have momentum, direction, and intention. Our research suggests that applicants to the Johnson School's MBA program want to be more successful in their careers, develop a network of contacts, become more effective leaders, function better in teams, and increase their wealth faster. In short, an MBA will prepare you to rise within your organization, increase your value in the marketplace, or help you change functions or fields. An MBA is credible—it is widely recognized and highly regarded. It is flexible—you can move among business fields over your professional career. And it is valuable—you can recover your investment quickly.

What is an MBA education like these days? What are some of the changes in curriculum in place or planned for? Where is the focus of the training now or where is it heading?

MBA education today is **intense**. The curriculum, programs, and related activities are innovative, dynamic, and intellectually

(continued)

demanding. At the Johnson School, orientation begins with leadership assessment, followed by a highly integrated core curriculum to
enhance your knowledge, skills, and perspective in foundation
areas, financial analysis, and managing people and products. MBA
education today also is **highly interactive**. There are very few situations in which you can succeed as a lone ranger. To be an effective
leader, you need to understand yourself and others. An MBA program fosters interactions, teamwork, and collaboration through
leadership assessment and experiential activities as well as team-
based projects. And MBA education today increasingly **prepares you
to hit the ground running**. For example, immersion learning is a new
model of management education that provides integrated, experiential, just-in-time learning. Students work on real-world problems
under real-world time pressures and are evaluated as they would be
on the job. A sound theoretical background is combined with hands-
on practical experience to prepare you to get results from day one.

**What type(s) of student seems to succeed the most from the
program?**

The business world is looking for leaders. I believe that the most successful MBAs not only master the analytical foundations in key
areas, but also are highly effective in working with and leading others. They exhibit a consistent pattern of taking initiative and engendering change—they size up situations to see how to make them
better, wherever they are. They balance academic and professional
achievements with activities outside of school or work. They are
comfortable taking calculated risks. They have a genuine desire to
leave a legacy that lasts beyond their involvement in an organization,
often by actively engaging others. MBAs need to have it all—technical competence, interpersonal effectiveness, and long-term vision.

**What courses in college and other experiences best prepare an
aspiring MBA?**

MBA students today have undergraduate majors in engineering, economics, business, social sciences, science and math,

humanities or other fields. I believe that the undergraduate major is less important than your passion and intellectual curiosity in pursuing it—what you learned and how it changed you.

MBA students today have significant work experience. On average they have about five years of experience, including significant responsibilities and accomplishments. Many are fluent in several languages and have traveled extensively or worked in various regions of the world.

It is important that you look carefully at what you have accomplished. There are many ways to demonstrate competence and leadership. Consider examples of leadership or initiative, some of which may not have been public or visible. Where have you had an impact? Consider your role in teams—where have you energized and led others?

In many ways, the best preparation for an MBA education is doing what it takes to become effective—taking initiative, taking risks, engendering change, performing well both academically and professionally, pursuing a variety of activities, and leaving marks that last. It is important to demonstrate courage, independent thought, and a willingness to be accountable for making tough decisions.

What tips would you offer to a prospective candidate in looking for the most appropriate MBA program?

There are many excellent MBA programs, but they are not all alike, even top programs. They differ in their size, intensity, flexibility, competencies, expectations, aspirations, attitude, and culture. It is important for you to assess how well you fit with a particular program. You are making an important personal investment decision and it is important that you get it right. The choice is somewhat analogous to choosing clothes off the rack—some programs look great but come without alterations and may not be the right fit for you; others look great and come with significant and important alterations to enhance the fit.

Use the school's website as well as those for various business periodicals to learn what you can about a program. Talk to

(continued)

graduates or others who might be knowledgeable about the program. It is particularly helpful to talk with people who know you and know the schools that you are considering. Then visit the schools and talk with current students, faculty, and admissions officers. Visiting the schools is an expensive and time-consuming process, but this is one of the most important investment decisions that you will make. Many schools will help you contact others who have been accepted to the program as well as alumni who may be helpful.

What are the core criteria the admissions committee considers in the selection process?

My response to question four includes many of the attributes an admissions committee looks for in the selection process—a consistent pattern of taking initiative and engendering change, sizing up their environment to see how they can make it better, a genuine desire to leave a legacy that lasts beyond their involvement, and so forth.

An admissions committee looks for a demonstrated record of achievement, career aspirations, breadth and depth of work experience, leadership, interpersonal and communication skills, decision making, and extracurricular and community involvement. It also carefully considers recommendations, GMAT scores [no number specified], TOEFL for international students, and prior academic performance at an accredited college or university with a minimum of a U.S. bachelor's degree or international equivalent.

In the final analysis, an admissions committee wants to know whether you "make things happen" or "add value to an organization." The committee wants to see results and the impact you had for your organization or a client's organization.

SVEN: *converting a passion for art into an MBA in the nonprofit field*

Sven's background and reasons for seeking an MBA degree illustrate several of our points. He was accepted to Yale School of Management's Master's Program in Public and Private Management, his target goal. How he arrived at this choice and gained admission is an interesting tale of a nontraditional business school candidate. With our counsel he turned his intellectual passion for art history into a career that distinguished him from the vast majority of candidates trained in the traditional business fields.

Sven's credentials were shaky for the traditional MBA programs in management, finance, accounting, and marketing. He had one year of work experience as an external affairs associate at the National Gallery of Art in Washington, D.C., followed by one year as a development associate at the Whitney Museum of American Art in New York. He then decided to gain exposure to the financial world by joining the sales force at Merrill, Lynch, Pierce, Fenner & Smith as an assistant in the sales and trading in equity and fixed-income markets. At the time he contemplated applying to graduate schools, he had only one year of experience in this area. Sven's score on the Graduate Management Aptitude Test (GMAT) was a 620, with a higher result on the verbal section. His college major was art history, and he graduated with a GPA of 3.5. He had taken only two quantitative courses and just micro- and macroeconomics in his undergraduate years.

Sven's original intent when he first came us was to apply to the usual contingent of the most competitive and traditional MBA programs: Harvard, Dartmouth, Columbia, Stanford, and Northwestern. We recommended adding Yale, Virginia, Cornell, Michigan, and NYU because his unique background matched nicely with their concentrations in arts administration and general nonprofit management. Once he reviewed the programs at the latter group of schools, he focused his efforts on applying to them, with special interest in Yale. Here are highlights of Sven's personal statement in response to this request from Yale: "Write an essay in which you discuss the principal elements of your educational and work experiences to date. Relate your background to your career objectives as a professional manager."

> When I entered college, I had no idea what to expect from the next four years. Unlike many of my new classmates, I had not yet devised a "master plan" for my life. I decided to take advantage of

the luxury of a liberal arts education, pursuing the myriad opportunities available as they arose.

My first significant academic decision was to major in art history. Having taken several classes during my first two years, I discovered that I not only enjoyed the subject but had an aptitude for the discipline as well. As the departmental required curriculum was quite broad, I gained exposure to many cultures and periods of history which I had not previously studied. By the time I was to graduate, I knew that art history had become more than merely a field of undergraduate study—it was a discipline that would enrich my life permanently.

The summer after my junior year I accepted an internship in Washington at the National Gallery of Art in its office of Special Projects. This office's mission was to promote the museum, a federally funded entity, to members of Congress, emphasizing its superior permanent collection and extensive national educational programs. An exciting combination of art, politics, and professional marketing, the internship opened my eyes to the many ways in which the art world interfaces with the public sector. My experience at the National Gallery that summer was a critical step in helping me to focus on my career objectives, as I sensed I had found my "calling" in arts administration.

When the National Gallery offered me a permanent position in the Office of Special Projects upon graduation, I eagerly accepted. I understood that I was choosing a career path that differed sharply from the majority of my classmates who were headed to law or medical school or high paying positions in the canyons of Wall Street. I felt confident, however, in my decision which was based on a passion for the arts and a desire to help bring them to the public more regularly and easily.

My first year at the National Gallery provided a greater understanding of the intricate and difficult process of keeping a non-profit sufficiently funded. Although the Gallery received an annual appropriation from Congress, more money was essential to cover the operating expenses and to underwrite the educational programs and public exhibitions that make the National Gallery one of the great cultural institutions of the world. In my capacity as a congressional liaison, I worked closely with the museum Director and the heads of the External Affairs and Treasurer's departments. My close contact with these talented and committed executives further influenced my career direction, as I made a commitment to prepare myself for a management position in a major non-profit arts institution.

As federal funding for the arts in general was dramatically reduced during my time at the National Gallery (including the proposed elimination of the National Endowment for the Arts!), it became evident to me that free-standing cultural organizations would have to manage themselves more like for-profit organizations if they were to survive. Museums could not plan for a permanent life, let alone necessary growth, if they were to depend entirely upon state and federal funding. In order to succeed as an administrative leader in any museum, I would need to be not only resourceful at raising funds on a continual basis, but also skilled in organizational and fiscal management.

These insights gained in a valuable year of training, influenced me to accept a position in the development office of the Whitney Museum of American Art in New York. My responsibility would be to raise funds for the museum's extensive exhibitions and arts education programs. My assignment was to present me with a stiffer challenge than I could have imagined. As a small museum by comparison to its mighty neighbors like the Metropolitan that concentrated on modern American art which appealed to a narrow audience, it did not enjoy a large and diverse support group.

My task was to write grant proposals for art exhibitions, educational programs, and the bricks and mortar needs of the museum. My efforts on behalf of the museum gained me direct exposure to many of the large charitable foundations and cultural affairs offices of major corporations and financial institutions. I learned painfully that it is not easy to raise money from groups that might have little interest in the arts and cultural activities per se or questioned the fiscal management of non-profit groups.

After almost a year at the Whitney, I felt it was time to leave the museum world temporarily to gain training in the competitive financial world. An essential ingredient in my career plan was to earn a degree from a graduate business school that would ready me for greater leadership in the management of a museum. Thus, I interviewed for and was hired as a sales assistant in Merrill Lynch's Private Client Group, which gave me an opportunity to learn the fundamentals of the equity, fixed-income, and commodities markets.

Once I felt I had grasped the basics of these complex financial fields, I accepted a new position at the Fixed Income Capital Markets Group of UBS Securities, the investment banking arm of Union Bank of Switzerland. As an analyst in the Capital Markets group, my responsibility is to learn how certain companies obtain financing and how and why they should issue debt to meet their financial needs. In analyzing balance sheets, income statements, and annual reports over the past year, I have been intrigued by corporate finance and the intricacies of the bond market.

The most beneficial aspect of my position at UBS has been learning the subtle and not so subtle reasons why individual companies succeed or fail. In a fiercely competitive environment, corporations must perform in the most cost-effective manner possible in order to survive. This business knowledge will serve me well in my future work in the non-profit management field.

After four years of eclectic work experience in both the public and private work sectors, I am eager to undertake graduate studies in business in order to build on the knowledge base I have begun to acquire. I look forward to learning the theory of management, fiscal decision making, organizational development, and financial planning so that I can return to an important arts organization and help it to move beyond survival as a regular plan of action to one of continuous growth and prosperity.

Sven chose as his recommenders the chair of the Art History Department at Princeton and the director of development at the National Gallery of Art. Their testimonies regarding his capabilities and promise as a future management leader in the nonprofit world played an important role in his acceptance to Yale.

The Growth of the Part-Time Student

One-half of all MBA students today study for their degree on a part-time basis. Almost always, this is because they are older students with major commitments to their jobs and families. Some others find that this is the only way they can finance the heavy cost of getting their MBA degree. Business schools are adapting more and more to the needs of the part-time learner. Some of the top schools now provide for this more flexible approach to study; they include, but are not limited to, New York University, Chicago, Northwestern, Berkeley, UCLA, Michigan, and Minnesota.

We have some words of advice if you are checking out a part-time MBA program. To ensure that you will get real value from the time and effort you will have to put in, be sure that

- A good percentage of the full-time faculty will teach you.
- All of the facilities and resources of the school are available to you at all times, from the library to the computer center to the counseling staff.
- The career and placement center and its staff are accessible.
- You can participate actively in the recruitment activities on campus.
- The classes that interest you are offered at convenient times.
- The statistics on the graduation rate, job offers, and starting salaries for part-time students in recent classes are commensurate with those for full-time students.

With every day that passes, more business schools are providing classes and degrees via the Internet. On-line instruction is the means for reaching a larger and more diverse audience of business students. If this is the only way you can get an MBA, you should be certain that any program you consider is fully accredited by one of the regional accrediting agencies. You need to ask many of the same questions as a part-time student. However, there are inherent disadvantages to distance learning that you need to consider. You will have little or no personal contact with your faculty and fellow students, both of whom are significant factors in the learning experience. There is little opportunity for collaborative projects and studying. You will not have access to recruiters from major companies and industries. You need to be very self-motivated and disciplined to study on your own and block out the time for your on-line classes. You will need to be very assertive in contacting and communicating with your professor via e-mail.

BUSINESS SCHOOL FORUMS

The Graduate Management Admission Council, the organization that sponsors the Graduate Management Admission Test and accredits business schools, sponsors a series of information forums in the fall of each year in major cities in every region of the U.S., as well as in Canada, Mexico and Asia. More than 100 of the major American and international graduate business schools participate by sending their admissions staff to interview students and present their programs. The admissions process is described and present business students are on hand to describe their experiences. Workshops entitled "Exploring the MBA and Assessing Yourself, Your Career and Options" and "Selecting the 'Right' Business School and Getting the 'Right' Business School to Select You" are presented by the GMAC staff. You can explore more than 500 MBA programs and learn where and when the Forums are held on the GMAC's website: www.gmat.org.

Ensuring Your Admission

A theme we emphasize throughout this book is the need to do proper research on the available graduate programs to discover which ones offer what you want to study, meet your personal needs, and will view you as an appropriate candidate. Visit those schools of major interest to meet faculty and students and to check out the resources for learning. This will help you get beyond name recognition to comprehend the tone of a school, from the intensity of the workload and pressure on students, to the friendliness factor, to student satisfaction. Sit in on one or more classes to get a sense of the teaching level and approach. Visit the career/placement office to find out if they are well staffed and have a comprehensive library for your future job search. Check out their role in helping you land a meaningful summer internship between your two years of study. Look for all the signals that indicate the school has not remained static in its curriculum and teaching methodology. The active use of computers and information technology, emphasis on an international business approach, encouragement of collaborative student projects, the use of current case studies, and a wired campus and classroom are key factors in the modern business school.

Many prospective applicants have changed their direction after making visits to particular business schools. Make every effort to interview recent graduates to learn what their feelings are about their education. Do they feel adequately trained for their work? Did they get help in their studies? Did their present job result from the school's recruiting program? Given the chance to do it again, would they attend the same school?

You can increase your odds of acceptance to a strong program if you have a defined area of study and career in mind, and you locate the most appropriate program. If, for example, you are seriously interested in information technology and its use in the business world, consider Duke, Dartmouth, MIT, Carnegie Mellon, UCLA, Illinois, Texas, and the University of California, Irvine. If your future lies in international business, you may want to apply to Thunderbird, Georgetown, Wharton, Columbia, Michigan, NYU, and Berkeley. A desire to learn about e-commerce might lead you to Vanderbilt, Chicago, Berkeley, Harvard, Stanford, Carnegie Mellon, Pennsylvania, MIT, and Rensselaer Polytechnic Institute, among other expanding programs. Do you see yourself as a future entrepreneur? If so, consider Babson, Southern California, UCLA, and Southern Methodist University as well as the top schools.

CATCHING UP

The technology revolution is shaking the ivory tower.

Colleges and universities, once slow to change, suddenly are running on Internet time. High-tech classrooms, visiting entrepreneurs, and distance-learning programs are common-place. And now the business school curriculum is being refashioned.

Dartmouth's Amos Tuck School of Business Administration, marking its centennial this year, calls itself the oldest graduate business school in the world. It has rolled out a new curriculum with technology as its core. Included will be the Tuck General Management Forum, requiring every first-year student to craft a business plan that will incorporate technology.

"We don't just want to be a repository of tradition," said Philip Anderson, associate professor of business administration, who will be teaching a technology course to first-year Tuck students under the new curriculum. "We want to start our second century by innovating."

From "Catching Up," *Boston Globe*, April 10, 2000.

As we have said about law schools, it does not make much sense to apply to top business schools when your credentials will automatically put you out of the running. The key ingredients are your college academic record, appropriate quantitative and economic courses, your results on the GMAT, and your employment or internship experiences. Although we are positive thinkers and encourage dedicated candidates to do their very best in applying to graduate schools, we know that weak credentials in the present highly competitive environment will bring only rejection. We encourage you to consider the good programs for which your credentials will mean acceptance.

PROFILES OF TWO TOP BUSINESS SCHOOLS

University of Pennsylvania, The
Wharton School, Class of 2001

- Total full-time enrollment:
  1,566
- Number of applicants:
  7,428
- Percentage of applicants
  accepted: 14%
- Female students in class:
  28%
- Minority students in class:
  7%
- Average GMAT score: 700
  (range 640–750)
- Average number of years of
  work: 6
- Average student age: 29

Employment, Class of 2000

- Average starting salary:
  $92,000
- Average signing bonus:
  $22,700
- Companies recruiting on
  campus: 152

Top Employers of Class:

- McKinsey and Company
- Goldman Sachs and
  Company
- Bain and Company
- Boston Consulting Group

University of Michigan
Business School

- Total full-time enrollment:
  1,939
- Part-time enrollment: 1,065
- Number of applicants:
  3,923
- Percentage of applicants
  accepted: 21%
- Female students in class:
  27%
- Minority students in class:
  11%
- Average GMAT score: 677
  (range 620–730)
- Average number of years of
  work: 5
- Average student age: 29

Employment, Class of 2000

- Average starting salary:
  $85,000
- Average signing bonus:
  $22,000

Top Employers of Class:

- McKinsey and Company
- AT Kearney
- Dell Computer Corporation
- American Express

(continued)

- Merrill Lynch
- Morgan Stanley Dean Witter
- Donaldson, Lufkin, and Jenrette
- Anderson Consulting
- Deloitte Consulting
- Booz Allen and Hamilton
- Diamond Technology Partners
- Ford Motor Company
- Chase Manhattan Bank
- Anderson Consulting
- Boston Consulting Group
- Goldman Sachs and Company

Minorities and Women Sought

Business schools have not done as well as law schools in attracting qualified minority and female applicants. According to the Graduate Management Admission Council, within their member schools only 8 percent of students are Black, 4 percent are Hispanic, and 25 percent are women. In contrast, international students are a significant presence in the MBA schools, making up 30 percent of the student body at Wharton, 35 percent at Berkeley, 31 percent at Yale, 37 percent at MIT, 35 percent at NYU, and 25 percent at Stanford. Every admissions director is on record as wanting to continue the increase in attracting and enrolling more women, students of color, and other underrepresented ethnic groups. The allure of American-style management training has constantly increased as international business has grown, and all of the best schools actively recruit students from outside the United States by on-site forums. Their argument is that these different groups, in combination, establish a diversity of opinions, perspectives, experiences, and values that add to the educational experience of each business student.

Several surveys of graduates' attitudes toward their business school experience reflect the greater dissatisfaction of women. A study entitled "Women and the M.B.A.: Gateway to Opportunity" was recently carried out by the Center for Education of Women at the University of Michigan. A survey of more than 1,600 male and female graduates at 12 top-ranked business schools revealed that women are more likely than men to be unhappy with the culture of their business school. It also confirmed that the proportion of women who enroll in the top MBA programs lags well behind the proportion who enroll in the top law and medical schools. Female enrollment at these top business schools averages 30 percent, compared to 44 percent enrolled in the top law and medical schools.

Fewer women than men felt that they could easily relate to their professors and the case studies they were required to cover. Also, 27 percent of the women and 45 percent of the African American women surveyed stated they found the business school environment overly aggressive and competitive. A full fifth of the women believed they were perceived by their instructors as less qualified than the men for professional business studies.

The positive finding is that the great majority of men and women reported their satisfaction with their MBA training and its value in the marketplace. Eighty-five percent of all the respondents believed their employers place great value on their MBA background. There is no questioning the need to encourage more women to consider a business education and career. Active recruiting of women and other minorities is a major recommendation to come out of this report. If you are considering a business career, you should feel encouraged to apply to the top schools if your academic background and work experience are strong.

HEUBLEIN'S BEER BUST

Heublein decided to acquire Hamm's. For all the smart marketing efforts, it proved impossible to make money on beer. In fact, losses piled up until Heublein had to sell the brewery. What were the problems management might have foreseen? Vodka is easy and inexpensive to make; it requires no high technology and no expensive aging process. Beer, by contrast, must be brewed under the supervision of an artful brewmaster with the right touch and the best equipment, and must be

(continued)

sufficiently aged in expensive tanks and warehouses. Hamm's equipment was outdated. To make a commercial success out of beer in a highly competitive environment, a clever marketing strategy like the one used for Smirnoff vodka was insufficient. Investment in new equipment was only the first step toward profitability. Success would have required years of patient development of a business totally unfamiliar to Heublein management. Heublein's executives did not realize this, and they suffered the consequences.

Who Gets In?

Competition for places in the best MBA programs continues to grow each year, but we urge you not to be discouraged if you have your heart set on working for an MBA. The level of many programs has been rising from good to outstanding. Strong candidates are enrolling in a greater number of business schools, while at the same time generous alumni and other benefactors have donated enormous amounts of money to many institutions for the advancement of their graduate schools. The old saw of a rising tide raising all boats on the water is true in the case of graduate schools. This is one of the reasons it makes little sense to rank business schools in a precise quantifiable order. Though there will always be a top 10 or 20 around, the individual schools within this construct change over time. What rejection statistics suggest is that many candidates overestimate their attractiveness to and qualification for a school and many other candidates are applying to their long-shot schools as well as to others that will likely accept them. We know that as long as there is a pecking order of business schools, candidates face a psychological barrier; they tend to despair and berate themselves when rejected by places where the competition is stiffest. Often they counsel themselves out of applying at all. This is unfortunate, for we find that those rejected by the top schools are often admitted to other excellent MBA programs.

ADVICE FOR THE PROSPECTIVE MBA FROM A
BUSINESS PROFESSOR AND PROFESSIONAL

Ervin Shames is the former chief executive officer of Borden Industries and Stride Rite Corporation; president and CEO of Kraft, USA, and General Foods, USA; and a visiting lecturer in marketing at the Darden School of Business at the University of Virginia. He is a graduate of the Harvard Business School, where he was a Baker Scholar. We asked him to respond to several of the important questions we have encouraged you, as a prospective graduate student, to consider. His comments are relevant to graduate education in business and to professional graduate school training in general.

What is the real purpose of an MBA education today?

There are five major functions to an MBA education. They are to teach: a. functional content, that is, the basic management principles and practices; b. the discipline of setting strategies against internal and external factors and information; c. analytical skills for making decisions; d. team skills and collaborative effort; e. sharper communication skills.

Is graduate training in business and management necessary?

No, it is not critical to have an MBA education, but it is highly desirable for several reasons. The actual content a professional businessperson needs to know will be learned more quickly. The curriculum, especially the case method of teaching, enhances the students' analytical skills and reasoning ability. There is also the very practical fact that prospective employers use the MBA degree as a screening device. The thinking goes like this: "Why wouldn't I hire a more experienced individual who has taken his or her learning to a higher level of formal training and proved the extent of his or her commitment to a career in business?"

(continued)

Do you consider it critical to attend a top ten graduate business school?

I do not think this is as essential as many young people considering graduate education do. From my experience in the corporate world, I would say that an MBA from any of the top 25 or so MBA programs would serve one well. After that it becomes more debatable as to the advantages of giving up a responsible job to spend two years in a learning environment that may not be too challenging and enriched. In order to get what you want and need out of the program, the faculty and students must be at a high level of expertise, experience, and ability. The resources for learning must also be first-rate, particularly the library and technological facilities.

What do you consider the best undergraduate majors for preparing for graduate business school?

Definitely a broad-based liberal arts education. Any academic discipline that will help a student to develop critical skills of thinking, writing, questioning, and communicating orally and in writing is going to ready a future business student and professional leader. There are three specific subjects that should be mastered: the principles of micro- and macroeconomics, accounting, and statistics. Any business student must have sound numerical and quantitative reasoning skills to cope with the demanding curriculum. These same skills are key to a successful career in virtually every field of business endeavor.

What tips would you pass on to a candidate for an MBA in picking an MBA program?

To my mind, there are two essential criteria that should override all others. First, understand the method of instruction and decide if it suits your learning style. The case study method requires active participation in class and accounts for 50% of the course grade typically. A reticent and less confident student may not do well in this classroom setting. Not unlike the undergraduate college experience, some students prefer lecture classes where there is less active participation and more emphasis on taking notes, reading the course material on one's own, and taking several major tests for the grade. Second, be certain the school has a strong faculty and curriculum in your specialty. Since all MBA students today have had an average of three to six years of work experience, they should have a pretty firm idea of what area of the larger business world they wish to pursue their career. Not every business school, not even the very top ones, will be equally strong in every specialty.

Are there any general observations you have for prospective business students?

There are several suggestions I have to offer. In the period between college graduation and graduate school, you should seek experiences that will allow you to demonstrate your leadership ability. More broadly, develop the credentials that will give credence to your skills. You cannot simply tell a graduate school that you have lots of potential to succeed in your studies and in the professional world afterwards. You must establish this credibility earlier. Also, after five years of working in a responsible job, the particular MBA pedigree will not matter—it is the performance on the job, the bottom-line results that will count. Thus, the business man or woman who is likely to rise to the top management positions has far more than the functional skills that might have served him or her well in lower- and middle-level positions. It is the ability to create and develop a strategic plan, to communicate effectively his or her goals and tactics, to get others to participate in implementing them, and to work in a positive and productive manner with team members that will win the day in every management situation. Successful leadership in any business or industry requires a high degree of self-confidence in order to stand by one's decisions. This degree of self-confidence is based on knowledge of people, the key elements of positive management, and the ability to learn new ideas and skill sets throughout one's career.

You can communicate by mail, telephone, or e-mail or on campus with a representative of the admissions office to review your credentials and the requirements for admission in the year you wish to apply. Remember that the sheer number of candidates drives the competition for acceptance, so you will need to know the trend line. You can also discuss the school's special concentrations and determine whether your background and interests are a match that will help your chances.

A SAMPLING OF SPECIALIZED MAJORS

Wharton School
Health care management
Insurance and risk
    management
Multinational management
Real estate
Human resource
    management
Operations and information
    management
Public policy and
    management

Harvard
Corporate strategy
Organizational behavior
    and human resource
    management
Corporate environmental
    management
Entrepreneurship
Environmental management
Nonprofit management

Manufacturing
E-commerce

University of Southern California
Business of entertainment
Service operations
    management
Technology development and
    e-business
Process consulting
Real estate finance/
    Entrepreneurship and
    venture management
Manufacturing operations
    management

New York University
Information systems/
    International business
Quantitative finance
Digital economy
Entertainment management
Media and technology

Summing Up

You should understand the many opportunities an MBA degree and the rigorous training required to obtain it can offer you. An MBA is likely to make you a front-runner in the competition for a top position in one or more of the many specialized fields of business. Although there are advantages to graduating from one of the very top business schools, you will find yourself attractive to business enterprises with a degree from any of the 25 most respected schools. Your chances for admission are greatly increased by three or more years of work experience, and you will take much more from the training with this experience. You will also help your odds by conveying a clear focus on why you want to enroll and what your goals are once you have your MBA degree. As with law school, be prepared to work many hours in an intense and competitive environment. Obtain the profiles of accepted candidates to the schools you are considering and apply only to the schools at which you have a reasonable chance to be accepted. If you are a woman or member of a minority group, you may have added appeal to a selective business school, but you must be qualified on all counts.

Medical School

Trends

A sea change has occurred in the health professions in recent years. This is most evident in the quantum growth of managed care by profit-driven companies, skyrocketing health costs, new discoveries in medicine and biology that are changing treatments as we understand more about how our bodies function, and the politicization of health delivery and research on human embryos. The extensive years of study and training and the cost required to become a medical practitioner make this choice of career an act of courage and conviction. More than 60 million Americans are enrolled in health management organizations today. This has dramatically changed the face of the medical profession. Doctors have had to cede much of their autonomy and authority to nonprofessional managers who make many of the decisions regarding the treatment of patients. In recent years, the federal government has not been generous to medical schools and hospitals, which have consequently been forced to make cutbacks in research, financial aid, and teaching resources. This has put considerable stress on the medical schools and their students.

If you are considering medicine, you should understand at the outset two significant factors:

1. You are likely to go into debt for as much as $100,000 by the time you are licensed to practice. The average debt load today is $90,000.
2. With private health care organizations pushing constantly for cost containment, the income of doctors has not kept pace with other major professions. In fact, many practitioners have experienced a decline in their income in recent years.

Another major change in the medical profession has been the extraordinary increase in the number of women enrolling in medical school. Only one generation ago, few places were given to women who wanted to become doctors. The medical schools were convinced that the long and expensive years of training would be wasted on women, since they were perceived as secondary earners within a family and responsible for bearing and raising children. Now women represent close to half of all medical students. Students of color and Hispanics are still grossly underrepresented in medical schools. Efforts are being made to address this issue through recruitment of college students and through scholarships to make it feasible for minorities to complete medical training.

With the emphasis on cost containment in the face of soaring medical expenses and the pressure from health management groups, more doctors are being trained today for primary care rather than specialized fields. More than one-third of all physicians are already in primary care, which means that they deal with a wide range of medical problems on the front line. They take care of a family's general health problems, referring on to specialists when necessary. We see more young people who want to go into general practice, because of their desire to work closely with their patients. Medical schools are weighing the desire for a career in primary care positively in their admissions decisions. You should consider carefully if you plan to train for a specific specialty. If your reasons are sound and can be explained to admissions committees in your applications and interviews, then go forward accordingly.

Many professionals with a medical degree are engaged in a variety of other fields today. Health management, public health, government agencies, hospital administration, teaching in medical schools, medical research, drug company management or research and development, and journalism are some of the avenues in which doctors put their expertise to good use.

There are 125 accredited medical schools in the United States, and they graduate 16,000 newly minted doctors each year. There are 22,320 training residencies at hospitals that need to be filled annually. The gap is a serious one, since hospitals rely heavily on residents to serve their patients. Medical graduates from other countries fill most of the additional spaces. The number of places in medical schools is unlikely to grow, because of the high cost of educating doctors, especially when many medical schools and their allied teaching hospitals are faced with serious financial difficulties.

DECIDING ON A CAREER IN MEDICINE

The Association of American Medical Colleges offers the following guidelines in considering your career choice:

First ask yourself what kind of future appeals to you. Do you want challenges and opportunities, a chance to make a difference? Many bright and motivated college students describe a "dream career" with the following characteristics:

(continued)

- *Opportunity to serve: Allows you to help people.*
- *Action: Does not tie you to a desk all the time.*
- *Respect: You are an important part of your community.*
- *Security: Allows you a good living with a secure future.*
- *Excitement: Changes daily, so it is hardly ever boring.*
- *Mobility: You are in demand wherever you choose to live.*
- *Flexibility: Gives you lots of career options from the same education base.*

Few occupations meet all of these standards. None meets them better than a career in medicine. Few fields offer a wider variety of opportunities. Most doctors' professional lives are filled with caring for people and continuously learning more about the human body. Every day in communities around the country, doctors work in neighborhood clinics, hospitals, offices, and even homeless shelters and schools to care for people in need.

But physicians also do many other things. Physician researchers are at work today developing exciting new treatments for cancer, genetic disorders, and infectious diseases like AIDS. Academic physicians share their skills and wisdom by teaching medical students and residents. Others work with health maintenance organizations, pharmaceutical companies, medical device manufacturers, health insurance companies, or in corporations directing health and safety programs. People with medical skills are in demand everywhere.

Admission Is Still a Challenge

As a result of the factors described earlier, the number of applicants to medical schools has dropped off in recent years by 20 percent. The Association of American Medical Colleges reports that 37,137 candidates applied for 16,303 places at the 125 accredited medical schools in the 2000–01 academic year. This contrasts with the peak year of

1996, when 47,000 candidates sought admission. The major reasons for this decline are as follows:

- There has been negative publicity about managed care and the loss of professional freedom.
- Historically, the offspring of medical professionals represented a significant portion of medical students. Today, fewer doctors encourage their children to consider medicine as a career.
- The competition at the undergraduate level to complete required science courses eliminates many prospective medical students. Many students need to work during the academic year to cover their high tuition and living costs. They find they cannot keep up with the intensive hours and workload in the premed courses.
- The strong economy in the 1990s created attractive job opportunities in fields where more money could be made with fewer years of higher education required.
- More than half of all college students will graduate with educational loans that have to be repaid. The prospect of incurring far greater debt is not an appealing one for many of them.

The decline in the number of applicants naturally improves the chances of admission for some, but the quality of applicants is still extremely high, and mediocre students are consistently rejected. It would be a mistake to assume that an average candidate has much chance of acceptance by an accredited medical school. There are major steps to take if you are to be accepted. However, we encourage anyone seriously committed to a medical career to apply. The majority of young adults we encounter choose medicine for personal and altruistic reasons rather than for future earnings and prestige. They purposely decide not to join their peers who head into investment banking, technology and the new economy, management consulting, or law. They recognize the hard work, persistence, focus, and emotional and physical vigor they must have to qualify for medical school and to complete their professional training.

Six Prepatory Procedures

Most applicants to medical school are self-directed. They know what it takes to get accepted, and they begin applying themselves in high school in order to be able to enroll in a good college or university known for preparing students for medical studies. They are aware they will need to excel in and outside of the classroom. Yet half of all who apply to medical school each year will be rejected, despite their efforts to complete the premed course requirements. Your chances of acceptance can be increased by carefully following these procedures:

- Study medical school admissions requirements carefully. Be certain that you have completed more than the minimum number of required science courses.
- Take advanced math, computer science, and psychology courses in addition to the laboratory subjects that are required.
- Enroll in an undergraduate college that is respected by the medical schools.
- Cultivate your premed advisor and follow your college's procedures for applying with his or her guidance.
- Apply to at least 10 medical schools of varying selectivity.
- Prepare an alternative plan for meeting your career goal at the same time you are applying to medical schools.

Let's look more closely at these procedures.

Study *Medical School Admission Requirements*

Medical School Admission Requirements is the annual publication of the Association of American Medical Colleges (hereafter referred to as the AAMC guide). It is indispensable to your planning. The AAMC guide can be found in public libraries and the career counseling center at your college. You can also gather a good deal of information that is in the guide on the AAMC website (www.aamc.org) and order the latest edition, which costs $25.00.

The guide discusses the nature of medical education, premed planning, the decision whether and where to apply to medical school, the Medical College Admission Test (MCAT) and the American Medical College Application Service (AMCAS) universal application, the application and selection process, financial information for medical students, information for minority group students, information for applicants not admitted to medical school, and detailed descriptions and requirements for admission of every accredited medical school in the United States and Canada.

You can directly contact the medical schools that seem appropriate once you have done an initial screening in the AAMC guide. Most schools have a website that can make your search for more detailed information easy and efficient.

Enroll in a Respected Undergraduate College

If you are bound for medical school you should aim to attend the most academically challenging undergraduate college, public or private, you can get into. This does not mean you should enroll in a place where you will have to compete so intensely with other students that there is a chance of not doing well in your studies. Your rule of thumb should be, "Where can I complete all the required courses for medical school and achieve a 3.4 GPA or better?" Many colleges and universities known for their premed program are not necessarily ranked in the top 25 or even 50 institutions. Literally hundreds of colleges send their graduates to medical schools every year. Much will depend on how well you perform in the required premed courses and in your major. One of the best criteria is to find out how medical school applicants from the particular colleges have fared in recent years.

Extracurricular accomplishment is also a factor in medical school selection. This includes not only the traditional athletic and club activities, but also those that are directly related to medicine: summer and part-time research and hospital volunteer work. Good colleges have active and well-informed premed committees that can guide students to these jobs or internships locally and nationally or recommend resources in their home communities.

The AAMC recommends that you ask these questions in choosing an undergraduate school:

- Does the school have a good faculty and a reputation for high academic standards? Is it accredited?
- Does it offer a broad range of courses in the humanities and in the social, behavioral, and natural sciences?
- Does it have strong science departments with good laboratory facilities?
- Does it offer all of the required courses you need for acceptance to medical school?
- Does the college have a designated advisor specifically trained to help students interested in the health professions?
- Does it have a good track record for having its students accepted to medical school?
- Does it offer extracurricular activities that appeal to you? Are there programs for volunteer work at local hospitals or clinics?
- Are there programs in which you can demonstrate leadership and compassion?
- Does it feel right to you? Are you comfortable with its size, location, social life, and general atmosphere?
- Is it affordable for you?

The AAMC advises, "As you select a college remember that just as in high school, a good liberal arts education is a key ingredient to becoming a physician. You'll need a strong foundation in mathematics and the sciences that relate most to medicine: biology, general chemistry, organic chemistry, and physics. But it's important for your college experience to be broad. Taking courses in the humanities or liberal arts will help you prepare for the 'people' side of medicine."

Take Advanced Math, Computer, and Psychology Courses

Medical school training is undergoing major changes in its approach. Computer literacy is a must for any student. Computers are used extensively to teach, to do experiments, and to study the body in virtual space. The large lecture halls and operations pits are ceasing to be the standard method of teaching and acquiring the vast amount of information necessary to becoming a doctor. The faculty will expect you to use your computer for much of your studies, from learning anatomy to diagnosing diseases. Communication with your teachers and participation in research projects will be carried out on the Internet.

Math is the language of the sciences and research. Without the requisite mathematical skills, you will be at a disadvantage in lab work and research projects. This is why medical schools require you to take a full year of calculus. A year of probability and statistics is also important to understanding and communicating about vital research projects and information on general medical issues.

The best medical practitioners have excellent relational skills. They are empathetic to their patients' emotional as well as physical needs. An understanding of how and why people think and behave as they do comes from the study of psychology. Be sure to include electives in the behavioral sciences in your undergraduate curriculum.

Cultivate Your Premed Advisor

This step is sometimes overlooked by candidates, who suddenly find themselves unsupported by a premed advisor they scarcely know. The premed advisor in the strongest undergraduate programs has an obligation to his or her institution to prevent weak candidates from applying to and being turned down by medical schools. The advisor is not a gatekeeper who wants to prevent you from meeting your goals, however. His or her role is to serve the qualified and ambitious student, the one who takes advantage of the advice offered on what courses to take and where and when to apply to graduate school.

It is easy for a premed student to overlook the fact that only one or two or more chemistry or other science courses offered at a particular school are rigorous enough to qualify as a proper course for medical school admissions. Your premed advisor will steer you in the right direction—provided he or she is aware of your existence. It is not a question of buttering up someone, but simply of being a known quantity who can be helped. It is still possible for an advisor who knows you well to withhold full endorsement of your candidacy, but it should only be because of a weak academic record, not because you have failed to meet the necessary requirements. Admissions committees look to your advisor to offer insights into your academic program and activities on and off campus that augment your statistical profile.

Apply to at Least 10 Medical Schools of Varying Selectivity

The great majority of medical schools require that you apply through the AMCAS procedure. AMCAS provides you with a common application, which you complete and return to them with your college transcript and personal statements. AMCAS forwards your application to all the medical schools you have designated. This procedure makes it easier for candidates to apply to a good number of schools to broaden their list of possibilities. We encourage applicants to fashion a list of medical schools, from the highly selective to the more likely, on the basis of their credentials. It makes no sense to apply to as many as 20 schools, which some candidates have actually done, if you are unlikely to qualify for admission to any of them. You should be able to develop an appropriate list with the help of your premed advisor and/or a close reading of the statistical data on each school included in the AAMC guide.

In evaluating your credentials, admissions committees review your college grades, with a breakdown of your performance in all science and math courses, and your MCAT scores, volunteer activities, caring for others, communication skills, emotional maturity, interpersonal skills, self-motivation, adaptability, sense of humor, physical health, and passion for medicine as a career. This is why your personal application, advisor and faculty recommendations, interviews, and work or internship experience can play vital roles in the decision process. By making 10 applications, you may well capture the attention of a particular admissions committee member who will strongly support your candidacy. As you study the curriculum and mission statement of a number of medical schools, look for signals that your strengths and interests match the school and thus might increase your odds of being accepted.

One last point: your official state of residency plays an important role in the process. Public universities accept few out-of-state applicants, as they are under great pressure to train qualified in-state residents, who are more likely to practice in their state once they have their medical degree subsidized through the tax dollars of state residents. Be sure to apply to any medical school in the state in which you have permanent residency, and do not apply solely to other public schools. Private universities aim to enroll as geographically diverse a population as possible. They enjoy the national reputation this brings to their school and the variety of backgrounds that naturally occurs. As we stated in the earlier discussion of law and business schools, you do yourself a disservice by limiting your applications to a narrow geographic area. You could miss out on a fine medical school that would consider your regional background a plus factor.

You can learn a great deal about medical school life and the issues that most concern students by contacting the American Medical Student Association via the Association of American Medical Colleges. They will enable you to get answers to your questions directly from present students.

Prepare an Alternative Plan for Meeting Your Career Goal

Many medical school applicants take out insurance by applying simultaneously to other professional health science schools. In case of rejection by all the medical schools, they may have a good chance of acceptance at a school of public health, dentistry, osteopathic medicine, physical therapy, pharmacy, occupational therapy, rehabilitation counseling, speech-language pathology, or nursing specialties. Any of these professions will provide you with outlets for your interest in helping others and working in a specialized, knowledge-based field, and your premed studies will stand you in good stead in these graduate programs.

Other alternatives to explore are master's or doctoral programs in related sciences, such as biology, biochemistry, anatomy, biomedicine, biophysics, cell biology, genetics, immunology, microbiology, molecular biology, neurosciences, pathology, pharmacology, and physiology. Any of these disciplines can lead to a satisfying career or can serve as a foundation for reapplying to medical school in the future. This can be a successful first step toward attaining a dual degree eventually.

Explore Postbaccalaureate Programs as an Option

What can you do if you are set on becoming a doctor and have little or no interest in alternative health-related careers? What if you come to the decision you want to be a doctor after you have graduated from college? Since both scenarios are true for thousands of individuals of all ages, a number of outstanding colleges and universities have created postbaccalaureate programs in the requisite sciences. What you majored in while an undergraduate or what you have been doing for a living since you left college does not matter. What does matter is that you are convinced that this is the direction in life you wish to take, and you are ready to put your full energies into intensive study of biology, chemistry, physics, and mathematics before applying to medical schools. We believe that this formal postbaccalaureate program is one of the best ways to prepare for and get accepted to medical school.

We have counseled many men and women to take this step, and we have had the pleasure of watching them gain acceptance to the medical school of their choice in time. Some of the most popular postbac programs are at Columbia, Bryn Mawr, Goucher, Georgetown, the University of Connecticut, Boston University, Tufts, Simmons, Brandeis, Rutgers (for in-state residents), NYU, the University of Pennsylvania, Pennsylvania State University, and the State University of New York at Stony Brook. The time required to complete one of these programs is normally one full year, but some students spread out the course work over two years to perform at a higher level.

Summing Up

Any of the 125 accredited medical schools will provide you with the necessary training to qualify you as a medical practitioner. Unlike law and business schools, there are no easy or safe medical schools that you can count on for acceptance. There simply are too few places available for the number of qualified candidates each year. You must meet all of the specific course and test requirements to be considered for admission for all of the medical schools. As in applying to other professional graduate schools, your grades, test scores, course program, and relevant experiences will play the major role in your consideration. If you do not have the proper credentials, consider other opportunities in the health professions or, if you have your heart set on a medical career, apply to a postbaccalaureate program.

Other Graduate School Options: Hunt Down Those Programs

At the beginning of this step we listed the major professions that require graduate training through at least the master's degree. We also mentioned that within each of these professions are numerous specialized fields for which one can train. Take education, for example, and you can easily imagine the extraordinary number of areas in which someone with a master's or doctoral degree can fashion a secure and satisfying career. The same holds true for almost all of the professions we have listed. Considering social work? You can work for a city, regional, state, or federal agency overseeing programs that assist people in need, or you can become a counselor or consultant in private practice, or work in a school or hospital. We can go on with examples ad infinitum. There are careers you probably have not thought of that would provide you with the challenge, the stimulation, the rewards, and the professional stature you are seeking. We will highlight a few to demonstrate the way to find what you hope for in your life's work.

Ministry, the Elusive Calling

For most people, the choice of career does not come easily, and the journey is not a straight line from Point A to Point B. We remind you that there are ample decision points to begin a new career. Graduate programs that will serve your needs in furthering your journey will be available to you at any time. Sometimes a small voice inserts itself in the process and takes several years to be heard. Such was the case with the following student at the Virginia Theological Seminary in Alexandria, Virginia.

BARBARA: *fulfilling one's personal destiny*

Take Barbara, for whom the journey to ministry took an unantici-pated route. Born in Minnesota, a graduate of Carleton College, she taught high school English for several years before marrying and moving about the country with her husband, who was in the military. They eventually settled in Alaska, where they lived in an Eskimo village. Her husband worked for the state public health service. Bar-bara and her husband adopted two local children, who occupied her full-time for their early childhood years.

When she returned to work, Barbara held increasingly important positions with state and local government, including being division manager of an Alaskan waste and water utility and administrative assis-tant to two of Anchorage's mayors. "If you have a good college degree and know how to write, you can do any job," she reported. "My last job was a really big undertaking, with a large budget and responsibility; I ran the parks, libraries, museums, and recreational programs. I even thought of running for mayor, but began to ask myself, What will hap-pen to me in the next part of my life and what do I really care about?"

Active in her church as a young person, Barbara reflected on an earlier desire to study for the ministry. At the Virginia Theological Seminary in "the lower 48" she was attracted to "an intentional wor-shipping collegial community of faculty and students." Her plan was to return to Alaska. In her original questionnaire she wrote:

> Parish life is where I want to be. That is where I see myself having an impact, through people. I am very much a people person. I can see myself getting a lot of energy from working with people of all backgrounds and needs. I cannot any longer imagine myself not taking this step into divinity studies.

For Those Interested in Journalism and Communications

It is hardly necessary to call attention to the explosion in the world of communications. We have created so many new ways to deliver infor-mation and entertainment to a larger and more diverse audience. Radio, television, the Internet, film, magazines, and satellite make it possible to communicate on any subject to a global audience at any moment we choose. The majority of you will have come of age in this diverse and fast-moving communications environment, and you take for granted all of the means for entertainment and communication. The career opportunities for anyone who has a creative imagination, is passionate about words, and loves to write or communicate orally are limitless.

A degree from a recognized graduate school of journalism is very useful, though not the only way to break into print or electronic media. Formerly looked down on by editors who had worked their way up, starting as copy boys on newspapers, or as gofers in television and radio stations, these schools are now visited eagerly by recruiters for newspapers, magazines, radio-television departments, government and corporate communications departments, and public relations firms. Various departments of the federal government send their employees to certain schools of journalism, for example Boston University's School of Public Communication or Syracuse's Newhouse School of Journalism, for training as public affairs officers. The training you receive at a journalism school is excellent preparation for a career in virtually every kind of organization in which strong communication and marketing skills are called for. We have counseled many people who have creative minds and take pleasure in communicating their ideas through words and images to consider a graduate school of journalism and communications. It can only expand the range of opportunities in this wide world of media we live in today.

In general, these are one- or two-year master's programs. Ph.D. programs are intended mostly for those who plan to teach in journalism or communications at the college level. Basic courses include news and feature writing, copyediting, headline writing, page makeup and graphic design, and television writing and producing. Among the electives are magazine writing and publishing, news photography, opinion polling, investigative reporting, and book, film, theater, and arts reviewing. Candidates interested in public relations can take courses in writing releases, planning a press conference, and product promotion.

If you are interested in the field and study the offerings of the major graduate schools of journalism, you will discover that they have a number of special programs that can meet your interests. New York University's School of Journalism offers master's degrees in such specialties as broadcast journalism, science and environmental reporting, business and economic reporting, journalism and Latin American studies. Indiana University's School of Journalism emphasizes public affairs reporting; their philosophy is to balance professional skills training with solid academic study.

Desirable preparation for journalism school is usually a bachelor's degree in history, English, political science, psychology, or sociology. The current demand for science and technology writers, business and medical reporters, and other specialized topics provides an opportunity for those who have majored in science, engineering, biology, chemistry, economics, or business to enter the fields of journalism and communications.

The Top Graduate Schools of Journalism and Communications

We have already established the point that there is no precise or scientific method for ranking graduate schools of any kind. There is a sense among deans in the discipline and the professional community which programs attract the most talented students and prepare them well for careers in the field. This is an alphabetical list of the acknowledged leaders in journalism and communications:

Boston University	University of Illinois
Columbia University	University of Iowa
Indiana University	University of Maryland
Michigan State University	University of Michigan
New York University	University of Minnesota
Northwestern University	University of Missouri
Ohio State University	University of North Carolina
Pennsylvania State University	University of Texas
Stanford University	University of Wisconsin
Syracuse University	

A Career in Words and Ideas

There is a long, honorable tradition of liberal arts graduates who wish to spend their lifetime around books and reading. Rather than become doctors, lawyers, business people, teachers, counselors, or even journalists, they have a passion for writing, editing, literature, biography, history, and, for some, the history and interpretation of technology and science. They would like to produce and publish books. You can think of editors and publishers as word masters with an eclectic range of interests. For such individuals, the field of book publishing is a professional beacon.

New York University has one of the oldest M.A. programs in book and magazine publishing in the country. A balance of studies in academic courses and professional subjects and internships prepares its students for careers after graduation. For 53 years, the Radcliffe College Publishing Institute has trained thousands of aspiring editors and writers in an intensive six-week summer curriculum. In 2001, this venerable program moved to Columbia University's Graduate School of Journalism. This change recognizes New York City's position as the book and magazine publishing center of America. Students will have opportunities to intern in the leading publishing houses with editors, publicists, and graphic designers. If your interests fit with the above description, investigate these two leading graduate programs.

LIFE IN TELEVISION COMMUNICATIONS

Al Briganti, executive editor of CBS News's *48 Hours*, shared this advice with us. He is a graduate of the Columbia University School of Journalism.

> As Dan Rather might say, working in the TV business today is a lot like trying to change a fan belt on a moving city bus. Mergers, radical new technologies, and government deregulation rou-

(continued)

tinely send shock waves of change through the communications industry. This is not a career for someone looking for stability in his or her life; but it can be enormously fulfilling and more fun than you can possibly imagine.

The first thing you have to do is be prepared to work hard and not get paid a lot of money. Though the big names on TV make millions, most entry-level positions pay a lot less than your friends on Wall Street or in law firms will be raking in.

On this career path there are a number of forks in the road where you will have to make important decisions on how to proceed. The first is whether you want to be an entertainer or a journalist. The lines may have blurred a bit in recent years, but serious broadcast journalists view the paths as mutually exclusive, and are annoyed by young applicants who do not understand that.

In the television business of the future, the roles of reporter, camera person, and editor are likely to merge. It will be helpful not only to be a good writer, but also to have some technical expertise, especially with computers.

Will a graduate degree in communications help? Yes, if it helps you refine skills that make you useful to your first employer. Look for a school that has a demanding writing program, and also has the latest television toys and electronic equipment. It is also important to find a graduate school that has strong ties to real newsrooms. Practical experience, including campus journalism and internships, will give you an edge in finding that first job and being able to do well.

In the end, the most important quality for a career in television broadcasting is what has gotten you this far in your academic career, namely, intellectual curiosity. If you really like to learn new things, you will be good at telling people about them.

Engineering and Computer Science Offer Many Choices

Of all college graduates, engineers and computer scientists seem best to know where they are headed. Yet even they should not lock themselves into preconceived notions of where they should continue to study without investigating a wide range of opportunities. The professions are becoming more blurred as the explosion of knowledge in many fields requires training that overlaps formal educational boundaries. Engineers and computer scientists turn into business entrepreneurs and corporate leaders in the expanding world of technology, or work with medical doctors to develop physical devices to help the handicapped or to replace parts of the body. An engineering degree does not oblige you to enroll in a graduate engineering program as a prelude to a career in technology. Here is a typical pattern these days: One-fourth of the recent graduates of the Thayer School of Engineering at Dartmouth went directly into business, while another fourth went to medical school, law school, or architecture school.

A report recently issued by the National Science Board, *Science and Engineering Indicators,* raises concerns about the steady decline in the number of American and international students pursuing graduate work in science and engineering. This could result in a shortage of skilled workers and researchers in the future to meet the needs of our increasingly technological society. Even the number of foreign-born scientists receiving master's and doctorates dropped by 15 percent several years ago, the beginning of a trend that continues. This group has traditionally represented one-half of all doctoral students in science research and engineering. The good news is that more women are now pursuing master's and doctoral degrees in technology and sciences. They account for 40 percent of graduate students in the field. Minority enrollment has remained static at only 5 percent of enrolled students, despite efforts to recruit candidates from the college ranks.

There are many reasons for this gloomy situation. In a market economy, the opportunities to earn handsome incomes in other professions have attracted many potential engineers and scientists. Instead of working as an engineer, for example, many enterprising men and women decide to jump into the business side of the new economy, or become lawyers and use their college education in science and engineering. We have seen the pendulum swings in the major professions over the years, and encourage those who enjoy and are good at solving technical problems, inventing new devices, or doing scientific research to pursue graduate work. Any time there is a shortage, the opportunities for those who are well trained become plentiful and exciting.

Despite the softening in the number of applicants for graduate programs, the quality of candidates is very strong, and you can be sure that the top engineering and science schools do not admit students they deem to be of substandard quality. MIT admits only 30 percent of all applicants; Berkeley, 26 percent; Cornell, 28 percent; Princeton, 25 percent; Michigan, 34 percent; and Stanford, a surprising 45 percent. Although these percentages are higher than for the top medical, law, and business schools, the applicants universally have outstanding science and engineering backgrounds in their undergraduate schools and average GRE scores in the top decile. Engineers as a group know what they want early on and prepare themselves well for graduate training.

In the list of top schools that follows, many public universities are represented. This is because only large research institutions with considerable facilities and faculties can carry on simultaneously advanced training of future scientists and engineers and advanced research projects. If you are seriously considering a graduate degree in any of the technical and scientific fields, you should cast a wide net that includes the great state universities. The American Society for Engineering Education provides valuable information on the nature of scientific education and career opportunities in different engineering specialties and profiles on all of the schools they accredit. Their website is www.asee.org.

The Top Graduate Engineering Schools

California Institute of
 Technology
Carnegie Mellon University
Case Western Reserve
 University

Cornell University
Duke University
Georgia Institute of
 Technology
Harvard University

Johns Hopkins University
Massachusetts Institute of
  Technology
Northwestern University
Ohio State University
Pennsylvania State University
Princeton University
Purdue University
Rensselaer Polytechnic
  Institute
Rice University
Stanford University
Texas A&M University
University of California,
  Berkeley
University of California, Davis
University of California, Los
  Angeles
University of California, San
  Diego
University of California, Santa
  Barbara
University of Colorado,
  Boulder
University of Illinois, Urbana-
  Champaign
University of Maryland,
  College Park
University of Michigan, Ann
  Arbor
University of Minnesota,
  Twin Cities
University of Pennsylvania
University of Southern
  California
University of Texas
University of Virginia
University of Washington
University of Wisconsin

The Many Careers in Education

The opportunities for a worthy career in education are many and diverse. The U.S. Department of Education and the various professional educational associations project a need over the next 10 years for 2.5 million new teachers. By 2009, large numbers of present teachers will have retired, while 20 percent more students will have entered our school systems. In addition to this dramatic shortage of trained teachers, significant numbers of guidance counselors, special education teachers, school principals, and superintendents are needed if we are to fulfill the national agenda of improving our schools at all grade levels.

All of our recent presidents have made education a major item in their platform. The Department of Education is presently engaged in a national campaign to publicize the need for more good teachers to give all of America's children a quality education and to keep the nation competitive in the world economy. For members of minority groups in particular, the opportunities in the profession are enormous, because of the growing recognition that they should have equal opportunities in the teaching and administrative fields. Further, students of color and ethnic minorities represent the fastest growing group of students who will enter our school systems in this decade. Role models are important if these youngsters are to succeed in school and, in time, take their place in the mainstream of American society.

In 1910, Simeon Baldwin, the chief justice of the Connecticut Supreme Court and also chair of the Board of Trustees of Hopkins Grammar School in New Haven, Connecticut, had the following to say on the 250th anniversary of this distinguished school in which one of us taught and from which the other graduated. His words have as much meaning today as they did nearly a century ago:

> And what life work is there which offers more? The main duty of every generation of mankind must always be to rear the next. What a man does in life is largely measurable by the way he has impressed himself on the minds of others when they are in the most impressionable stage. They will live after him and he will live in them.

Teaching is not the whole story. An education degree can lead to a career in administration, special education, guidance and counseling, language training, curriculum development, educational psychology, and consulting to school systems, the government, and companies. As we are fond of explaining to hundreds of individuals we have counseled on careers in education, one of the beauties of this profession is the ability to zig and zag over a lifetime. Virtually all educational administrators, consultants, and writers, college admissions deans, and student personnel directors began their careers as classroom teachers. They moved on to a more advanced specialty or leadership role as they grew professionally and discovered areas beyond the classroom that appealed to them. It is relatively easy to return to a graduate school of education to study for a higher degree as your career goals move to a next level. Many teachers and administrators, in both public and private education, continue working as they pursue an advanced degree in special education, an academic subject, educational administration, or reading and literacy, for example. Many schools help their teachers pay for part-time advanced study.

When you adopt education as a career, you become valuable to businesses, government, consulting firms, the military, publishers, Internet-based and communications groups—in fact, to any organization with an educational focus or component. For example, high-tech companies have multimillion dollar education departments that train users of hardware and software. The U.S. State Department has its own language schools, at which employees are taught fluency in a number of languages. Arthur D. Little, the well-known consulting firm in Cambridge, Massachusetts, is licensed to grant master's degrees in management to executives who take courses offered by staff engineers, scientists, management consultants, and human resource experts.

We include here a partial list of universities, arranged alphabetically, that offer highly regarded programs at both the master's and doctoral levels in the many fields of education. Only a handful of the top private universities have outstanding faculty and training, while a larger number of public universities can provide you with a prestigious advanced degree that can launch you on a successful career. The opportunities for scholarships, fellowships, and internships at these universities are many and generous.

Another plus for the average graduate student in education: Once you're admitted to a major institution, you have access to all of its resources for interdisciplinary study. This allows you to combine a professional degree with pursuit of an academic interest in art, psychology, music, history, science, language, management, or any other subject you would like to specialize in. Educational training should not be conceived as limited to dry techniques of teaching, administering, and counseling. Most graduate students today combine several different disciplines to prepare for their careers. You will have a great deal of flexibility once you enroll in your top university program.

Highly Rated Graduate Schools of Education

Arizona State University
Boston College
George Washington University
Harvard University
Indiana University, Bloomington
Michigan State University
New York University
Northwestern University
Ohio State University
Pennsylvania State University
Stanford University
Teachers College, Columbia University
Temple University
University of California, Berkeley

University of California, Los Angeles
University of Colorado
University of Georgia
University of Illinois
University of Iowa
University of Maryland
University of Michigan
University of Minnesota
University of North Carolina
University of Oregon
University of Pennsylvania
University of Texas
University of Virginia
University of Washington
University of Wisconsin
Vanderbilt University

A CAREER IN THE FOREIGN SERVICE: FOR THOSE WITH AN OUTSTANDING LIBERAL ARTS BACKGROUND

Dr. Frederick Quinn, a senior officer in the Foreign Service for 32 years, provided us with this overview. He worked closely with the late David McClelland, former head of the Social Relations Department at Harvard University, in designing new approaches to Foreign Service recruitment that would not discriminate against women and minorities and would provide accurate predictors of skills needed to function successfully in an overseas environment.

If you like living abroad, with fairly frequent moves from country to country, and working on challenging problems, some of which

never seem to be fully resolved, then the Foreign Service just
might be the career option for you. Each year, the Department of
State selects about 300 Junior Officers, and a comparable number of specialists, to work in embassies and consulates overseas. The average age of such entering employees is 27 to 35,
and the salary is in the $30,000 to $50,000 range, depending on
previous experience and education.

Most Foreign Service Officers will tell you it is not the money
that attracts outstanding college graduates. It is the constant
excitement of dealing in the foreign affairs arena. At a given
American embassy on any Monday morning, a Political Officer
might be interviewing a regional governor about North–South
political tensions; the Economic Officer could be meeting an
American business delegation weighing whether or not to invest
in that country's telecommunications expansion effort; the Public Affairs Officer may be suggesting whom a visiting journalist
might want to interview; the Administrative Officer will be looking at an alternative site for the proposed American School to be
relocated in the capital city; and the Consular Officer will be por-
ing over an in-basket filled with visa applications, deciding who is
eligible for travel to the United States and who is not. The entire
embassy might be preparing for a cabinet officer's visit, or for
the arrival of a congressional delegation to discuss such bilateral
or multilateral issues as trade, arms sales, terrorism, or economic assistance programs.

The work is challenging. Your portfolio could include human
rights issues, work with the local scientific community on issues
like AIDS or environmental questions, seeing that a jailed American receives fair treatment by the local officials, and helping
American businesses find a level playing field on which to compete in local markets. American Officers serve in more than 160
countries around the world, and many of them are places where
health and climate conditions are less than optimal, telephones
don't always work, and resiliency of personality is a must for

(continued)

survival and success. American-style amenities are not always available. For all its fascination, the cross-cultural life has negative as well as positive aspects.

A recent job analysis survey identified the following skills as essential to success in a Foreign Service career: proper English usage and a knowledge of American society, culture, history, political cultures and life, the U.S. Constitution, world geography, history of international relations, and global political and social issues. Foreign Service Officers should also have a basic familiarity with accounting, statistics, and mathematics, skills in interpersonal communications, and familiarity with basic management and economic principles.

The Department of State also has intern and fellowship programs, and numerous opportunities for specialist employment, for example, computer, office management, security, and related technical skills. A 24-hour Foreign Service Career Information Line, (703) 875-7490, will answer many questions about the recruitment process.

A wealth of information on Foreign Service Careers and details on the written and oral examination process is available on the Department's website, www.State.gov/careers, complete with audio and video segments.

Where to Look for Program Options

We have discussed a few programs at random simply to prime the pump of your imagination. Now it is up to you to do some exploring.

- Begin in your college library. If you are out of school, use the public library or Internet to look at a variety of graduate school catalogues.
- Review the reference materials on career opportunities and the U.S. Department of Labor's annual report on employment trends and salaries.
- Talk to people in your field of interest. Find out where they did their graduate work and where people are now doing their training.

- Read the education pages of newspapers and magazines that feature articles on careers and graduate schools and the degrees they offer.
- Search the Internet to learn about careers and where to prepare for them. Every graduate school of note has its own website that will enable you to discover its strengths and requirements for admission.
- Consult faculty members who have specialized in the academic discipline you are considering. They are excellent sources of information about graduate programs in their specialties and the strengths and weaknesses of programs at various universities. Faculty advisors can discuss career options and employment outlooks in various careers for persons with advanced degrees.

The most comprehensive directory of graduate degree programs in all academic and professional disciplines is *Peterson's Annual Guide to Graduate Study,* a six-volume index of graduate programs. It lists graduate programs in various disciplines and specialties within disciplines, and has two-page summaries of some individual programs. The GRE/CGS four-volume *Directory of Graduate Programs* identifies graduate programs in specific disciplines and specialties. It indicates the highest degree offered, the number of degree candidates enrolled, prerequisites for admission, and financial aid. Both of these publications list the home websites of the graduate schools for your further research.

We have gathered a list of websites, as well as printed books and directories, that will help you in your research on any of the major careers, graduate schools, and financial aid resources. You will find this in the Bibliography at the end of this book.

Concluding the Exploration

In Step Three we have led you to explore a number of graduate opportunities open to qualified present and past college students. Some are like inlets on a strange coastline that you simply pass by during an expedition. If you have no medical aspirations, for example, you perhaps skipped the pages on medical schools. If you read everything in this step, you probably perceived a common thread that runs through all graduate school admissions: Every graduate school depends on recruiting and enrolling new students every year, and the top institutions set demanding admissions standards that put American graduate education at the summit of the world's universities. Nowhere else will a student find such an enormous variety of graduate programs and the resources of faculty and facilities to provide a world-class education. Nowhere else is it as feasible for the ambitious person to enhance a career or enrich life for himself or herself by earning a graduate degree.

Recently, Cindy, a young woman with a bachelor's degree from Pomona College, came to see us. After three years on the marketing staff of a Texas-based software firm, she found herself, as she put it, "somewhat illiterate about corporate management." She was not drawn to business school training and an MBA degree. Weren't there other opportunities available to her? There were, but Cindy had not yet done enough exploring.

We recommended that Cindy complete the Myers-Briggs Type Indicator and Strong Interest Inventory as part of the career transitions counseling we provide for individuals at the beginning of their journey. The findings of these inventories and a personal session with us indicated that her interests and personality fit nicely with the field of counseling and psychology. We recommended that she consider applying to several master's programs in industrial psychology. This profession calls for an understanding of the environment of the corporate world and psychological behavior and types; it is a field that actively seeks more women for vital positions. After researching the field through reading and interviews with professionals in the field, Cindy applied and was admitted to several top programs. She enrolled in Columbia University. Cindy reported back to us that her first year of studies was demanding but exhilarating. After completing her two years of study, Cindy entered the field of executive management recruiting with one of the largest firms in the country. She wrote us recently to tell us about her work and how well she is doing. Her interests and the skills she'd learned in her graduate program positioned her well, she observed.

ADVICE FOR PROSPECTIVE ARCHITECTURE
AND DESIGN GRADUATE STUDENTS

We asked Karen Van Lengen, dean and Edward E. Elson Professor at the School of Architecture at the University of Virginia, to respond to several questions that individuals considering a degree and career in architecture should ask:

What do you think are the important questions a person should ask him- or herself, and a university, when considering a graduate degree?

Is this what I really want to do?

Who does best in a graduate architecture program, and what does the graduate admissions committee primarily look for in applicants?

Usually students who have a basic understanding of the discipline of architecture through either prior work experience or some undergraduate training. However, the students with a broader and more comprehensive arts and sciences background usually perform better in the long run, so we try to find students who have a combination of these two qualities.

What criteria make for a strong graduate program?

Diverse and accomplished faculty, a strong student body, focused leadership at the administrative level, and complementary programs which can augment and support the particular graduate program that a student selects. Programs with double degrees are often preferred now, as they provide students with more professional alternatives and offer a more comprehensive education.

How important is a graduate degree from an architecture school today (versus a B.Arch. or B.F.A., for example)?

A graduate degree in architecture is now the preferred professional degree over the old bachelor of architecture. A bachelor of

(continued)

fine arts is not a professional degree; one cannot sit for a licensing exam in most states without having a professional degree.

How important is a portfolio for a student with interests in art, architecture, and design?

At the undergraduate level we do not require a portfolio; however, if a student has prepared one, it often helps us to gauge where he or she is in the area of visual arts. At the graduate level it is very important to demonstrate some experience and interest in the general field of design.

The multiplicity of career and graduate school options is overwhelming to many prospective graduate students. The exploration process may seem like being on a superhighway lacking exit signs to guide you. In reality, the signs are there, but you have to look behind the obstacles on the highway that hide them. You, like thousands of individuals we have guided, will find that a diligent search that uses all forms of help can be thoroughly rewarding.

Step Three Checklist

- Explore beyond the small handful of top professional degree programs you have heard of. Be sure not to overlook the many excellent universities that can prepare you for the career you have determined is your future.

- Always get profiles of the most recent entering classes in programs you are considering and compare them with your academic and nonacademic credentials to see where admission opportunities lie for you.

- Explore beyond conventional degrees for unique degrees and training that may give you a special advantage, from specialized or emerging professions to combined-degree programs that give you greater choices in your life.

Look for career options and degree programs in the major directories and websites. Talk to people in your college, from faculty to career advisors to working professionals, to be certain the direction you are considering is appropriate to your personality and aptitudes.

STEP FOUR

Determine Your Academic Qualifications

How Good Is Your Bachelor's Degree?

As we mentioned earlier, anyone with a bachelor's degree can get into a graduate school somewhere. Many colleges and universities are actively seeking out potential graduate students, because they need to fill their enrollment for revenue purposes, justify their programs, or increase the selectivity of their applicant pool. Inevitably, whatever the value and prestige of such programs may have been, they are now diminished, even though the faculty and instruction may be adequate. Less qualified students drag graduate schools down. Beware of enrolling in programs that seem easy to get into. The program you want should make demands on its applicants. Rather than try to fill their programs with mediocre students, the better institutions close down those programs that are not attracting their desired enrollment. A number of prestigious universities have, in recent years, closed graduate programs in dentistry and nursing and academic subjects for which there is little interest, rather than lower the overall standards of its graduate student body. Be certain when investigating specific graduate departments to check the history of enrollment size and qualifications of enrolled students in the past few years. This will give you an indication of the direction and strength of the program.

We are assuming that you are not a mediocre student, but there are degrees of excellence. To understand where you fall on this scale, you should evaluate the course content of your undergraduate curriculum and your grades in key courses. Many potential graduate school candidates underestimate their qualifications, because they think that their overall GPA is average or below average. This may be true, but graduate admissions committees look particularly at your performance in the last three years of college and in those individual courses that relate directly to the intended field of study. Many students do not do well in their first year of college for all the obvious reasons: adjustment to being away from home, getting used to the academic demands of their instructors, taking courses that are required and not of immediate interest or pleasure. How you performed in your major concentration in your junior and senior year will send the important message to admissions committees. Conversely, you may have achieved a high GPA but failed to take or did poorly in specific courses that a graduate school expressly requires as a foundation for the work in their discipline.

It is a mistake to conclude that after college, your educational record is fixed once and for all. The fact that you have completed undergraduate work and received your B.A. or B.S. does not mean that your record cannot be improved by taking extension courses in subjects that will strengthen it. Bear this in mind as you read this step: It is never too late to enrich your undergraduate record, no matter how long ago you graduated. Just your willingness to continue your education and improve on it will impress admissions officers and faculty reviewers, providing the work you have done is meaningful and of high quality.

Undergraduates reading this step may have time to alter their curricular plans to meet the desires of admissions committees. It is not necessarily sufficient to graduate with a high GPA; graduate schools will be unimpressed if they find that you have taken courses they consider to be lacking in intellectual rigor. A demanding curriculum is essential if you are to have a chance for acceptance to the top programs, no matter what field you are considering.

DOUG: *going from teaching to medical school*

Doug graduated from the University of Rochester with a B.A. He was clear from the start of his undergraduate studies that medical school and a career as a physician were his ultimate goals. Doug planned his college program and extracurricular commitments accordingly. He did his homework on the procedures for applying and where he thought he had his best chances for acceptance. His major was the history of medicine, a self-designed major. His cumulative GPA was 3.42, and he made the dean's list in his last two years of study.

In his final year of college, Doug worked with his premed advisor, filed the AMCAS application, took the MCATs, and diligently wrote a personal statement that he believed helped define his interests and goals. The results were disappointing: He was rejected by all 15 of the medical schools to which he applied! The list included one public university in his home state and 14 private university programs. They included New York Medical College, Tufts, Emory, Tulane, George Washington, Rochester, Vanderbilt, Northwestern, Albert Einstein, and Mt. Sinai Universities.

When Doug turned to us for advice on what went wrong and what he might do to improve his chances for acceptance in another round, we studied his curriculum carefully. The list of science and math courses on the AMCAS application highlighted the strong emphasis and academic success in his social science subjects rather than in the sciences. Although Doug completed all of the necessary lab science courses to qualify for medical school admission, he had four C grades. In addition, he had not undertaken any science in his junior or senior year. Naturally, this had an impact on the admissions committees' view of his preparation, as did his MCAT performance. His combined score was only 27 out of a top score of 45.

We reassured Doug that he had many strengths that, in time, admissions committees would find appealing. Throughout his high school and college years he had had significant experience in volunteer work that was relevant to medical studies. His résumé included the following:

- Instructor/Volunteer with the American Red Cross for four years. He taught Red Cross Health and Safety classes to a variety of age groups. He conducted practical and written exams, and prepared lesson plans and demonstrations.
- Emergency Medical Technician (EMT) and Driver, Pre-Hospital Trauma Life Support, and Hazardous Material Management

certifications. He provided advanced life support care, and coordinated efforts of emergency/rescue personnel both in his suburban hometown and in this university town.

- Red Cross–certified HIV/AIDS volunteer for six years.

Doug was not about to give up his dream of becoming a physician. Together we determined that there were two particularly worthy options that were of interest to him. The question was, which served him better for medical school admission? The first was an invitation to enroll in his state university's postbaccalaureate program. This was a well-regarded two-year curriculum that boasts a 90 percent success rate in admissions to medical schools. Because Doug was a state resident, the tuition would be affordable, another concern, since he had accumulated educational loans that would have to be repaid in the future. The other option, one that appealed strongly to him, was to participate in the Teach for America organization. This program would place him in an inner-city middle school in New York City, where he would teach introductory science.

For a number of sound reasons, and with our encouragement as to the benefits he would gain, Doug decided to commit to the teaching position. He would continue his commitment of service to others, this time youngsters whom he could potentially inspire to want to continue their education. He would enhance his own knowledge of science by having to teach life sciences to seventh and eighth graders. He could relearn Spanish, which he had enjoyed immensely during his high school years, since 90 percent of the student body at the school he was assigned to spoke Spanish. Another critical component of this plan: Doug could take chemistry and biology courses at one of the nearby universities to ready himself for medical school and prove to admissions committees that he was well prepared to handle the heavy academic demands. He would likely perform better on the MCAT this time around. Once Doug made this decision, it was as if the weight of a Mack truck had been taken off his shoulders. He could see clearly what a wonderful combination of experiences he was about to launch into. He almost forgot that this was all about going to medical school in the future.

To fast-forward the story, Doug taught for two years in Spanish Harlem in the middle school that he came to regard as his home. He developed into an outstanding teacher, he helped design middle school science curricula, he became fluent in Spanish (he had little choice, he claimed), he realized that he had had a significant influence on a large number of disadvantaged boys and girls, and last but far from least, he recognized his own strengths and courage to accomplish all that he had set out to do. This included attaining A and B+ grades in four lab science courses over the two years.

Somewhere in his demanding schedule, Doug made time to study for the MCAT with a far stronger foundation of knowledge. As a result, he improved his scores enough to put him into realistic competition for the limited spaces in the medical schools.

Now better prepared to reapply to medical schools, Doug decided to concentrate on schools in the greater New York area. His reason was compelling: Because of his teaching experience he decided he wanted to become a primary physician and practice in a community like the one he had taught in. The stories of children coming to school each day not only undernourished but also deprived of any health care, and thus carrying numerous illnesses that went untreated, convinced him that he would dedicate his career to working in this community. With his Spanish fluency, he felt that he could work successfully with Spanish-speaking families in the inner city. Consequently, Doug focused on five medical colleges in and around New York City. In time, he was admitted to three of them. The following is the personal statement that Doug crafted after several rounds of discussion with us and that he sent with his applications. The sincerity and commitment to medicine and people in need that pervade this essay are contagious. The admissions committees perceived that here was an outstanding primary care practitioner in the making.

Angie is a tall, awkward thirteen-year-old who has yet to understand the importance of raising her hand before speaking in class. Like most of her classmates at this overcrowded, predominantly Latino middle school in upper Manhattan, she is reading far below grade level and English is her second language. Her demeanor, however, belies any sense of the low self-esteem that one might expect of a low-functioning student. Before every science class she greets me with a wide smile and an enthusiastic, "hello!"

Angie has been in my science class for the past two years, and she has always struggled academically. One day several months ago I was giving a lesson about the different parts of an animal cell when Angie volunteered information without raising her hand. To my surprise, she asked a very thoughtful question dealing with cells. This moment was, as it turned out, the mark of a new beginning in her education for Angie as both she and I realized that she could be a strong student. She is now one of the first students to grasp difficult concepts, is an eager participant in class discussion, and is scoring high marks on her exams. Angie's misplaced and unsolicited comments now consist primarily of two declarations: "I'm so smart!" and "Mr. B., I love science!"

There is an abundance of Angies at Intermediate School 143. They are children whose bright personalities and adolescent dreams are often extinguished by the myriad tragedies and difficulties that fill their lives. They are Richard, whose mother was stabbed to death in his native Ecuador. They are Tara, who has been ill with an undiagnosed disease. They are Danielle, who has attempted suicide and often comes to school high on marijuana. They are Luis, who accompanies his mother to the hospital as her translator during school hours. When these children talk about their neighborhood, they speak of crack-heads and shootings and illness and dying as if they were a natural part of the landscape.

As a teacher, I have tried to instill in all of my students a sense of responsibility for their own education and a sense of possibility for their future. In the process, I have come to realize that these resilient early teenagers are children in need of encouragement, affection, and an opportunity to affirm their intelligence. Perhaps it is because of their hardships, many of my students have exhibited an amazing capacity to return the support and love of their teachers. When my father passed away during my first year of teaching, I received letters from students telling me that "time heals everything" and "no matter what happens, the person that you love will always be in your heart."

The relationship that I have developed with my students has made the decision to re-apply to medical school a difficult one. My twelfth grade writing instructor recently wrote me a letter in which she advised me that once you have been a teacher, nothing else really comes close to being as important or as satisfying. Medicine, she continued, is probably the only exception. Over the past two years I have developed an understanding of the parallel roles that doctors and teachers play in the lives of their "patients." The most effective teacher is the one who provides his students with the skills necessary to become a responsible, life-long learner. The most effective medical doctor is one who communicates with his patients about their well being and equips them with the knowledge to care for themselves.

Ultimately, both are educators striving to empower those in their care. Teaching has secured my commitment to young people like Angie and to the community in which I have lived and taught for the past two years. I am now eager to combine that commitment with my intellectual fascination with the human body and my desire to meet the challenges of a career in medicine.

Undergraduate Curricula for Candidates in Medicine and Allied Health Fields

Premed programs require 10 terms of science and math: 2 terms each of basic chemistry, organic chemistry, biology, and physics, all with lab work, and calculus. These should be completed by the end of junior year, the same year you take your medical aptitude tests. Competitive colleges make it difficult to get into their premed programs, or use organic chemistry traditionally as the "screening out" subject, and are unlikely to recommend those who do not do well in their science and math courses. Falling below a 3.0 GPA in the premed portion of your curriculum usually means that you must make up lackluster performance by taking additional science courses, on the grounds that some medical school will be impressed by your diligence and the breadth, if not depth, of your scientific foundation.

Some medical schools also require, and all of them strongly urge, that applicants have taken some combination of English, behavioral or social sciences, and humanities courses. The idea is to train physicians who have an understanding of the patients they will be treating and know how to communicate with them effectively. Compassion comes from understanding motivation and behavior, and this comes from studying history, literature, psychology, sociology, anthropology, and foreign languages. Details on such requirements and recommendations are laid out in the invaluable volume *Medical School Admission Requirements,* published annually by the Association of American Medical Colleges (AAMC), which we discuss in Step Three.

But what about the choice of a major? No medical college specifies a required major, and the AAMC cautions against picking a major you think will enhance your admissions chances, especially one of the sciences. "Medical schools are most concerned with the overall quality and scope of undergraduate work," they state in *Medical School Admission Requirements.* Notwithstanding this recommendation, typically two-thirds of applicants will choose to major in the life sciences in their undergraduate school. Study the table on the next two pages carefully. It shows that nonscience majors were just as successful in gaining admission as the science majors; those majoring in health-related technical subjects such as nursing, pharmacy, and medical technology were less successful.

We encourage those starting their college careers to seriously consider majoring in a nonscience subject, for the breadth it will add to their education. Many seasoned doctors lament the fact that they concentrated so heavily on the sciences in college that they missed out on the opportunity to learn what the humanities and social science disciplines had to offer them. Those of you who contemplate a medical career after college without having had premed training should not worry that your major was in economics, history, or some other nonscience major. The medical and health professions need the widest variety of talents, and those who have done well in any major subject are just as strong candidates as the biology and chemistry majors once

Acceptance to Medical School by Undergraduate Major
1999–2000 Entering Class

Undergraduate Major	Total Applicants		Accepted Applicants	
	No.	% of Total	No.	% of Major
Biological Sciences				
Biology	14,249	37.0	6,137	43.1
Microbiology	1,041	2.7	431	41.4
Physiology	558	1.4	212	38.0
Science (other biology)	1,061	2.8	510	48.1
Zoology	735	1.9	327	44.5
Subtotal	17,644	45.8	7,617	43.2
Physical Sciences				
Biochemistry	2,389	6.2	1,172	49.1
Biomedical engineering	368	1.01	212	57.6
Chemical engineering	321	.8	173	53.9
Chemistry	2,110	5.5	1,020	48.3
Chemistry and biology	314	.8	128	40.8
Electrical engineering	173	.4	81	46.8
Mathematics	225	.6	99	44.0
Natural sciences	204	.5	91	44.6
Physics	188	.5	88	46.8
Science (general)	176	.5	70	39.8
Subtotal	6,468	16.8	3,134	48.5
Nonscience Subjects				
Anthropology	329	.9	182	55.3
Economics	340	.9	193	56.8
English	463	1.2	244	52.7
Foreign language	279	.7	142	50.9
History	414	1.1	244	58.9
Philosophy	184	.5	95	51.6
Political science	254	.7	131	51.6

(continued)

Acceptance to Medical School (continued)

Undergraduate Major	Total Applicants		Accepted Applicants	
	No.	% of Total	No.	% of Major
Psychobiology	304	.8	168	55.3
Psychology	1,802	4.7	769	42.7
Sociology	195	.5	85	43.6
Subtotal	4,564	11.8	2,253	49.4
Other Health Professions				
Medical technology	170	.4	31	18.2
Nursing	267	.7	72	27.0
Pharmacy	193	.5	48	24.0
Subtotal	630	1.6	151	24.0
Mixed Disciplines				
Double-major science	869	2.3	433	49.8
Double-major/nonscience	1,487	3.9	834	56.1
Interdisciplinary studies	221	.6	130	58.8
Premedical	563	1.5	204	36.2
Preprofessional	139	.4	66	47.5
Subtotal	3,279	8.5	1,667	50.8
Other (includes nonreported majors)	5,944	15.4	2,623	44.1
Grand total	38,529	100	17,445	45.3

they complete these required courses through the postbaccalaureate programs described earlier.

Yale Medical School, for example, states, "The medical faculty has no preference as to a major field for undergraduate study but recommends that students advance beyond the elementary level in their field of study." The University of California, Los Angeles, says it "gives preference to those applicants who present evidence of broad training and high achievement in their college education and possess, in the greatest degree, those traits of personality and character essential to success in medicine." Stanford University states that "an undergraduate major in any field is acceptable, provided the candidate presents a record of outstanding achievement. Breadth of education and/or experience in the humanities and social sciences and knowledge of a foreign language are desirable."

What we have said about prospective medical school applicants applies in general to those contemplating dental schools, veterinary schools, and other advanced professions in the health sciences. Naturally, future clinical psychologists should take psychology courses, but they, too, need not feel obligated to major in psychology. Those contemplating a public health career would do well to take courses in government, geography, economics, and sociology. Here again, admissions committees will be looking at your level of academic achievement and intellectual curiosity to discern the likelihood of your succeeding in the demanding programs of their particular schools.

In brief, there is no complete prescription for getting into medical school or any school in the health sciences field. The best preparation over and above the required science and math courses is a broad liberal arts education. Also consider an emphasis on communication skills, since it is increasingly important that medical professionals be clear in their writing or speech in dealing with their patients and the public.

The Myth of a Prelaw Curriculum

Some colleges do offer a prelaw curriculum. We do not necessarily recommend taking it, because such courses merely dabble in the study of professional law and can add little to the student's reading and analytical skills. *The Official Guide to U.S. Law Schools* offers this counsel:

> Unlike the premed curriculum that contains specific courses, some obligatory, there is no recommended set of prelaw courses. Law schools prefer that you reserve your legal study for law school and fill your undergraduate curriculum with broad, diverse, and challenging courses. Prelaw courses that introduce you to

broad legal principles may present you with enough information to decide whether you want to continue with a legal education, but they are rarely taught with the same depth and rigor as actual law school courses. A prelaw curriculum that is designed to encompass a broad array of liberal arts courses, however, can be excellent preparation for law school. Be sure you know precisely what is meant by prelaw when choosing your undergraduate course of study.

Much law school literature offers little advice as to an appropriate undergraduate curriculum for applicants. Yet such open-endedness should not lead you to think that anything goes. Courses in photography, studio art, home economics, health, or physical education, although practical and worthy, count for nothing when applying to law school.

The law school candidate should take courses in writing, literature, history, political science, psychology, and economics. It is wise to also include accounting, statistics, and computer science. Public speaking or rhetoric is key training to have prior to beginning law studies. Science courses are optional, but may prove useful in that some fields of law today relate to medical issues, environmental concerns, technology copyright, patent disputes, industrial accidents, and the social responsibilities associated with such controversial topics as abortion, cloning or surrogate pregnancy, and biological research on pre- and postnatal humans.

What does this add up to in curricular terms? A smorgasbord of liberal arts courses with the major left up to the individual. The important thing is the depth and intensity of study. Almost any challenging liberal arts program is good preparation for the enormous amount of reading and case analysis that has to be done in any qualified law school. You can major in science and engineering, philosophy, linguistics, math, biology, Russian literature—there really is no limit, so long as you stick to the intellectual training you will receive from the liberal arts, and remember, these include science.

Again, what are undesirable are undergraduate courses that superficially survey aspects of the law. You can major in business and take liberal arts courses as electives. But leave the law courses to the law schools. Think of getting ready for law school as a matter of

1. Learning to read critically,
2. Learning to write and speak clearly and forcefully,
3. Reaching an understanding of human institutions and values upheld by the law,
4. Becoming a creative thinker who can bring original solutions to problems of law.

Admission to law school can be highly competitive, and your grades will make a significant difference. To cite an extreme case, Stanford's most recent law school class admitted only 474 applicants from a pool of 3,824. Those offered admission had GPAs of 3.65 to 3.90. Their LSAT scores averaged 165 out of a top score of 180. The Stanford catalogue states,

> Admission to Stanford Law School is based primarily upon superior academic achievement and potential to contribute to the development of the law. Competition is severe: the 178 members of the Class of 2002 were selected from among 3,824 applicants. The largest part of each class is drawn from the upper 4 percent of their undergraduate colleges and the upper 4 percent of the LSAT pool.

Stanford goes on to say that other factors are taken into account, including applicants' nonacademic talents, experiences, and accomplishments. Like every top law school, Stanford declares its goal of increasing the diversity of entering classes by encouraging racial minority students and those of other ethnic and social backgrounds who will broaden the perspectives brought to everyone's legal education.

We worry that some potential applicants misjudge the academic competition they are up against. Doing extremely well academically is the sine qua non for admission to a great law school. If your record suggests that you are out of the running for the likes of Stanford and the other law schools listed on page 88, you can still improve it to the satisfaction of other excellent, accredited, but less competitive schools. Consider taking additional courses over the summers if you are still in college, or in an extension program that is convenient to you if you are presently working. Remember that the average age of those enrolling in law schools continues to rise every year, which indicates that successful candidates have done a variety of things, including in many cases taking postbaccalaureate academic courses, to increase their appeal to the admissions committees.

SAMUEL: *using the liberal arts as a springboard to an elite law school*

At first glance, there appeared to be little likelihood that Samuel would have difficulty in attaining his personal goal for graduate school and career, given his exceptional academic performance and his many leadership roles and activities in a top undergraduate college. What was not apparent were the various stages and levels of confusion Samuel experienced regarding his future plans. His election to Phi Beta Kappa and his test scores were the result of a good deal of effort and focus. His intellectual and social interests were diverse. Here is a case where much exploration was called for to determine which career direction to take and then how to pursue that goal to its successful conclusion.

When Samuel first met with us, he was engaged in a number of intellectual interests to which he felt he could devote his professional life. Everything from ethical issues in medicine to teaching, politics, and research and teaching in religion and philosophy appealed to him. As a result of ongoing conversations with us, the particular attraction of the study of law became more apparent. He was encouraged to accept the invitation to study and intern for a summer in Israel after his junior year, because it presented him with an opportunity to study the unique legal system and the religious history and heritage of this nation. Upon further discussions with us when he returned home, Samuel recognized the extent of his fascination with issues and dynamics of the law and the various ways he could apply his intellectual aptitude within this profession.

On the basis of his outstanding grades and a LSAT score in the 97th percentile, Samuel was encouraged to apply to 10 of the top law schools. He was admitted to all of them and entered Harvard Law School in the class of 2003. The personal statement that Samuel presented to the elite law schools to which he applied illustrates the level of thinking and experiences that appeal to selective admissions committees. His writing reveals the kind of mind that can cope with and enjoy the study of law:

> The Bible describes law as a straight line and justice as a curve. Some of us walk forward throughout life, never deviating from the straight path. Black and white, right and wrong, legal and illegal. Others look past what is written and determine what is correct, just, and take a detour from the straight path. Those that can combine the straight and the curved, law and justice, evoke my admiration.
>
> The Israeli Supreme Court building juxtaposes the straight lines and curves. The justices of the court seek to unite religious law and civil law in a nation defined by its Judaism. The justices also seek to create a unique and modern set of legal precedents by studying and citing decisions of the courts from other nations. This combination of tradition and modernity allows for a nation that has been divided since its birth to remain physically united and generally at peace.
>
> This past summer I spent six weeks in Israel, exploring the nation physically and obtaining a great sense of the intangible elements of the culture. Throughout my time in the country, I was taught about two ethnic groups that populate Israel, Jews and Arabs, both Christian and Muslim. Within the Jewish community alone, there are disputes between Ultra-Orthodox and secular and Ashkenazim (European) and Mizrachim/Sephardim (Mediterranean and Oriental). The dispute between the Palestinians, Palestinian Arabs living in Israel but without citizenship, and the Jewish population is well documented. Added to these disputes is the dissension between Israeli Arabs, non-Jewish citizens of Israel whose ancestors lived in the region, and the Jewish citizens.
>
> My interest in the state of Israel stems from my childhood lessons in Hebrew and Sunday school. Judaism has always played

an important role in my life and the idea of visiting Israel began to develop into a dream and life goal when I was twelve years old. I wanted to see all the places and structures I had read about and I grew jealous of my peers who had already gone. I decided that before I left college I had to travel to the Jewish State. Never did I imagine that with all the beauty and grandeur of this ancient land, the Supreme Court would make the biggest impression on me. Upon entering the building, my excitement built and I began to question how a nation caught up in such a struggle could maintain legal order.

The first leaders of the nation understood that the establishment of universal laws would lead to a rift. Therefore, criminal matters were placed in the hands of the state. Marriage and divorce remained under the domain of the religious leaders. Ultra-Orthodox Jews retain the right to employ the Beth Din, or religious court, in their affairs. The government of Israel does not force itself on the religious affairs of the Muslim, Druze, or Christian communities.

Freedom of the individual is held in high regard in Israel. Just as one has a right to practice his or her own religion and have these matters ruled on by a religious court, one also retains the right to protect oneself from the government. The Supreme Court of Israel has two functions. The Court rules on appeals from all district courts—every alleged criminal is guaranteed one appeal according to the law—and it serves as the High Court of Justice. Anyone, citizen or non-citizen, may file a *bagatz* which states that a ministry of the governments has infringed on his or her civil rights.

Without a written constitution and without a bill of rights, everyone in Israel still possesses the ability to protect his or her civil rights. Each person can petition the Supreme Court and, if the petition is accepted, can not only defend himself or herself, but can alter the future of Israeli law. The High Court of Justice allows for the hard, straight lines of law to be rounded and smoothed into curves of justice.

As president of my college fraternity and in other leadership roles, and simply in daily life, I attempt to place justice above black and white, right and wrong issues. I take into account the circumstances surrounding an action and I do not stay bound by that straight line of law. I have learned from my experience in Israel that justice is the goal and law is the path.

TANYA AND NICK: *clerking for a judge—two who made it*

Among the career choices open to young people, few are more interesting for those who make the law their profession than clerking for a judge. Many municipal, most state, and all federal judges have clerks assigned to their chambers. Generally these are bright recent law school graduates who spend a year working for the judge. In some cases, a federal judge who might have two clerkships will have a permanent clerk, referred to as an "elbow clerk," someone who stays with the judge for several years. In most cases, the clerks will stay for a single year.

Each judge uses a different method of selecting clerks. In Judge Peter Messitte's case, two hundred applications come to him each year for two openings. The judge asks his two current clerks to make a preliminary cut of the applications, winnowing the number down to seven or eight who are invited to interview. The judge and the two clerks conduct the interviews and grade the candidates on potential ability to function in a complex and demanding setting, adaptability of personality, knowledge of the law, and level of communication skills.

A native of Montgomery County, Maryland, and graduate of Bethesda-Chevy Chase High School, Judge Messitte graduated from Amherst College and the University of Chicago Law School. He served two years as a Peace Corps volunteer in Brazil, where he learned to speak and read Portuguese. After practicing as an attorney in suburban Maryland, he was elected a county circuit judge, and was named a federal judge in the early 1990s.

The 800 federal judges each receive several hundred clerk applications annually. "While the positions do not pay extraordinarily well, they are obviously prized by the top law graduates," Judge Messitte notes. "Generally, people apply in their own region, or in the region where they eventually want to practice. The exposure you get in this kind of setting is tremendously varied. You will be exposed to the best kind of lawyering, and sometimes to bad lawyers as well." Messitte instructs his clerks to look for candidates from six or seven major law schools, but not to exclude outstanding individuals from other schools as well.

"Basically, I divide my cases in half and I say to one clerk, 'The odd numbered cases are yours' and to the other, 'You get the even numbered cases.' 'You have to stay on top of them, read the mail as it comes in, you have to know everything about that case and keep me advised. You are the ones in contact with the lawyers, there will be motions coming in all the time.'" Clerks are also asked to prepare bench memos for the judge, flagging the facts of the case and the applicable law. Clerks either draft routine opinion or, once the judge has fleshed out his own opinion of the case, do the necessary research to complete the opinion. Both during and following the case, Judge Messitte will sit down with his clerks and discuss how he and they see the case progressing.

Tanya was a left-side hitter in college volleyball at Rice University, but that is not what got her the highly coveted job as Judge Messitte's clerk. Tanya grew up in El Toro, California, in a family of health care professionals. While in high school, she participated in a moot court competition. The experience took hold, and she became fascinated with the prospect of a career as a courtroom attorney. She graduated from Rice, having majored both in English and economics, and headed off to Harvard Law School. In law school, she taught a Harvard undergraduate course in economics, and worked for three years with a prison legal assistance program, representing inmates charged with disciplinary infractions that ranged from stealing a piece of cake to stabbing the warden.

Tanya's goal, when her clerkship ends, is to join the Department of Justice honors program as a career criminal prosecutor. Three areas interest her: organized crime, violent crime, and public integrity, which involves the prosecution of corrupt officials. "When liberty is at stake, everything is heightened and a little more intense," she reflected.

Nick is the second clerk in Judge Messitte's chambers. A New Englander, he attended public schools, where he was active in debating.

He graduated from Dartmouth as a government major and served on the student judiciary panel. Two years with an international strategy consulting company convinced him that law school was the right direction to take. After a year at the University of Chicago Law School, he transferred to Harvard, enabling his wife to pursue her career as a professional writer-editor in the Boston area.

Nick found law school intellectually challenging and learned that litigation was the field in which he wanted to practice. "I had seen transactional attorneys at work in the business world and knew this was not what I wanted to do. So I applied for clerkships both in Boston and in Washington. Judge Messitte's was the first offer I received, so I accepted it right there and then." Next year, Nick will join a major Washington law firm as an associate, where he hopes to do a variety of things, from white-collar criminal defense work to appellate work to employment law.

"I will let my interests be pretty wide and see where it leads me. The experience of being a clerk in a federal court has shown me a great deal about lawyering, what goes on in a court, and what constitutes good and bad law practices. It really has been an opportunity to get into the trenches of litigation and see what takes place. Judge Messitte helps a lot in this regard. He really looks at himself as a mentor and a teacher. Not every judge is like that."

Undergraduate Curricula for Candidates for Business Administration Programs

Business schools do not lay out a recommended curriculum for prospective applicants. One of the attractions of an MBA is that anyone with a good solid liberal arts background and degree has an excellent chance for acceptance to a top business school. The rule of thumb, once again, is that the stronger your undergraduate record, the more prestigious the business school you can and should apply to.

All MBA programs admit applicants with bachelor's degrees in any solid academic field. The important factor is not what you study so much as how well you do in your courses. One top MBA program states, "Our school looks for candidates whose analytical and organizational abilities, communication skills, motivation and leadership indicate potential for successful careers in professional management." Another top-10 school emphasizes, "When evaluating an academic record we consider the level of success achieved and the quality of the undergraduate programs pursued." Still another declares, "The faculty believes that solid preparation in English, history, economics, and social sciences is desirable. Adequate preparation in mathematics is essential for strong performance in the School's program. While specific courses in mathematics are not required for admission, the faculty strongly recommends that admitted students successfully complete an introductory calculus prior to matriculation, either in college or in a post-college extension program at the collegiate level."

SALLY: *converting communication skills into an MBA*

Sally had established an outstanding record at Stanford University as an undergraduate. She graduated with a major in the history of art with a 3.6 GPA. She scored a 640 on the GMAT, which she took in her first year out of college. In love with words and creative idea development, Sally took a position after graduating with Young and Rubicam advertising agency. Sally quickly was recognized for her abilities and work ethic, and thus was promoted in her second year to an account executive. When she came to us to discuss her plans to apply to graduate business school, she was counseled to wait another one or two years on the basis of her limited, though significant, work experience to date. This surprised Sally, but she took this counsel to heart and decided to accept a new job. In time, we received the following letter from her:

> When I first visited you one and a half years ago, I was a newly promoted Account Executive at Young and Rubicam, San Francisco. From that time, I continued to work on the Golden Grain businesses for another year. I was responsible for all of the daily client contact, reporting directly to a management supervisor. Overall, I felt that I received excellent training and established a strong foundation in management and leadership skills.

As we had discussed, the time would come when it would be helpful to consider job experience outside of the advertising world. This led me, after a lengthy search, to my current position as Marketing Director at The PeaceWorks, Inc. Based in New York City, PeaceWorks is a small, start-up company with a unique and ambitious mission: we are for-profit and for peace. Our objective is to foster joint ventures designed to promote tolerance and coexistence between people of different cultural backgrounds. Our first initiative is a line of gourmet foods manufactured cooperatively by Arabs and Israelis in the Middle East. My responsibilities include supervising the development and execution of all national consumer and trade promotions, as well as the production of all brand-related materials. I am also leading efforts to source new products from the Middle East.

Now, with more substantial work experience, I would like to pursue an MBA. I believe that I am a stronger and more qualified candidate for graduate school than when we last met. I am ready to move forward and feel the timing is right.

Sally wrote the following statement in her application to the Amos Tuck School at Dartmouth. On the basis of her broader work experience, letters of recommendation, and outstanding writing, Sally was accepted to Tuck and four other top business schools.

Upon receiving my undergraduate degree from Stanford University, I began a career in advertising because I wanted to work in an environment that fostered both business and creative challenges. I sought a position at a small agency where I knew that there would be immediate opportunities for substantial responsibility and client contact. I was hired by MM and A, a creative boutique in San Francisco known for its outstanding and unconventional management team. As an Assistant Account Executive, I received a crash course in account management in a dynamic and somewhat chaotic environment. I worked on two different accounts and contributed to a number of new business pitches.

After gaining a good deal of experience in this group, I moved to a much larger agency, Young and Rubicam. In less than a year, I was promoted and became one of the youngest Account Executives at the firm. I successfully handled four different packaged goods accounts. I acted as the liaison between the various departments within the agency, including creative, media, production and traffic, and our clients. My responsibilities included everything from strategic development and project management to marketplace analysis and budget/profit projection. While at Young and Rubicam, I received excellent training in the rigors of diplomacy, management and teamwork. I felt confident that these skills would enable me to tackle new and different challenges outside the industry.

As I approached the end of my third year in the advertising industry, I sought an opportunity that would offer an international perspective in a truly entrepreneurial environment. After reading about various start-ups, I discovered The PeaceWorks, Inc., a small socially conscious company that fosters joint ventures between people of different backgrounds. The company's mission and its products are described in a later statement in this application.

I was immediately attracted to PeaceWorks for four compelling reasons. First, I believed in the company's mission to promote tolerance and coexistence via joint economic ventures. Second, I sought the challenge of this unique business model, which requires all projects to be socially conscious and profitable. Third, I knew that in a company of ten people I would have the opportunity for substantial responsibility, including the development of all consumer and brand related materials, national promotions, and new products. Fourth, I was attracted to the international scope and global vision of the company.

As a Director in the company, I have been faced with a number of strategic dilemmas. For instance, our products are currently available in five of the eight channels identified for potential distribution. Current thinking for this year's sales plan falls into two differing camps. I believe that we should focus our efforts on increasing sales in the five existing channels of distribution. Due to our limited resources and the opportunity to increase performance, I believe that we can leverage our existing business and realize tremendous growth within these five channels. Others in my organization believe that we should concentrate on expanding our network to include all eight market segments. They maintain that the remaining three untapped outlets for distribution represent enormous sales potential.

While at business school, I would want to acquire the tools that would enable me to assess such a scenario in a systematic fashion. I hope to establish a better foundation in the business fundamentals of finance, statistics, decision making analysis, and long range planning so that not only would I be able to answer the tough questions but also to know what are the proper questions to ask.

I believe that the Tuck School would provide the ideal forum for this pursuit. I would gain from the program's emphasis on general management and expertise in the technological tools so critical to business planning today. I would also benefit by the exposure to the diverse backgrounds and ideas of my fellow students. I believe that I would contribute, in kind, to the community as a skilled communicator and team player. I am creative and compassionate, and anticipate incorporating these qualities in my work, and in doing so, to influence my classmates.

Upon graduation from Tuck, I will seek the challenge of an international career in marketing and small business management. I would like to work in an environment that fosters a global perspective and allows me to utilize my foreign language skills. Initially, I anticipate gaining experience with an established company and, in time, perhaps to launch a venture of my own that addresses the needs of people around the globe while financially sustaining itself.

We need not belabor the point about academic preparation for admission to a good MBA program. The essentials are these:

- A bachelor's degree from an accredited college or university.
- An undergraduate program of significance, with few non-academic credit courses.

- Strong undergraduate performance, with a GPA above 3.0.
- Demonstration in course work of good communication skills.
- College-level math, taken while in college, or afterwards if missing from your transcript.
- Strengthening of any weakness in your academic record by course work taken after college. Besides calculus, courses in probability, statistics, microeconomics, and macroeconomics are key subjects to complete.

Undergraduate Curricula for Candidates to Other Graduate Schools

Having covered the big three professional programs, we will now focus on the entrance requirements for schools of engineering, science, education, government, communications, architecture, and the arts.

Engineering Programs

Only graduates of engineering schools or graduates with a bachelor of science degree qualify for advanced training in these fields. The first hurdle for engineers is being admitted to a good undergraduate college of engineering. Then they must complete the rigorous program in a chosen concentration: Civil, mechanical, chemical, electrical, aeronautical, marine, environmental, computer, mining, industrial, architectural, and nuclear engineering are some of the special fields in which an engineer can concentrate. Some undergraduate programs take five years to complete the bachelor of science in engineering degree, whereas most bachelor of science degrees require the traditional four years to complete. We counsel prospective engineering majors to research very carefully the collegiate programs they are considering, to understand not only the requirements for admission but also how many courses and how many years of study are required.

Anyone who earns a bachelor's in engineering needs little guidance about further academic training. Even high school students who are strong in math and science tend to know how to go about pursuing an engineering or science degree. Some who start an undergraduate program find they are not cut out for such studies and transfer into other programs, but those who finish are usually qualified to do graduate work.

Admission to graduate engineering programs is often really a matter of your being guided and recommended by present faculty members to institutions·where they have contacts or know which are the best programs in each of the engineering specialties. There is a considerable old boy network among engineers, and this is true of scientists, too. We urge engineers and scientists who want to take their education to the next level to focus more on the reputation of the faculty and funding for research and facilities in their field than on the overall prestige of the university. This will result in the optimum training and career opportunities.

Science Programs

The college science major in biology, physics, chemistry, zoology, or astronomy does not follow the kind of professional path laid out by engineering schools. Many such majors, after graduating, go into non-scientific fields like banking, law, communications, consulting, and corporate management. Instead of a graduate degree in science, they may opt for one of the professional degrees in law, business, or the health sciences. Those who wish to follow a research career at a university, a corporation, a foundation, or under government auspices must go on for at least a master's and, preferably, a doctorate in their discipline.

Here again, the undergraduate faculty plays the principal role in advancing scientific careers. Science professors realize that the majority of students in a given class have no intention of doing graduate work in science. In addition to teaching, they wish to identify and encourage the potential future scientist, often to the point of calling a student's attention to his or her aptitude for science and stimulating an interest in a scientific career. As we indicated earlier, graduate work in an academic discipline requires the support of one or more academicians in the discipline a student wishes to pursue.

It should be made clear that the science student seeking faculty support will not get very far merely on charm or manipulation. Scientific accomplishment in college is quantifiable, much more so than accomplishments in the so-called soft social sciences or humanities disciplines. Conversely, good scientists are not likely to be overlooked today since there is a shortage of talented Ph.D.s needed to strengthen the United States in its continuing efforts to compete economically against other countries that support scientific education programs more heavily.

The undergraduate science major should give serious thought to any faculty suggestion to consider graduate training. The lure of immediately higher pay in business and industry is an understandable temptation. In the long run, the compensation paid to highly trained scientists is not inconsiderable. Ph.D.s in science may earn as much in the private sector, if this is their goal, as MBAs and lawyers. Most important, they have significant choices and control of their career.

Nonscience Graduate Programs

Admission to academic graduate programs in fields outside science and engineering is best achieved by a challenging liberal arts curriculum in which the student shows a capacity for superior intellectual work. Since no grade lower than a B is considered passing in graduate school, quality graduate programs are usually open only to those with a GPA of 3.4 or higher. It is easier to begin a nonscience academic program than to finish with a doctorate. Those who seek a Ph.D. are very strong students with a passion for their subject. Satisfying the requirements for a master's degree is within the reach of students who have neither the drive nor the scholarly qualities needed to earn a doctoral degree.

What you major in as an undergraduate can be less important than the strength of your academic record. You can major in English literature or classics or psychology and get a master's degree in history, economics, or education, for example. We have advised many students to begin their graduate studies in a master's program to build their intellectual credentials and confirm that they have enough interest and drive to undertake four to five more years of study to complete doctoral studies.

Admission to nonscience graduate schools depends heavily on faculty recommendations. Those seeking acceptance to an academic school immediately after graduating from college should rely heavily on their faculty in determining the schools to which they ought to apply.

We offer a word of caution: You should have a clear objective in mind and a full awareness of the potential usefulness of the graduate degree in finding a job or increasing a capacity such as writing, painting, or acting. The key question to ask is, How is this degree regarded outside the university or, for that matter, within it?

A case in point: A French teacher with a doctorate in that subject was unable to get a job other than that of a part-time language teacher at the university at which she had earned the degree. In such positions, the rate of pay is about one-fourth that of full-time faculty, and you cannot participate in the health and pension programs of the university. After several years of this exploitation, to call it what it is, she gave up this position and became a full-time instructor in a large museum, where she lectured on French literature and history as a background for the study of art. This is not an isolated incident. Universities are increasing the number of part-time instructors as a means to keep their budgets reined in and maintain flexibility in the size of their staff.

To avoid disappointment after earning a graduate degree in an academic field, try to make sure in advance that your hard work will have a satisfactory payoff. We encourage you to get answers to the list of questions we lay out in the introductory chapter before you commit to particular graduate training.

It's the Degree, Not the College, That Counts

How often we hear smart high school seniors assert that they are applying to colleges that will ensure them admission to the best graduate schools. It is a fundamental mistake to say that any college degree by itself is an assurance of graduate admission anywhere. To prove this to yourself, look at the list of colleges attended by the students in the graduate classes of prestigious institutions. You will find that the students usually come from more than 200 different undergraduate colleges. It is the quality of the education you receive from a strong college and your ability to make the most of it as evidenced by your grades and participation in internships, research, and extracurricular activities of note that will ensure your acceptance into the top graduate schools in all of the professional and academic disciplines.

We address this issue at length in *The Hidden Ivies,* in which we indicate the proportionately higher rates of acceptance to the top graduate schools from outstanding colleges other than the Ivies. We carry the point further in *The Public Ivies,* discussing the honors programs and research opportunities and facilities available to public research university students. A problem often overlooked by students and their parents is that it is much more difficult to attain an impressive academic record in a highly competitive college. It is also more of a challenge to gain recognition from the topflight faculty who invite students to carry out research or independent study projects under their aegis. An honors prep school graduate at Harvard complained to us that he found it almost impossible to get an A in the Philosophy Department. He did not even apply to the grad school at Harvard. He went on to Fordham University to pursue a doctorate in philosophy. Had he gone to Fordham as an undergraduate chances are he would have earned As in his major. Then he might well have been admitted to the Ph.D. program at Harvard.

Graduate schools want the best candidates from whatever quality institution they have attended. To do well in an environment that enables you to thrive in your studies is the key that will open the graduate school gates for you.

Ways to Beat the Competition

Given the large numbers of strong liberal arts graduates, how do you guarantee yourself acceptance to a worthy graduate school, aside from getting as many As as possible? First, look for an academic specialty that you enjoy and for which you have natural aptitude. Second, do not fall prey to the popular fields of the moment if you have little or no interest in them. Third, consider additional courses to take that will complement and enhance your profile. We offer some examples that made the difference in the appeal of recent college graduates:

Languages: If you are fluent in a foreign language, you have an edge on the competition applying to many graduate schools. As the globe shrinks, the ability to speak and write in another language will be of immense value in business, communications and media, and government. Graduate admissions committees recognize this and are likely to give you added consideration.

One way to become fluent in a foreign language is to arrange to spend a semester or year of study abroad. Another approach is to take a break between college and graduate school in order to work in a foreign country. There are jobs available with government and businesses needing bright college graduates who want to live in another country.

International Affairs: This usually involves a reading knowledge of one or more foreign languages and a strong background in history and economics. The job opportunities in international organizations for those with specialized knowledge are many. Again, graduate schools are looking for people who can bring a broader dimension to the classroom and will be highly desirable candidates in the job market upon graduating with their advanced degree.

Communications: There is a premium placed on the ability to express yourself clearly in writing and in spoken presentation. Any encouragement you get as an undergraduate on your written work is a sign that you may be talented in this regard and should think of adding some communications study to your curriculum. We recommend courses in journalism, writing, public speaking, rhetoric, and debate. You might later combine graduate studies in business or law or science with studies in communications or journalism.

Computer science: You need not be a math, science, or engineering major to do well in computer programming or information technology. The capability to use computers and many different software programs to accomplish your ends is valuable in every field of endeavor today. Thus a prospective historian or political scientist with computer expertise may be more attractive to a graduate school than a competing applicant without it.

Combined undergraduate majors: Colleges have not only made it easier today to complete a dual or combined major, but they actively encourage strong students to combine several academic disciplines. We have included several case studies of students who did a double major purposely to prepare for graduate studies. One young woman we counseled combined Russian language with child development and went on to complete a doctorate in child psychology. She is now an expert in the field of child development with a particular understanding of the Russian system of child care.

With a little imagination you can discover all sorts of ways of standing out without necessarily being the most brilliant member of your class. Put together a combination of academic majors that demonstrates originality of thought, and you will stand out in the pack of candidates. Beating out the competition academically may be a matter of thinking creatively and presenting yourself to admissions committees in a special light.

Step Four Checklist

- Examine your undergraduate experience in light of the expectations of particular graduate programs.

- If you discover any weakness in your record, consider taking courses now to strengthen it.

- Remember that premed students need not major in science, that there is no such thing as a prelaw curriculum, and that you can major in anything and be admitted to an MBA school.

- In applying to engineering school, rely on undergraduate faculty to steer you to the right program.

Nonscience academic graduate programs are usually open only to students with high GPAs and signs of potential for advanced research and writing. Admission to programs at the master's level is easier than admission to doctoral programs and may meet your goals or can prepare you for the Ph.D.

Develop complementary specialties or pluses, such as a language skill or computer literacy, that will make graduate programs want to accept you.

STEP FIVE

Prepare for Graduate School Tests

The Importance of the Tests

The scene is familiar yet dreaded by many: a classroom full of people frantically filling in little boxes or circles for three to as many as six long, intense hours. They are not high school students taking their College Boards, but adult men and women from the age of 21 to middle age, sitting for graduate school admissions tests: the Graduate Record Examination (GRE), the Law School Admission Test (LSAT), the Medical College Admission Test (MCAT), the Dental Admission Test (DAT), or the Miller Analogies Test (MAT).

Scores on these tests provide admissions committees with vital criteria by which to judge applicants' suitability for graduate studies. Virtually all professional and academic graduate schools state outright that the two most important criteria for selections are college grades and standardized test scores. To be sure, other criteria guide admissions decisions—recommendations, nonacademic accomplishments, work experience, and the quest for ethnic, gender, racial, and geographic diversity—but mediocre or poor test scores can cast an enormous shadow over a candidate's file. Candidates for academic programs seeking certain fellowships, in addition to acceptance to a graduate program, must submit their GRE scores.

The Importance of Test Preparation

We cannot overemphasize the importance to graduate school candidates of spending many hours leading up to the test date in preparing for the required test. Those who prepare well do well on the day of the test; it's that simple. They have done their homework by taking a number of practice tests against the clock, scoring the tests, and studying the results. They have become familiar with the kinds of questions to expect and are used to the time constraints of the tests and the pressures imposed. They also learn the basic, but key, strategies for getting as many correct answers and as few wrong answers as possible.

Given the dramatic changes in the format of several of the graduate tests from paper-and-pencil to computer-based assessment, it is all the more critical that you understand what you will face the day you sit for the test. Further on, we describe the differences between the paper and computerized tests and the different strategies for taking each.

When you prepare intelligently, you discover your weaknesses and can drill to overcome them. Mistakes made on the verbal sections of a test suggest the need for vocabulary drills and a review of grammar. There always is a need to read as much as possible to enlarge your vocabulary and be comfortable comprehending and analyzing the complex reading passages found on all the graduate entrance tests. Candidates taking tests with mathematics problems and quantitative reasoning sections (the GRE, GMAT, MCAT, and DAT) may need to review fundamental mathematical concepts, rules, and operations unless thoroughly familiar with them because of recent college math courses. We have heard far too many laments of intelligent men and women who flub the math sections because they could not recall the most basic rules and operations needed to arrive at the correct answer.

The amount of time needed for test preparation depends on the individual. Fifty hours might be sufficient for a student still in college, while twice that amount might be necessary for the candidate who has been out of college for a few or many years. Those of you who will be taking the GRE for doctoral studies or the MCAT for medical school face the additional challenge of preparing for the individual subject tests. You must prepare, since no amount of natural aptitude for test taking makes up for a less than thorough grasp of the subject material.

The Official Guide to U.S. Law Schools, in discussing preparation for the LSAT, puts the issue well: "It is impossible to know when an individual has prepared enough, but very few can achieve their full potential by not preparing at all." The same can be said for all of the graduate entrance exams.

How you choose to prepare for graduate tests is again dependent on several factors: your natural ability to take tests; your educational background in math and English; and your knowledge base in any of the subject-based tests. Some individuals spend hundreds of hours preparing on their own or with a professional tutor and gain little from the effort, while others do less preparation and score well. Not everyone has the aptitude to think quickly and respond to questions that demand one specific answer; some are slower readers who understand any materials put before them but need to reread passages at their own pace; others do not think effectively under stress. We can state from our years of experience that almost every graduate school candidate we have encountered improved his or her scores with practice and preparation.

Some individuals of considerable intelligence and knowledge do badly on tests simply because they are not familiar with the particular test format. Smart as you are, you haven't time when the clock is running against you to puzzle out the way the questions must be answered, to scratch your head and think, "What do they want?" Only those who know what the examiners want by practicing on tests can expect to score well. This is in the nature of these tests.

The producer of the GRE General Test offers this advice on preparing for the test:

> GRE General Test questions are designed to measure skills and knowledge gained over a long period of time. Although you might increase your scores by preparing for a few weeks or months before the test, last-minute cramming is unlikely to help. The following information will help guide you if you devote some time to preparing for the test.
>
> - Become familiar with each type of question used in the test, paying special attention to the directions. If you thoroughly understand the directions for each question type before you take the test, you will have more time during the test to focus on the questions themselves.

- Research suggests that practicing unfamiliar question types results in improved performance and decreases the likelihood of inaccurately low scores.
- Use official GRE publications and software to familiarize yourself with questions used on the GRE.

This sound advice from the professional test makers holds true for every one of the graduate tests. A common trap in which many aspiring graduate students get caught is not allowing enough preparation time. Too many individuals know that they need to study beforehand but fall easy prey to the excuse that they are too busy with their school work or their job is so pressured they cannot fit any studying into their schedule. To this we have one response: Find the time if you are serious about applying to graduate school, and do not apply until and unless you have prepared for the entrance test and scored well on practice tests.

How Preparation Pays Off

In this step you will learn something about the nature of the tests and why we urge you to prepare rigorously for them. The reward for the work we propose should be a good test score and also a good start on the academic road you choose to follow. Prepping for tests, though not necessarily a great deal of fun or pleasure, stretches the mind and helps get you in mental shape not just for the tests, but for the formidable demands graduate studies will make on you. We have indicated already that if you are a college graduate with an average academic record, one of the ways you can compensate is to achieve high test results that can persuade an admissions committee that you indeed possess good reasoning ability and logical thinking processes and are highly literate.

The Rationale behind the Tests

Why another round of tests? Isn't a bachelor's degree sufficient evidence of capability to accomplish graduate studies? It isn't, because the difference in the training at a highly selective public or private university and that of a marginal college is so great that no admissions committee can measure the comparative merits of candidates from such different institutions. Without national standardized tests, the selection process would have to be achieved by admitting only top candidates from major universities that are well known to the admissions staff.

The rationale for graduate tests is the same as that for the SAT, which came into active use after World War II, when thousands of high schools began sending students to college for the first time. Admissions officers were faced with the impossible task of distinguishing well-prepared from inadequately prepared students educated in schools they knew little about. The SAT, and later the ACT, provided a benchmark, enabling admissions committees to compare thousands of students academically in an objective fashion. The good student from a country high school who scored in the top 10 to 20 percent on the test could be predicted to be a better academic prospect than a Phillips Exeter Academy student who scored in the middle range of all college-bound students.

Originally, there was a determined effort to identify the intellectually talented students from across the nation who might otherwise go unnoticed by the colleges and universities. We purposely avoid a discussion of the merits and flaws of this kind of standardized testing, a complex issue, because these tests are here to stay for the foreseeable future and will be used by colleges and graduate schools that enjoy the luxury of selecting their class from a large pool of talented applicants each year. To take a philosophical or political stand that the tests are flawed in assessing what they purport to measure or are sexist and racist will only prove frustrating within the context of your applying to the graduate schools of your dreams. Several of the most prestigious graduate professional schools that dropped their test requirement a few years ago have reinstituted the requirement, because they needed the additional quantifiable factor in choosing from far too many highly qualified candidates. Again, entrance exams are likely to be around for as long as any of you are likely to apply to a graduate program.

As graduate school applications expanded dramatically in the baby boom years of the 1960s and 1970s, administrators of graduate tests began to adopt the same format as that of the College Board's ubiquitous SAT; the tests are made up of multiple-choice questions that test verbal skills, math skills, and/or knowledge of course content. In fact, the GMAT and GRE are created and administered for the College Board by the same organization that developed the SAT and the SAT II content-based tests, the Educational Testing Service (ETS) in Princeton, New Jersey. The LSAT, MCAT, DAT, and Miller Analogies Test (MAT) have separate administrations: The LSAT is administered by the Law School Admission Council/Law School Admission Service in Newton, Pennsylvania; the MCAT, by the American College Testing Program in Iowa City, Iowa, under contract to the Association of American Medical Colleges; the DAT, by the American Dental Association; and the MAT, by The Psychological Corporation.

Each of these graduate tests is designed for distinctly different admissions committees. The GMAT tests aptitude for studying business theory and problem solving; the GRE tests aptitude for the intellectual processes required to do advanced reading, writing, and research in an academic subject. They both include verbal and math questions to test reasoning ability. The LSAT tests aptitude for the kind of skills required in law studies; it focuses on verbal and reading aptitude, logical thinking, and deductive ability and has no math questions. The MCAT and DAT test aptitude for studying first-year medical and dental courses. In addition to verbal and math questions, called reading skills analysis and quantitative analysis, there are questions that test a core knowledge of biology, chemistry, and physics subject matter, as well as the ability to solve problems in these three sciences. The DAT questions test for knowledge of biology, chemistry, and organic chemistry. The MAT is a test of mental ability presented entirely in the form of verbal analogies; it tests a store of general information on a wide range of subjects by means of the different types of analogies that must be completed.

WHAT THE MCAT MEANS TO MEDICAL SCHOOLS

Here is how the Association of American Medical Colleges describes the usefulness of the MCAT:

The MCAT is a standardized examination comprised of multiple-choice questions and a writing assessment, designed to help admission committees predict which of their applicants will perform adequately in the medical school curriculum. It provides these committees with a standardized measure of academic performance for all examinees under equivalent conditions. The test battery was developed by medical school admission officers, premed instructors, medical educators, practicing physicians, the AAMC, and a group of testing experts under contract to the AAMC.

Scores on the MCAT provide ancillary information on candidates' ability. Each school establishes the method by which the scores achieved on the MCAT are factored into determining whether candidates can reasonably be expected to accomplish the academic work necessary to progress through a school's curriculum. The range of acceptable MCAT scores varies among schools. MCAT scores are given greater attention when evaluating the academic records of candidates from colleges that are unfamiliar to an admission committee. Comparing MCAT scores with grades earned provides an estimation of such candidates' academic accomplishments in relation to candidates from colleges that are familiar to the committee.

Academic graduate schools requiring thorough knowledge of a particular subject require candidates to take one of the GRE Subject Tests. Since April 2001, these tests have been offered only in biochemistry, cell and molecular biology; biology; chemistry; computer science; literature in English; mathematics; physics; and psychology. If you are well prepared, you can do well on these tests, proving to graduate school faculties that you possess a solid foundation of knowledge in the discipline you wish to pursue at the graduate level of study.

TAKE HEART, LIBERAL ARTS STUDENTS

The newest test developed by GRE is the Writing Assessment, and it is offered independently of the GRE General and Subject tests. The purpose of this new test, developed at the request of the graduate school community for a performance-based assessment of critical reasoning and analytical writing, is to expand the range of skills assessed by these two traditional tests. According to GRE, the Writing Assessment "can indicate your ability to make a successful transition to graduate level work; highlight academic strengths that are not captured by other tests or in your personal statement or writing samples; contribute meaningful information that helps distinguish you from other candidates who present otherwise similar credentials."

The Writing Assessment consists of two analytical writing tasks: the first asks you to present your perspective on an issue, the second to analyze an argument. This means that you are not tested on specific content or required to respond to multiple-choice questions that call for a single right answer. This assessment gives you freer range to express your ideas, opinions, and analysis of a complex topic. As the GRE describes it, this test "assesses your ability to articulate and support complex ideas, analyze an argument, and sustain a focused and coherent discussion. It is not a test of specific content knowledge, and there is no single best way to respond." The liberal arts student who has enjoyed a rigorous, well-rounded educational training should view this particular test as a welcome opportunity.

The Writing Assessment is so new that you will need to check with the graduate schools you are considering to find out whether they require the test or will accept the test results in considering your application. You should be aware that this test is offered only on computer as a separate test, and it can be taken year-round at all ETS-authorized computer-based testing centers.

Given the hundreds of academically outstanding applicants each year, admissions committees at highly selective graduate schools have to judge them on the basis of other qualities—proven leadership capacity, communication skills, evidence of integrity, maturity, emotional stability, purpose and focus—and by such other means as interviews, essays, and faculty recommendations. In making decisions among hundreds or thousands of good but not outstanding applicants, most admissions committees find that test scores together with GPA are critical.

Hence one can understand the anxiety in that room full of adults being tested once again like schoolchildren. For they are competing against thousands taking the same test in centers and at computers all over the United States and abroad. Anxiety in itself is not a bad thing when combined with a measure of confidence. The two may seem contradictory, but just as the best actors suffer momentary stage fright or the lawyer enters the courtroom with a sudden rush of doubt in his ability to argue his case, so the most prepared applicant cannot help fearing that a trick question or a careless mistake may be his or her undoing.

The motto to paste on your mirror is, Prepare! Prepare! Prepare! Although the subject matter differs, the principles of preparation are the same for any graduate admission test: Sharpen your verbal, reading, and (for all but the LSAT and MAT) math skills and sharpen your test-taking skills in general. In addition, since the GRE Subject Tests are best taken soon after finishing courses in the subject, it may be necessary for someone who has been out of college for a time to repeat a survey course or retain a knowledgeable tutor to prepare for the test.

Summaries of the Major Entrance Tests

Graduate Record Exam (GRE)

General Section: verbal, quantitative, analytical skills (2 hours, 15 minutes);* Writing (computer-adaptive test): issue and argument writing sections (1 hour, 15 minutes); Subject: varies according to requirements (2 hours, 50 minutes)

*Beginning October 1, 2002, a writing section will replace the analytical skills section.

Scoring scale: 200 to 800 on each section

Dates: open (except for the subject tests, which are offered
as paper tests in November, December, and April each year)

Graduate Management Aptitude Test (GMAT)

Verbal, quantitative, and analytical sections (3 hours, 30 minutes)

Scoring scale: 200 to 800

Dates: open

Registration deadlines: open

Computer-adaptive test

Law School Admission Test (LSAT)

Reading comprehension, analytical and logical reasoning sections
(five 35-minute sections, four of which are counted toward your
score)

Scoring scale: 120 to 180

Writing section (30 minutes): The essay is not scored, but it is sent
to the law schools to which you apply

Dates: six times each year

Medical College Admission Test (MCAT)

Verbal reasoning, physical and biological sciences, writing sections
(5 hours, 45 minutes)

Scoring scale: 1 to 15 for each section, J (low) to T (high) for the
writing sample

Dates: twice a year, in April and August

Dental Admission Test (DAT)

Survey of Natural Sciences (90 minutes), Perceptual Ability Test
(60 minutes), Reading Comprehension Test (90 minutes), and
Quantitative Reasoning Test (45 minutes)

Scoring scale: 1 to 30 on each section

Dates: open

Computer-adaptive test

Miller Analogies Test

100 analogies (50 minutes)

Scoring scale: 0 to 99 percentile basis

Dates: open (given on an as-needed basis only at Controlled Test
Centers located on college and university campuses throughout
the United States)

THE TOEFL
(TEST OF ENGLISH AS A FOREIGN LANGUAGE)

If your native or first language is not English, you will be required by
every graduate school to take the TOEFL. Some graduate programs
also require you to take the Test of Spoken English (TSE). Short of a
personal interview and evaluation, this is the best means for admissions committees to decide if your English skills are strong enough to
meet the demands of the curriculum with which you will have to contend. The ETS administers both of these tests.

The TOEFL is a computer-based test, similar to the GRE and GMAT.
It includes four sections—reading, listening, writing, and language
structure—and takes four hours to complete. The test is available
to take throughout the world on a flexible schedule since it is a computerized test. You must adhere to very specific requirements to be
allowed to sit for the test, because of concerns about cheating. Be
certain to read the instructions before going to a test center; these
can be found in the TOEFL/TSE booklet published by ETS or on their
website.

The TSE tests your ability to speak English. You are required to
respond to questions orally that are presented in written and recorded
form. Your responses are tape-recorded for grading by a team of trained
teachers. The test has no written portion and takes 30 minutes to complete. You need to be sure that a test center near you is equipped to
administer this test. Again, check with ETS for the center nearest
to you.

How to Prepare for Graduate Tests

Getting Information about a Test

As we have noted, preparing for a graduate admissions test is essentially a matter of becoming so acquainted with the nature of the questions you will be asked that you won't be nervous or lose valuable time in answering them during the actual test situation. The first thing to do is get hold of one of the following publications appropriate to your field:

The GMAT Bulletin of Information
The GRE Bulletin of Information
The Official Guide to U.S. Law Schools: Prelaw Handbook
The Medical School Admission Requirements Handbook
DAT Preparation Materials
The MAT Information Book

The GMAT and GRE bulletins are published by ETS and distributed free to every college's counseling and career center. They can also be obtained by contacting the ETS.

For GMAT information, contact:

GMAT
Distribution and Receiving Center
225 Phillips Boulevard
Ewing, New Jersey 08628-7435
Phone: (609) 771-7330
Website: www.gmat.org

For GRE information, contact:

GRE-ETS
P.O. Box 6000
Princeton, New Jersey 08541-6000
Phone: (609) 771-7670
Website (GRE Online): www.gre.org

The Law Package and the Official LSAT Sample Test Book can ordered by contacting:

The Law School Admissions Council
Newtown, Pennsylvania 18940
Phone: (215) 968-1001
Website: www.lsac.org

For MCAT information, contact:

MCAT Program Office
P.O. Box 4056
Iowa City, Iowa 52243
Phone: (319) 337-1357
Website: www.aamc.org/students/mcat/start.htm

DAT Preparation Materials is available free to dental school applicants by contacting:

Division of Educational Measurements
American Dental Association
211 East Chicago Avenue
Chicago, Illinois 60611
Phone: (800) 621-8099
Website: http:www.ADA.org

The Miller Analogies Test information is available at most colleges' career and counseling centers or by contacting:

The Psychological Corporation
555 Academic Court
San Antonio, Texas 78204
Phone: (800) 622-3231
Website: http://www.tpcweb.com

Getting Help in Preparing

The question we are asked invariably by those facing entrance tests is whether they should prepare on their own, take a formal course, or work with an individual tutor. We often respond using the analogy of a physical training course at the gym for someone who has decided to improve his or her physical health. Some people can motivate themselves to work out regularly and learn a routine by reading materials, others need the support and energy of a group training session, and still others know they will not succeed in meeting their goals without the direction and encouragement of an individual trainer. You must decide what will work best for you to achieve the score you know you need to be considered for admission to a selective graduate school program.

There are several well-established commercial test preparation centers available throughout the country, the most notable being Kaplan Test Centers and The Princeton Review. Many college campuses make group test preparation courses available through their career placement office. There are also tutors who make a profession of guiding individuals through the steps to be ready for the tests. The advantages of each are probably apparent to you, but let us point out what we have observed in counseling prospective graduate students over the years.

Group Courses Several of the commercial companies have years of experience preparing many thousands of students, which enables them continuously to refine their prep materials. They also provide practice materials and computers at their centers. They have locations in all major cities and near most of the major colleges and universities. The actual classes can be large and distracting, and the quality of the teachers can be inconsistent. Before committing to a commercial course, be sure to check on the experience and knowledge of the person who will be teaching you. In general, these courses are expensive, but they may well be the best way for you to learn how to take entrance tests.

Individual Tutors Experienced individual tutors will focus their training on your unique academic background, knowledge base in the relevant subjects, and your particular style of taking tests. Your tutor should then devise a program that will address your strengths and weaknesses, as well as serve as a motivator to keep you on track in your study and practice. Your professional working schedule or academic studies may be so intense that you need to devise a flexible schedule with a tutor rather than prepare within the constraints of a structured group course schedule. The advantages of this approach are obvious, but the challenge is to find the right tutor for you. He or she has to be knowledgeable and experienced, and convenient to where you attend college or work. The rates for individual tutoring vary greatly, so ask what the charge will be and compare this to other tutors' fees before you make a commitment.

Self-Preparation A good many people have found that they can prepare for the tests on their own. They have the motivation to work diligently on a regular program, using the many practice materials readily available that will guide them through each step of the way. They can study with printed workbooks, interactive CD-ROM computer materials, or on websites of the test prep companies or the sponsors of the real tests. We suggest that you first check the practice materials made available by the test producers. A number of the graduate school admissions testing programs are now giving away their own test preparation software and materials for free to any and all students. If you are still in college, you should also look over the sources your career center provides. If you are out of college, go to any of the large booksellers, and you will find several shelves of study materials that can meet your needs.

Whichever method of preparing for the test you decide to use, get started in plenty of time so that you can cover all the parts of the test and review math or a subject you may have forgotten. Many an applicant to graduate school has expressed his regret, after taking a test, that he had not given enough time to getting ready for it. Draw up a realistic test study schedule and then systematically follow it. This is difficult, we know, especially for those of you who are working in a demanding job that allows for little flexible time, but you must do it in order to compete against those who are preparing diligently.

How much time should you allow yourself for such a selectively taught course in test taking? The average student preparing on his or her own will benefit from 8 to 10 hours a week over the course of six to eight weeks. Just taking one practice test requires three to four hours; the test must be scored and the results studied to find your weak points; then you must work to overcome weaknesses—in grammar, organization of an essay, in calculation, in science problem-solving, in analytical reasoning, or in evaluation of basic facts and knowledge of a subject.

If you are working with a tutor or taking a group course, you will have commitments of six to nine hours a week just for classroom learning. You must carve out time each week to review and practice the lessons you have just taken. The bottom line is to figure out when you are most able to commit this amount of time to readying yourself for the graduate test. This can then help you to determine your schedule for taking the real test and applying to graduate school.

Here is one schedule that we suggest you use to track your progress in preparing for the real thing:

Name of Test _____ Target Date to Take Test _____

Week	Time spent on test	Time spent reviewing and drilling	Practice score
1	_____	_____	_____
2	_____	_____	_____
3	_____	_____	_____
4	_____	_____	_____

(and so on)

When taking a test, you must replicate test conditions, using an alarm clock or timer to signal the end of a test section. Do not take a portion of the test and return to the rest of it later. This is self-defeating, because you are not rehearsing the exact conditions of the actual test, which is a continuous process that calls for a sense of the overall test content and the stamina and concentration you will need to complete it successfully. You cannot leave a test room during the examination. It is therefore absolutely imperative that you assure yourself of an uninterrupted three, four, or five hours (for the MCAT) to understand what it will take to maintain a concentrated and steady pace during the test. Think of this process as you would if you were a marathon runner. You could not prepare yourself to go the full distance if you trained irregularly and only by doing short runs rather than extended ones. You would not have the ability to pace yourself properly and to have the psychological confidence that you could go the full distance.

Though we encourage you to concentrate your fullest efforts on the first attempt at a graduate test, you should realize you can retake the test if you feel that more preparation time will result in a significantly higher score. On average, admissions committees will give talented and interesting applicants the benefit of weighing only their better score. If you have a disappointing experience the first time round, consider retaking the test later on, but do so only if you have an idea of what you need to study or practice to improve your score, and are sure that you will commit the necessary time to preparation.

Some Test-Taking Tips

- Get a good night's rest before test day. Do not stay up late to do last-minute cramming.
- Arrive at least an hour before the test to get comfortable with your surroundings; it really makes a difference in how you perform.
- Leave plenty of time to allow for traffic delays or losing your way, either of which is every test taker's nightmare.
- Bring a reliable watch so that you can keep track of time throughout the test without having to look up continuously.
- Be sure to bring your admissions ticket and an authorized personal identification, typically your driver's license or passport.
- Bring several sharpened number 2 pencils and erasers for paper-based tests.
- Take time to read all test directions carefully, even though you will be familiar with them from doing sample tests.
- Be certain of the consequences of answering questions incorrectly or omitting an answer. Before you decide to guess on some

questions, know whether you have points deducted from correct answers for an incorrect one.

- Never hurry through a question. Do not skip and skim. This is a graduate-level exam that calls for in-depth analysis and thought.
- Plan the time you will spend on each section based on the requirements of the test and your experience with practice tests.
- For paper-based tests, if you finish a section ahead of time, go back and review your answers. Do not look ahead to another section.
- For paper-based tests, answer time-consuming questions after you have answered those you can do quickly.
- If you're allowed, stand up and stretch every so often to keep your body from tightening and allow oxygen to reach all parts of your body.
- Do some deep breathing at the beginning and throughout the test to keep yourself relaxed and alert.

A New Age: Computer-Adaptive Tests

We have referred several times to the GRE, GMAT, TOEFL, and DAT as computer-adaptive tests. This is a very recent innovation of the ETS and the American Dental Association, and is certain to confuse many of you who plan to take any of these tests. We offer an explanation of this test format and the ways in which it calls for different test-taking strategies.

The name of the testing format, "computer-adaptive," reflects the nature of the test and how it differs from the old-fashioned paper-and-pencil test. The test is programmed to adapt to your responses from the outset. At the beginning, you are presented with questions of moderate difficulty. Your answers quickly determine what next level of difficulty is presented to you. If you answered incorrectly, the computer adapts accordingly and presents less challenging questions next. If your first answers are correct, the next sequence of questions will be more demanding. That's right, showing your ability will reward you with tougher questions. You cannot skip any questions and return to them later, as you can with the paper-based tests. The computer demands an answer before it can program the next question. You also cannot return to an earlier question to change your answer. A sign should be posted at the door that says, "no erasers needed here" as a reminder of the difference between the two test formats.

Since the computer adapts to your level of ability, you can find yourself dealing with an easier (relatively speaking) or harder set of questions throughout the test. The test is designed so that everyone gets 50 percent of the questions correct. Your final point total will be affected by the degree of difficulty of your test questions since they are weighted according to their difficulty. Answering easier questions successfully will not necessarily give you a higher score. ETS states that although no two people will have the exact same test, their scores can be compared because the nature of the questions and the levels of difficulty are factored into the calculation of the score. ETS claims that the questions and scoring are generally the equivalent of the old paper-based test but the computer test is not simply a computer screen version of the earlier paper tests.

There are several advantages to computer-based tests. If you feel you did poorly, you can cancel your test at the end of the session (before you learn your score), and your test results will not be forwarded to any graduate school. Another advantage is that you can learn the results immediately, which leaves you that much more time to decide if you should retake the test at a future time and if you have picked the right level of selective graduate schools to apply to. Official results of your testing are available within two weeks to be sent to those institutions you have designated on your registration form. Since the test administration and scoring is more efficient for ETS, you can sit for the test every month of the year. This, of course, gives you greater flexibility in planning your own preparation schedule.

For those who are facile with computers and accustomed to using them for all of their academic or professional work, this format may well be an advantage in taking graduate tests. For those who have limited experience in using computers, the computer-based test may be disorienting and uncomfortable. Besides the inability to go back to earlier questions or to omit answers, there are several disadvantages to the computer format that need to be mentioned. Since you are working on a computer screen, you often have to scroll up and down to review a reading paragraph before answering a question, or to see some graphs and charts in their entirety. You also cannot underline or mark key sentences for your own reference as you consider the correct answer.

Before you start the actual test, a tutorial is provided to acquaint you with the use of the computer. Clearly, if you are accustomed to using a computer on a regular basis you will have no difficulty in mastering the technique of taking the test. If you are not a regular user of a computer, you should take several lessons from a computer-literate roommate or friend well before the day of the test. In any event, you will have the opportunity to complete the full tutorial in the test room before you have to begin the test. There is good news for those of you who are not good at typing: the entire test requires only that you know how to point and click with the mouse. Before you arrive at the test center, be sure to read the description of the computer-based test and the strategies for executing the test in the GRE and GMAT information booklets. This will prove very useful to you.

If You Have a Disability

Since the passage of the Americans with Disabilities Act, all colleges and universities have had to avoid possible discrimination in admissions by meeting the needs of those with physical or learning disabilities who are fully qualified. This ruling applies also to test taking. All of the testing organizations presented in this step will make any necessary accommodations to enable an individual to perform at his or her full capability. If you are physically handicapped and need to take a test in a different setting or need assistance in answering paper-based or computer-based tests, apply for special testing with procedures outlined in every test program's registration form. If you have a learning disability and need extended time to complete the test or need a testing room with no distractions, you can qualify for these accommodations by documenting your learning need.

We can reassure you that you will not be negatively affected in the selection process because of any of these factors. In fact, we have been witness on many occasions to admission of handicapped individuals in part because of the courage and strength they have shown in overcoming their disability to succeed in their studies. Just be careful in following the written procedures each test organization requires for you to qualify for special testing. With regard to the testing service's indicating that you took the test under nonstandard administration or conditions, changes are afoot. ETS recently announced that, as part of a settlement, they will no longer indicate on their test reports that a student has taken the GRE, GMAT, TOEFL, or Praxis tests with accommodations for a learning disability.

Think of the Tests as a New and Rewarding Experience

Much of what we have said here may seem elementary, and it is, but thousands of people taking graduate admission tests perform below their capability because they fail to prepare for them meticulously. Attention to detail is one requirement of those pursuing graduate study; another is possessing the organizational skills to know what test you have to take and when you will best be prepared to take it.

Look on graduate tests as a new experience since you are at a turning point in your life, having already made the really difficult decision to go to graduate school to prepare for or to advance your life's work. Taking a test is a relatively small part of the whole undertaking to move yourself forward. Though we make no claim that preparing for and taking demanding tests with so much riding on the outcome is a bundle of fun, we encourage you to recall some stressful experience in which you had to overcome your initial trepidation, but felt a great sense of accomplishment and satisfaction once you met that challenge. You might have spent days in the wilderness camping, or climbed a high peak, or canoed white-water rapids, or biked hundreds of miles, or learned to ski when steep hills scared you to death. Remembering how you dealt with the challenge should make sitting in a room, well-prepared to tackle a test, less intimidating to you.

Almost all the people we have counseled come away from the testing process with a new confidence in their ability to meet the intellectual demands of the test, and feel they have learned a good deal of information or techniques that will carry over once they begin their graduate studies. You will have the same experience if you follow the advice we have presented.

Step Five Checklist

- You must prepare for graduate tests, whichever one you need to take and in whatever format it is presented. Few do well who do not prepare.

- Familiarize yourself with the nature of the test by taking practice tests and working on subject matter or verbal and quantitative skills. Take advantage of the easily available resources to prepare for the tests.

- Keep a record of the practice tests you take and note the time you spent studying. From this, project when you will be best prepared for the actual test.

- Consider if you are best served by taking a preparation class or using an individual tutor.

- Spend 40 to 80 hours preparing for the test. That is what your competition will be doing.

- Take advantage of special test accommodations if you have a physical or learning disability.

- Think of the test as an opportunity to gain knowledge and confidence.

STEP SIX

Write Strong Personal Statements

The Significance of Personal Statements

Candidates for graduate school are asked to include with their application one or more personal statements, each consisting of a few paragraphs stating their motivations for graduate study, plans after graduating, aspirations, interests, accomplishments, or anything else that seems relevant to an admissions decision. Sometimes an admissions committee wants your personal reaction to a hypothetical scenario—how you would react to an employee's refusal to do something you requested, or, conversely, how you would deal or have dealt with an order from your boss that you regard as unethical or harmful to others, for example. What could be more disarming than an invitation to talk about the most important person in the world, yourself, and what you have accomplished thus far in your life, or to give a personal reaction to a trying situation?

Yet the best of us can choke at such an opportunity and, after writing something, wonder: Is this what they want and do I really have anything of importance to say? A natural reaction to be sure, but one that is obviously counterproductive if allowed to dominate your thinking as you compose the statement.

Just what members of an admissions committee want is to a certain extent impossible to know, since they are strangers to you. You can be sure of some of their expectations. No law professor, doctor, or Ph.D. going through candidates' folders is saying things like, "Hasn't told us about his childhood," or "Hasn't said why she went to college so far from home," or "Doesn't even mention honors courses," or "Why not say how much he expects to make as doctor or businessman?" Nor are these busy and astute professional educators looking for the kind of essay you wrote when applying to undergraduate college. If they are not looking for any one thing in particular, how can you ever write something that will make an iota of difference to your acceptance or rejection?

Put yourself in the chair of an admissions committee member for a moment and consider the task to be carried out: reading the personal statements of dozens upon dozens of candidates, who have already been screened as possible admits on the basis of their high grades and test scores. In spite of their high statistical profiles, one-half or more of these excellent candidates must be rejected. How can personal statements help experienced faculty members and professional admissions deans decide whether to vote for or against each applicant?

You will note that nothing is said about grading personal statements. All judgments are subjective, and no grading scale is used to react to each applicant's essays. Some members of the admissions committee may be more impressed by a personal statement than others. When there is considerable disagreement about the content and point of a particular statement, other criteria become more important in understanding the candidate's virtues and strengths to arrive at an admissions decision.

We have already presented you with cases of applicants who had a story to tell the admissions committees of the graduate schools they wished to attend. You should be reassured that their essays and statements, which proved successful, were the result of many hours of writing and rewriting. None of them were capable of creating such presentations in one or two sittings. With hard work, you too can and will fashion essays that will influence committees positively.

MATTHEW: *an MBA candidate with a low GPA but extensive experience*

Matthew, an MBA candidate, had a mediocre 2.7 GPA at the University of Virginia and a very high GMAT score. He managed to gain acceptance to Columbia, Cornell, the University of Michigan, and

UCLA. Only Harvard and Amos Tuck School at Dartmouth turned him down.

Matthew is the son of the owner of a substantial chain of hardware stores. His father holds an MBA from Harvard. There was no problem about Matthew's prospective career, but he wondered how effective and influential he would be in his father's expanding business. Using Harvard's questions as a basis for self-examination, he began with rough drafts, worked to improve them, and ultimately was able to prepare cogent personal statements. Take the subject of his weak academic record:

> I graduated from the University of Virginia with a BA in history. That event remains the highlight of my undergraduate career. Instead of studying hard, I hardly studied at all. This attitude towards my studies was borne out in my grade average—a lofty 2.7, a remarkably mediocre achievement accomplished chiefly through long hours of neglect. Instead of concentrating on my studies, I managed to indulge myself in everything from scuba diving to heavy option stock trading. Though I was very successful at these endeavors, my grades suffered.

Having got this confession off his chest, Matthew then wrote a lengthy description of his work experience. It began:

> Upon graduating from college, I started work in the family business and experienced a remarkable and unexpected turnaround in both my attitude and confidence. I suspect the reason for this change was a combination of maturity, fear, and my having the opportunity to focus my energies and achieve concrete goals. In any event, I am proud of my accomplishments in business, and I am keenly aware that I still have much to achieve.

Matthew went on to explain in detail his experience in the company, how he learned a number of advanced computer software programs to help update the business, and how he rose to head a staff of 25 sales and financial record-keepers in one year. Next he described his solution to a problem of expanding inventories:

> I put together a core team of eight employees who represented operations, research, purchasing, distribution, and billing. After a few months, it became clear that inventory was swelling due to inaccurate demand forecasts and sharp increases in speculative buying. We then set out to construct a sophisticated inventory management system that produced more accurate product demand forecasting. The project proved so successful that we are now considering packaging the software program for commercial sale.

An additional personal statement described how he won the annual Young Leadership award from the Society for a Better Community for his work in helping to open 19 new independent stores with strong minority participation.

Finally, Matthew had to respond to the question every graduate business school asks candidates: "Why do you wish to get an MBA degree and how do you plan to use it in your future career?" By now, Matthew had had enough work experience to respond with clarity and vision:

> For me, an MBA is of great importance in determining the future of our business, which must expand, but the question is how? Through acquisition? Or should we diversify into a different industry like computer technology? And how will we finance expansion; through a public offering or borrowing? I am eager to acquire the tools to help answer these and other questions by means of the training a graduate business school will give me.

A confident, responsible, happy young man comes through in Matthew's personal writing, which helped get committees to look beyond his poor college record. It was clear from the details and examples of his work experience that Matthew was ready to take full advantage of the MBA curriculum and that he could contribute to class discussion and group projects.

One of the positive side effects of the personal statement is that writing clarifies your own ideas and feelings about a graduate program. It forces you to examine your motives in light of your record. If it is an honest evaluation, you will benefit from it.

There Are Many Marginal Candidates

We purposely include among our case studies good but not outstanding students, typical of many graduate school applicants who possess great potential. In a sense, all applicants to top graduate schools are marginal, because of the intense competition for limited places in an entering class. Just the numbers—academic GPA and test scores—place many candidates in the category called Possible Admit by the admissions committees. The personal statements may just turn the tide for any applicant to any quality graduate school.

This is why we ask you to devote more attention to the personal statements and the responses to specific, brief questions than you might otherwise think necessary. Writing is not easy even for professional writers, who spend as much time or more rewriting their essays or stories as they do on a first draft. You are not asked to compete with masters like Henry David Thoreau, John Updike, E. B. White, or any of your favorite authors, but graduate schools do expect you to be able to write clearly, logically, and with a modicum of grace, originality, and imagination. If you already have this capability, then you may think that Step Six requires less of your time. However, you may need guidance in selecting appropriate topics to write about, and in finding the tone and style that will convince a committee of strangers that you are a candidate they should have in their program. If you have doubts about your writing skills, our suggestions, combined with practice, can help you to improve and gain confidence in your ability to write winning statements. Not surprisingly, the more you write, the better your writing becomes, and the easier it is to say on paper what you have in your mind.

AMY: *writing about a disability*

At our insistence, Amy rewrote her major statement four times to get her story presented as it deserved to be. She had quite a story to tell. In eighth grade, she learned that she had Turner's syndrome, a chromosomal disorder that limits physical growth to five feet or less and affects traditional processing skills on standardized tests and written exams, but has no effect on intelligence. Her GPA of 3.2 at Northwestern University is highly commendable but not brilliant. Her MCAT composite score placed her at the median for all candidates for medical school. Nevertheless, Amy was admitted to six excellent medical schools, including Tufts, New York University, Boston University, and the University of Rochester. Her deeply moving essay made a difference in her selection. We present it in part:

> When I found out I had Turner's Syndrome, I ran. I disassociated myself from the situation and attempted to run my life as if nothing had happened. This was not possible. In preparing for medical school, I have discovered the ability to face consequences and find channels for change.
>
> I have not only formed deep relationships with people, but have also become able to talk to my family. I now have the ability to express what I have gone through. As I began to experience relationships with people outside of my family, I realized that for me science will be an indispensable tool, a method that I can use to do something about the issues I care about most.
>
> In this past year I have discovered areas that not only interest me, but to which I can devote my life. I work on turtle brain cells in an attempt to establish a connection between two types of neurons.

Amy goes on to spell out the sophistication of the research she has carried on under the tutelage of a highly regarded medical researcher at Northwestern who recognized her talent and commitment to science.

In this personal explication, Amy honestly conveys her original dismay at discovering her illness and how she eventually overcame self-pity and anger by making a commitment to a scientific usefulness to humanity. The contrast between her slightly above average academic performance and average test scores and her intense and compassionate convictions is striking and compelling.

Essays for Graduate School Differ from College Admissions Essays

When you applied to college, the essay that you sent with your applications was an attempt to bowl over the admissions officers with your individuality. You tried to show your uniqueness by writing about an unusual experience. If you were creative, you let that come out in humor, eloquence, and graceful and poetic expression. You also tried to show you would fit into campus activities and sports, and you would be a constructive force in college. Your essay was designed to demonstrate what you could offer to the institution.

Your extracurricular achievements in college can look good on your graduate school application, but to build an essay around them will work only if they are related to what you plan to do after you have secured your graduate degree. Being captain of the baseball or field hockey team is an unlikely basis for a personal statement. Having nearly completed college or perhaps already having a job or an internship, you indicate that you are a mature individual. Your personal statement must reflect this maturity and show how your record and accomplishments have led to personal growth. Admissions committees look for evidence of such development, because it suggests you are capable of further growth under their tutelage. The personal statement can be helpful in projecting the future of a candidate: Will he or she be a good or great doctor, lawyer, teacher, editor, architect, captain of industry, government expert, or economist?

Your account of your junior year abroad is of no interest to a medical school admissions committee if you do not relate it to your prospective career. You may have been head of your fraternity or sorority or started a new club on campus, but that cannot by itself make an MBA committee sit up and take notice. Again, you have to show somehow that this accomplishment bears on your professional career. The experience you choose to write about can demonstrate a talent for leading others, and organizational and communication skills that are likely to make you a successful businessperson in the future. As another example, your eagerness to study abroad and master another language will underscore your determination to work in a multinational company.

WHAT KRISTEN MOSS, THE DIRECTOR OF ADMISSIONS AT HARVARD BUSINESS SCHOOL, LIKES TO READ IN A PERSONAL STATEMENT

My favorite applications are the ones that "dance." You read them, and this individual, whoever he or she is, and whatever he or she has done, jumps off the page. . . . You are not just a resume—you will bring a unique perspective and set of talents to our community. Help us to understand what you will bring.

From *Business Week* Online, August 23, 2000.

Cleverness in a personal statement can be counterproductive. What opened the eyes of weary professional readers of college applicant folders only annoys graduate admissions officers and professors who screen to discern which qualified students will be a pleasure to teach and to prepare to carry on their own profession.

Spend as much time as you need thinking about your topic before you actually begin writing. Consider your responses to these large questions which only you have the answers to:

- What are your primary goals in life?
- What matters most to you in your life?
- In what ways do you think of yourself as being unique?

- What obstacles or hardships have you overcome to get you where you are at this point in your life and how have they defined who you are and where you want to head?
- What are your major strengths and how do they relate to what you want to do?
- In what ways will you enhance the professional field you are preparing for?
- What specific examples can you describe that illustrate your personal set of values, ethical standards, and code of behavior?
- How does your academic performance in college, and your volunteer or work experience, explain who you are and why it makes sense for you to pursue graduate studies and a career in the profession you are considering?
- How will your talents and personal characteristics contribute to success in this professional career?
- What have you accomplished in your schooling or work or volunteerism that you are proud of?

With someone who knows you well, brainstorm answers to these questions and your choice of topic. Remember that the personal statement should not be a rehash of your background and activities that appear in other parts of the application. Your goal is to flesh yourself out in a way that convinces an admissions committee that you will be a successful member of their school and their profession. If you can settle on the direction of your statement, then starting the writing process will take you to your destination.

Finally, the college admissions officer is a generalist seeking to admit a number of different academic types to satisfy all the academic departments of his institution. In one essay, he may spot a future ecologist and in another, a doctor. In contrast, the graduate admissions officer is a Johnny-one-note, looking for new students for the one or few programs of that school. He or she is extremely focused. The best personal statement in applying to graduate school is one that says in effect: I will be a credit to this graduate school while attending and in my career afterward. I am focused on what I want to accomplish in my career and am determined to meet all the demands of the training to achieve this goal.

ANDY: *a medical school applicant whose goal is to work with children*

One young man seemed certain from an early age that his greatest desire was to work with children in his future. Throughout his high school years, he actively engaged in a peer tutoring program, helping middle school youngsters, and coaching Little League teams during the summer months. The direction in which this interest would take him was uncertain into his early college career. The field of medicine did not occur to him at first, as the sciences did not intrigue him as much as the study of history, mathematics, and economics. We encouraged Andy to pursue his general intellectual interests in his undergraduate years at Yale and to explore internship opportunities in several fields related to working with children. With this sense of confidence that he could be flexible in choosing his undergraduate courses and extracurricular activities, Andy enjoyed his college experience.

While majoring in econometrics, a heady combination of economic theory and mathematical analysis, Andy decided to fulfill the six courses in sciences that would qualify him for entrance to medical school, should he choose that direction. He worked diligently to complete these subjects with A and B+ grades. His overall GPA was excellent, a 3.65 over the first three years. His MCAT scores were right on the median for medical school applicants. He used his summers to intern with a pediatrician, volunteer at the university's hospital, and work in a research laboratory. When Andy returned to us for counsel toward the end of his junior year, he had decided to apply to medical school to train for a career in pediatrics. The challenge was to show the medical admissions committees that he was committed to this field, even though he had majored in a social science, one which could give the impression that he really wanted to head toward a Wall Street career.

Andy had to present a thoughtful, articulate, and convincing application to gain the attention and respect of the medical admissions committees. He needed to fight for the opportunity to interview with a committee member to state his case directly. In addition, a review of potential recommenders concentrated on those teachers and supervisors who would confirm his talent and his passionate interest in helping children in a medical setting. Here is his completed personal application to the University of Connecticut, his first choice of medical school:

"Question 1: Describe your motivation to pursue a career as a physician."

I enjoy problem solving. My two favorite courses in college have been Organic Chemistry and Econometrics. Both classes centered on determining an unknown, given certain limited pieces of information. I have recently interned in both a pediatric group practice and a hospital setting, and I found that this same principle applies to pediatrics. The process of discovering the causal factors of a child's symptoms and determining what courses of treatment need to be applied captivated me. During my internships, I observed a few difficult cases where a child's history and current symptoms were presented and it took several days before the diagnosis was made. I found this complicated and critical process of solving such a problem an exciting challenge and opportunity. My experiences thus far in the field of pediatrics have shown me that this is a field that will provide both the intellectual stimulation I seek and the opportunity to help young people to get well on a highly personal basis.

"Question 2: Physicians will face considerable challenges in the future. What do you see as the most significant issue the medical profession faces in the next 40 years?"

It is almost inconceivable to contemplate that 6.3 million American children are currently considered to be living in extreme poverty. These unfortunate children are born into poverty-stricken families, many of whom are single parents and many who are addicted to drugs and/or alcohol. I saw first hand the faces of many of these children while working at Yale–New Haven Hospital.

The social plight of a critical mass of young boys and girls in this country is out of hand and is becoming progressively worse. It seems that doctor-patient relationships are deteriorating due both to managed care companies that reduce the time allotted to doctors per patient and, in many instances, a language barrier that makes communication and access to assistance by those in need difficult or impossible. Changes in our present system must be made to allow for easier medical care for the disadvantaged members of our society. The managed care groups must be encouraged to strike a balance between their emphasis on profits by limiting treatment and serving the needs of all our populace.

The growing language barriers in our society also need to be addressed. I witnessed at the hospital I worked in the importance of crossing this barrier by communicating in Spanish wherever possible. I have committed to studying introductory Spanish in my senior year of college because I believe this will improve my ability to develop a rapport with many of the patients I expect to treat as a physician. The government and the medical profession, in tandem, must work towards a goal over the next forty years, starting immediately, to make preventive and curative medicine available to all who are in need of care.

"Question 3: Describe your experiences in the health field and what insights you have gained about problems you will face as a physician."

Over the past two years I have attempted to confirm my decision to pursue a career in pediatrics. Last summer I interned with my pediatrician from my childhood at a small group practice. This past summer I volunteered at the Yale-New Haven Hospital emergency room and this summer I shadowed a pediatric rotation at the same hospital. From these experiences I learned that an essential part of dealing with children is to gain their trust from the beginning. I learned how important it is to help them overcome their fear of being in a hospital or even a doctor's office. I also learned that personal communication with the patient is an enormously important part of medical practice. As described above, it is likely that in working in an urban hospital center the odds are great that language can be a barrier to serving a good portion of the patients in need. I believe I already have the skills to work with children because of my years of teaching, coaching, and tutoring. I am working on developing better skills in assisting disadvantaged and multicultural populations.

"Question 4: Describe your participation in research. How did you benefit?"

I have spent a good part of my past two years involved in clinical practice observing and learning what are the especial dynamics of this activity. As a result of this emphasis in addition to the constrictions of my academic major in econometrics, I have not had the time to pursue a laboratory research position. I have, however, had quite a bit of research experience in analyzing problems, developing a working hypotheses, collecting and analyzing data, and making an informed resolution of the problem through my academic major and summer internships. I am confident that I can bring these skills to the science setting in graduate school.

Partly on the basis of his personal statements, Andy was invited to interview with several members of the admissions committee at the University of Connecticut School of Medicine. This gave him a further opportunity to make his case that training to become a pediatrician in primary care was his goal. Andy was admitted to the medical school where he is now concentrating in pediatric medicine.

Revise, Revise, Revise

College students may or may not have the opportunity to rewrite their papers in the interest of improving the text. Their manuscripts typically come back to them marked with comments like "not clear," "inconsistent," "poorly organized," "weak expression," "punctuation," "spelling errors," "too subjective," "not true," and "missing the point." Such corrections will not have much impact on students, especially if the grade is disappointing. They are most likely to grumble, and then file the paper and forget it. Does this sound familiar? The corrections, instead of being a learning experience, are likely to be taken as an annoyance, or an insult. And if papers are graded A without comment about weaknesses in the writing, students naturally have no way of knowing that they could improve their expression.

Learning to write clear English is like learning to play the piano: it takes practice, and you must go over a piece of prose until it is reasonably smooth. This means drafting and redrafting, which is tedious but essential. A renowned book editor in New York told us that one of her authors was recently likened to several of the greatest American writers of the early twentieth century on the basis of her latest book. What the critics did not know was that the writer worked on 14 significantly different drafts to polish her writing.

We recognize that a majority of applicants to graduate schools have been away from the formal educational environment of college in which writing is a fundamental part of the learning process. We hear expressions of anxiety frequently regarding their ability to write quality personal statements since their jobs do not call for this kind of written expression. E-mail, telephone conversations, and brief memoranda are the means of communication on a daily basis. If this is your situation, you should consider purchasing a good primer on proper writing and expression skills before you start the application process.

RESOURCES FOR THE WRITER

Choose the Right Word: A Contemporary Guide to Selecting the Precise Word for Every Situation, by S. I. Hayakawa. New York: Harper-Collins, 1994.

The Elements of Style, 4th ed., by William Strunk Jr. and E. B. White. Upper Saddle River, NJ: Prentice-Hall, 1999.

Essays of E. B. White. New York: Harper and Row, 1977.

Grammatically Correct: The Writer's Essential Guide to Punctuation, Spelling, Style, Usage, and Grammar. Cincinnati, OH: Writers Digest Books, 1997.

Line by Line: How to Edit Your Own Writing, by Claire K. Cook. Boston: Houghton Mifflin, 1985.

Modern American Usage, A Guide, by Wilson Follett. Revised by Erik Wensberg. New York: Hill and Wang, 1998.

On Writing Well: An Informal Guide to Writing Non-Fiction, 6th ed., by William K. Zinsser. New York: HarperCollins, 1998.

Roget's International Thesaurus, 6th ed. New York: HarperCollins, 2001.

Webster's New World College Dictionary, 4th ed. New York: Hungry Minds, 1999.

Work on the Lead

Two things to aim for in a personal statement are:

1. An arresting, attention-getting lead sentence or paragraph.
2. Clarity of expression.

Let's take the lead sentence. You are competing with hundreds or thousands of other applicants for the admissions committee's attention. Once those who are unqualified are eliminated from consideration, the committee readers look for something that first sparks and then holds their interest. In a society so exposed to media of all kinds, newspapers, magazines, and sprightly ad copy, even educated university people come to expect all writing to be immediately rewarding. Our boredom thresholds are low. Imagine having the duty of reading thousands of statements all on the same subject!

Here is how the Associated Press started a story of an unusual woman:

Colina, Chile—Leontina Albina does not expect much from her children on Mother's Day. She did not raise the fifty-three of them to be like that.

A *Boston Globe* story started this way:

> San Francisco—Last January there were bad vibes in the Haight-Ashbury neighborhood here. The merchants and residents were fed up with the trash and litter caused by transients. The Summer of Love had chilled into the Winter of Discontent.

You can similarly pep up personal statements by avoiding the obvious opener:

> I first wanted to be a doctor when I went with my father on his hospital rounds.

Instead, why not use:

> "Can't you reduce the pain, doctor?" the young man asked. "Not without side effects that will complicate your recovery," the doctor replied. This was my first exposure to the hard side of medicine. When as a high school boy I saw my gentle father refuse to sedate a patient after a gallbladder operation, I thought to myself, "I want to be as gutsy and caring as Dad. I want to be a surgeon too."

An applicant to several top journalism schools opened her personal statement with:

> Four years on a metropolitan daily have taught me one thing: I need time to develop the skills I simply cannot learn on the job. You cannot expect busy editors to drop everything to coach your reporting or analyze weaknesses in your copy.

These are not brilliant ideas, but they beat:

> I want an MBA in order to learn the accounting procedures necessary for an entrepreneurial success.

And:

> After five years as a member of the working press, it is time for me
> to take a year off to polish my journalistic skills.

You, too, can write a good lead. Abandon the chronological account and search for something significant in the series of observations you plan to present to the committee. Ask yourself, "What is important in what I am going to say?" rather than, "When in time should I begin my statement?" Thus, if you are proud of earning a Phi Beta key, do not begin with a history of all the As you earned; begin with the moment you learned you had been invited to join the illustrious fraternity of scholars. Then you can describe how hard you worked to achieve this distinction and what it meant to you.

You can easily develop the habit of noticing how reporters do this in the newspapers or on television. They seldom respect chronology except in adjunct, sidebar material. They report first that an earthquake devastated India, killing thousands of inhabitants of rural villages. Then they work back to the details of the exact location of the earthquake's center, its recorded force, and when it actually occurred. The lead, the headline, presents a few significant facts with little regard for chronology.

E. B. WHITE: MASTER ESSAYIST

Here are three examples of E. B. White's classic style and technique for drawing the reader into his essays:

> *For some time now I have been engaged in dispersing the contents of this apartment, trying to persuade hundreds of inanimate objects to scatter and leave me alone. It is not a simple matter. I am impressed by the reluctance of one's worldly goods to go out again into the world.*
>
> From "Good-bye to Forty-Eighth Street," in *Essays of E. B. White*

> *On the day before Thanksgiving, toward the end of the afternoon,*
> *having motored all day, I arrived home and lit a fire in the living*
> *room. The birch logs took hold briskly. About three minutes later,*
> *not to be outdone, the chimney itself caught fire.*
>
> From "Home-Coming," in *Essays of E. B. White*

> *I am lying here in my private sick bay on the east side of town*
> *between Second and Third Avenues, watching starlings from the*
> *vantage point of bed. Three Democrats are in bed with me: Harry*
> *Truman (in a stale copy of the* Times*), Adlai Stevenson (in*
> Harper's Magazine*), and Dean Acheson (in a book called* A
> Democrat Looks at His Party*).*
>
> From "Bedfellows," in *Essays of E. B. White*

A question asked by most graduate business schools in their applications reads like this:

> Describe a personal or professional characteristic that distinguishes your candidacy for admission and how it will enhance the learning of your fellow students.

Many an applicant has faltered in completing his or her application when confronted by this challenge. They ask themselves, "How on earth can I figure out what I have to offer a group of smart, experienced students?" The best rule of thumb is to keep your response simple and centered on a trait or strength that has come into focus through your self-assessment.

SALLY: *a strong communicator*

Remember to begin with a strong, declarative, and attention-getting opening sentence. Here, as a fine example, is what Sally wrote in her business school application:

I am a confident and skilled communicator. My current and previous professional experiences have presented different challenges in this area.

Working as an Account Executive in advertising tested my communications skill. As the liaison between the agency and our clients I often found myself in sensitive situations. It was my responsibility to represent our clients' interest and make sure that we delivered upon their objectives. At the same time, I needed to support the agency's mission to produce high quality, creative advertising. Although not mutually exclusive, these two objectives were often at odds with each other.

Let me present a typical example of such a situation. A meeting to review work for a new print ad would typically include me, a creative team consisting of an art director and a copywriter, and members of our client's team. After reviewing for the group the strategy and the objectives for the assignment, I would turn the meeting over to the creative team. Together, the copywriter and art director would present the work and explain their vision for the concept and how it might look when fully produced.

After reviewing the conceptual plan, we would then look to the clients for feedback. Their reactions were sometimes overwhelmingly positive. On other days, their responses would be less favorable. At this moment, my role as a diplomat would begin. I had a responsibility not only to defend the work, but also to determine how it could be changed. For instance, when reviewing the image of a six-year-old girl in the print ad, we would receive a wide range of reactions. One client might comment that the girl looked too old, while another client might offer that the girl seemed to be too young. Then the agency's art director would respond in defense that the girl was perfectly rendered.

In order to give clear direction to our creative team prior to adjourning the meeting, I always needed to get to the core of the issue. Requests for change had to be very specific; otherwise, we could end up solving one problem and creating another. I learned to ask very precise questions: "Why does the girl appear too young? Is it her hair? Her clothes? Why does the girl appear to be too old? Is it her facial expressions?" Only through careful discussion could we arrive at sound conclusions that satisfied the client team. Once we reached a resolution, I also needed to ensure that this decision would be acceptable to our creative team.

In my present position as Director of Marketing, I communicate with our current and prospective trading partners on a daily basis. Such conversations require patience, sensitivity and sensibility, as often neither party has the benefit of speaking his or her native language. The ability to communicate effectively also demands respect and understanding for our respective cultures and business practices. In a single day, I have spoken with contacts in Israel, Mexico and Jordan. While I am proficient in Spanish, my Arabic and Hebrew language capabilities are limited, to say the least, thus putting my communications skills to the test.

How I express myself and the words that I choose greatly define how my friends and coworkers perceive me. Ultimately, I believe that my communication skills will largely determine my future opportunities as a leader. After all, my ideas are only as good as my ability to express them.

Sally's closing comment can serve as the theme of this entire step. We encourage you to read it again after you have written and rewritten your own personal statement. Does yours meet the test that Sally lays out here?

Aiming for Clear Expression

The second element to be conscious of in your revision is that everything you write makes sense. Will your thought be clear to someone else? You know what you have in mind, but there is many a slip between a thought and an expression. A good guide to clear expression is *The Elements of Style* by William Strunk Jr. and E. B. White, a brilliant essayist and writer for the *New Yorker* for many years. Another marvelous reference source to keep at your desk side is *Choose the Right Word*, written by S. I. Hayakawa, a leading professor of linguistics for many years. This book will help you to weigh subtle differences in the meaning of words, so you can convey precisely the message you wish to your readers. It is also a good idea to show your writing to someone else for comment. When you hear that something is not clear, clarify, clarify, clarify.

EDWARD: *a future airline executive*

Edward began his undergraduate education in the School of Engineering at Cornell University. After a full year of studies with less than stellar grades, he realized he was in the wrong field. His natural aptitude in mathematics and enjoyment of science had led him to believe he would prosper in the study of engineering. Jim transferred into Cornell's School of Hotel Administration after a review of his real interests and strengths. In this program he could concentrate on finance, accounting, marketing, and international economics, subjects he realized were of genuine interest to him.

Upon completing his undergraduate degree, Edward took a position with American Airlines as an analyst in the company's management program. During the course of two years, he rose to more responsible roles in the area of fiscal analysis and management. He decided to apply to four of the top MBA programs at this juncture. Three of the schools turned him down and the fourth placed him on their waiting list, ultimately denying him admission.

Edward came to us to discuss what he had done incorrectly and what he could do to enhance his odds for admission in the future. It was clear to us that his overall GPA, which was under 3.0 at Cornell, hurt him. He had not persuaded the admissions committee with his résumé and personal statements that he had gained the exposures and the insights to take full advantage of their programs. In his favor was a high showing on the GMAT, growing responsibility within his department at American Airlines, and numerous community service and leadership roles during his college days.

We encouraged Edward to remain in his position for at least one more year since he was promised a significant promotion that would gain him a number of new skills and challenges. He would then be able to present a more cogent argument in his statements and supervisors' recommendations that he was prepared for the rigors of graduate studies. Edward's new position was as a senior analyst and team leader, with supervisory responsibilities for ten staff, many of whom were older and had MBA training. One-and-a-half years later, Edward was accepted to Northwestern's Kellogg School and Pennsylvania's Wharton School.

Edward's response to the traditional question asked by virtually all of the top business schools presents a forceful picture of him as a successful future businessman. His tone of confidence and goal direction is considerably stronger than that conveyed in his previous applications. And notice his opening line.

Question: "Briefly assess your career progress to date. Elaborate on your future career plans and your motivation for pursuing a graduate degree at Kellogg."

My career ambition is to be the CEO of a major international air carrier and guide that airline through controlled, strategic expansion to become the industry leader in safety, innovation, service, and profitability. From my training to date, I see no incompatibility among these objectives. My progress to date, motivation for pursuing a graduate business degree, and future plans all stem from a determination to achieve this goal.

My business and educational experiences provide an excellent foundation of management skill sets. I have held job assignments and internships overseas, had continuous interaction with senior management, and strengthened my analytical skills through extensive financial and marketing analysis at American Airlines. My success at American has earned me an evaluation in the top 5% of the company's employees for four consecutive years. Additionally, I have received three job promotions since joining American, which makes me the fastest rising undergraduate in the department's history to reach a Senior Analyst position.

My responsibilities as Senior Analyst cap a fascinating career in the Yield Management department where I am directly managing a group of 10 analysts, gaining airline consulting experience, and helping to return a bankrupt Latin American airline (Aerolineas Argentinas) to profitability. While living for three months in

Argentina, I strengthened my understanding of international business dynamics while I reorganized the Sales and Marketing groups at the airline. Upon my return to Dallas headquarters, I hired a 15-member group and, recently I have enhanced my experience in managing groups of talented individuals and working with senior management at Aerolineas.

I now recognize that when I originally applied to Kellogg two years ago my background was insufficient to warrant admission. Having accomplished the goals I set for myself as described above, I now believe the time is right for me to perfect my business skills by studying under the faculty at such a premier business school. Kellogg's superiority in teaching marketing management, in particular, will allow me to continue my upward path in the management track in the airline industry. Other courses and faculty will enable me to complete the broader training I will need to head a major corporation eventually. I would take some of the specialized courses available in Northwestern's Transportation Center, although my primary objective is to learn major business concepts and techniques from other industries that can be applied to airline management.

Upon receiving my business education, I plan to re-enter the aviation industry and progress as quickly as possible through the tiers of management responsibility. Throughout this process, I see myself gaining valuable practical and strategic experience while using the skills I have learned in business school. I would plan to relocate to an international site where I can help to rebuild a mid-sized international airline such as Aerolineas Argentinas.

While I believe that business career paths are often influenced by the happenstance of timing and personnel availability, ultimate career success is not. Thus, I will anticipate reaching my goals through ever increasing job responsibility with an end goal of managing a major transportation company. I am confident that once I reach that level my earlier experiences at American Airlines, a business school education, and upper management training will have properly readied me to succeed in leading a company to new heights and transforming the industry as a whole.

A Powerful Personal Statement

We conclude this step with an example of a personal statement that derives its power from the emotional sincerity and clarity of the story.

ALEX: *finding a profession out of family problems*

Alex was admitted to the School of Social Welfare at the University of Wisconsin with a fellowship. His story affirms that you should not be afraid to share with an admissions committee the events in your life that have made you who you are today and what you stand for.

> My early childhood in Mississippi, where I lived until the age of eleven, was characterized by domestic tension brought on by father's weaknesses—he was a poor farmer, drank too much, and quarreled frequently with my mother. As a result, I grew very close to my mother, sympathetic to her struggle to keep her family going through menial work. I listened to her hopes that I would become a doctor someday. After her divorce and remarriage when I was ten, we moved to Wisconsin, where my stepfather became a modestly successful salesman of printing services. I excelled in high school and was determined to become a surgeon. My mother had become a practical nurse and continued to encourage my medical ambitions.
>
> But things did not work out exactly as planned. I was admitted to Oberlin College, where in my freshman year I got into an advanced peer counseling class. This is when I began having doubts about becoming a doctor. Among other things, I was trained to counsel students on the abuse of drugs and alcohol, as well as on eating disorders. I also had some success in helping addicts in the city during vacation as an intern counselor. At the same time, some negative experiences with overbearing and selfish doctors gave me further pause about a medical career.
>
> My parents were disturbed when I announced my change of heart, but I felt relieved, because I knew that my future lay in helping people the way my mother had helped me in childhood, by caring. I began to study psychology and sociology, and one of my professors introduced me to the career of social work. As I pro-

gressed through college with good grades, my parents became more understanding and appreciative of what I was preparing for—a career of social service.

I know I need to do graduate work to complete the training that will allow me to work with and help individuals, families, and groups of people in need. In the meantime, I have a job in a halfway house that I enjoy. I believe that in time I will be able to make a significant contribution to the live of many unhappy people.

Step Six Checklist

Recognize the importance of personal statements in applying to competitive graduate schools.

Do not rely on broad-based topics or originality for its own sake, both of which are encouraged on your college entrance applications.

Use sample essay questions from graduate school applications of interest to you to practice writing effective and revealing statements.

Do not begin writing until you have played with ideas for topics in your head. Answer for yourself the questions we have raised until you are satisfied that you know what you should focus your writing on. Brainstorm with those who know you well as part of this critical exercise.

Work on the lead sentence or paragraph after studying leads used by top journalists or essayists.

Rewrite your statements, show them to someone for comment, and polish them to complete this assignment.

STEP SEVEN

Make Your Nonacademic Experience Meaningful

ROBERT: *the value of significant work experience*

"Discuss your professional objectives, both short and long range, and how your past experiences have contributed to the definition of those objectives. Be as specific as possible about the kinds of positions you seek." Applicants to the Stern School of Business at New York University must answer this question.

Robert, at 26, felt that he was ready to profit from an MBA program such as that offered by NYU. He had performed erratically at first in Vanderbilt's intensive engineering school, but eventually finished with a 3.2 GPA. Given that he had to compete against others who had maintained high averages for four years, his prospects for admission to a competitive MBA or law school, his other choice, would not have been good until he gained worthwhile work experience.

He set out do a number of things. He took a full-time job with a small telecommunications manufacturing company in Newark, New Jersey, where he had clerked during summer vacations. He was made export sales manager at first because of his familiarity with the company, and then was promoted to head purchasing agent. While working, he took courses in advanced computer programming and information technology at Rutgers University. He also made time in his busy schedule to take a course in conversational French at a language school in New York.

At the end of two years, he went to France, where he joined the sales department of a large telecommunications firm for one year. He also took a course in French civilization at the Sorbonne. The next year found him in London working for a financial organization in their telecommunications underwriting division. Robert was now convinced that he wanted to build a career in the international marketing of telecommunications equipment. This was based on the exposure he had in his three jobs to the critical role telecommunications technology played in virtually all businesses in Europe and the U.S.

In response to the question on NYU's application, Robert was now ready to conclude his personal statement:

> The knowledge acquired from the variety of activities I have described on this application has progressively helped to define my professional objectives, which, in the long term, relate to the international marketing of equipment within the telecommunications industry, an industry that relies heavily on technical and engineering knowledge. Such acquired knowledge has also made me better appreciate my short-term goal, which centers upon a structured education in management. It is this appreciation, together with the confidence with which I can state my long-term objective, that drives me at this point in time toward seeking such an education, a quality education, which I know to be fully obtainable at NYU.

Robert was accepted to NYU, where he performed with great success. And why not? He showed that he could come back from modest scholastic work, was committed to continued study in fields that absorbed his interest, could gain fluency in a foreign language, and could make marked progress as a young man in the competitive world of international business. Professors teaching management love this independent type of student, one who has had practical experience and has a defined career goal. They know that Robert will have no trouble landing a good job with an international company and will be a credit to NYU.

Other graduate schools also appreciate the value of meaningful, relevant experience. Engineers who have worked in factories, science

majors with commercial laboratory experience, sociology and psychology majors who have interned in public agencies or health clinics,
education majors who have interned in a local school or tutored children, and communications majors with journalism experience have a
strong appeal to graduate admissions committees. Why? Because
graduate school is in a sense just another part of the real world of
practical striving and working with people of many different backgrounds. Experience usually brings with it flexibility, a capacity for
rolling with the punches, and dealing with setbacks and accepting
criticism from supervisors. These character traits are helpful when
you go through rigorous graduate training.

Robert's case and all the case studies we present throughout this
book are good examples of how focused experience can determine a
career objective. Compare them to the case of a very bright Harvard
graduate with an M.A. in English, who has been teaching for years,
and now finds he wants to make more money than he will in education. "I'm thinking of getting an MBA," he said to us recently. Well,
we told him, he might get into some kind of unimpressive graduate
program that was looking for students, but he really needed some
experience in management to make professional education in a
respectable university accessible and useful to him.

"But I thought that the MBA would land me a management position," he said.

Not necessarily. Why would anyone pay him a high salary simply
because of two years of graduate school when he had absolutely no
experience, except for teaching English to high school students? The
idea that a graduate degree alone will land you a well-paying job is a
false conclusion drawn from reading the reports of starting salaries for
MBAs that appear regularly in the media and in the graduate schools'
own literature. What the statistics do not tell you is how much experience these graduates have already had, or what the quality of their
degree is.

To work first and then go to certain kinds of graduate schools is now
a more common practice than heading directly into professional training from college. It is not as vital a factor in admissions decisions for

medical, law, and Ph.D. programs in the arts and sciences as it is for business schools, where experience is particularly appreciated and taken into account by admissions committees. The maturity that comes from working, traveling, or interning will always come through on applications and in interviews. We noted earlier the advancing median age of entrants to all of the major professional schools today. Though many law schools are filled with college graduates who have not held any significant jobs other than summer employment or internships, most top law schools would like you to have some experience in the so-called real world.

Duke University's Law School Prospectus states, "Grades, quality of undergraduate institution, and LSAT scores are among the most important criteria in admissions decisions. The committee also heavily weighs demonstrated leadership, community service, graduate study in another discipline, work experience, and other information indicating academic and professional potential."

The University of Virginia's Law School makes the same point this way: "The LSAT and GPA remain the primary determinants for admission. However, the committee takes other elements into account, including the maturing effect of some years away from formal education; employment during the undergraduate years; significant personal achievement in extracurricular work at college or in a work or military situation."

Stanford's Law School states, "In evaluating individual files, the faculty considers both the record of undergraduate and graduate education and the applicant's nonacademic experience and aspirations. Recent classes included many persons who have chosen to study law in order to enhance their contribution to fields like finance, academics, computer and natural sciences, medicine, the arts, and government based on their training and experience."

To underscore the important role significant work experience can play in the admissions process, consider the statistical profiles of highly selective law schools. If you do not meet this profile, other factors will have to come into play for you to have any chance for acceptance.

Other factors being equal, the candidate with a record of meaningful experience inside and outside of college will often be chosen over

PROFILES OF SELECTIVE LAW SCHOOLS

UNIVERSITY OF VIRGINIA SCHOOL OF LAW

3,368 applicants

   975 admitted to first-year class

   353 enrolled

GPA for those between 25th and 75th % = 3.54 to 3.83

LSAT for those between 25th and 75th % = 162 to 168

15% minority

43% women

47 states represented

236 undergraduate schools represented

50% residents of Virginia

DUKE UNIVERSITY SCHOOL OF LAW

3,418 applicants

   236 enrolled in first-year class

GPA for those between 25th and 75th% = 3.33 to 3.75

LSAT for those between 25th and 75th% = 162 to 168

26% minority

46% women

46 states and 14 foreign countries represented

204 undergraduate schools represented

STANFORD UNIVERSITY LAW SCHOOL

3,824 applicants

   474 admitted first-year class

   178 enrolled first-year class

GPA for those between 25th and 75th% = 3.65 to 3.90

LSAT for those between 25th and 75th% = 165 to 170

31% minority

45% women

47 states and 8 foreign countries represented

138 undergraduate schools represented

the person who lacks exposure to situations for which professional schools prepare students. Unlike undergraduate education, training in all of the professional fields is just that, highly professional in orientation, directly related to activity outside the university, activity that is an essential part of the machinery of society.

STEFAN: *finding the specialty graduate program*

Stefan's story is similar to that of many young college graduates in search of a career that will have meaning for them. While in high school, he demonstrated a natural talent and enthusiasm for writing. The quality of his class essays and feature articles for his school paper was at a level well above that of the average school writer. Counseling with us in his senior year regarding the right college to attend led Stefan to set his sights on Vanderbilt University, a school well known for its English faculty and tradition of turning out outstanding writers.

Stefan enjoyed his four years at Vanderbilt as an English major, writing many stories and articles for campus publications and honors seminars. The issue became what to do with this passion and talent once he graduated. After several forays into the world of book publishing and fundraising for a museum proved unfulfilling, Stefan took stock of his natural assets and personality. This led him to research graduate programs that would enable him to combine his writing ability with a stimulating and challenging career that allowed for self-expression, initiative, and financial security. Based on his related work experience, he focused in on a unique program at Northwestern University, which was very interested in him as well because of his related work experience. Here is a letter Stefan sent to us as he neared the end of his two years of graduate training:

> I haven't spoken to you for some time and I wanted to give you an update on my status. I am about to graduate with my Master's degree in integrated marketing communications from the Medill School of Journalism at Northwestern. The past two years have been a long haul, and I can hardly believe this long awaited day is here. My search for the right training has come to fruition.

I definitely feel good about my decision to enroll in this special program, as the program offered me a comprehensive education in the marketing communications field through innovative strategies and perspectives on the areas of advertising, direct marketing and public relations.

I spent my summer interning at General Motors in Detroit, where I worked in executive communications. As you may remember, I hope to incorporate creative and fresh writing into my future career, so this was an ideal match. I had opportunities to develop a communications plan, generate correspondence, and edit speeches and other important materials for the chairman and vice chairman of the company.

I now face the search for a position in the field of my choosing. I want to work either in-house for a large organization in corporate communications or as an outside source in communications consulting. Thank you for helping me to sort out what I really wanted to do with my life.

The Changing Applicant Pool

Applicants with good college records are usually startled when graduate schools they believe should admit them because of their academic performance in fact reject them. Graduate applicant pools are changing in the same way the undergraduate applicant pool is changing: There are more good students competing for a relatively stable number of openings in the more prestigious and popular schools. Undergraduate colleges that once were considered "safeties" now can pick and choose their entering classes from among the upper ranks of high school students. And what is true at the college level is true at the graduate level. The "baby boom echo" is having a resounding effect on graduate enrollments as larger numbers of well-prepared college students move on from college to graduate education. This trend will become even more pronounced over the next two decades.

In these circumstances, admissions committees feel that the more mature and experienced candidate has a better understanding of his or her profession and is more aware of what he or she is committing to. Such a candidate is usually more committed (hungrier is perhaps a more apt description), is focused on realistic objectives, and has more seriousness of purpose. We should add that many college seniors we encounter are dealing with the burnout factor; they have spent sixteen years in a formal educational environment with few or no other experiences to relieve the constant demand of taking tests, writing papers, and studying.

The general axiom is that the more professionally related experience a candidate has had, the less significance will be given to his or her test scores or college academic record. We underline this factor as one of the most important changes that have occurred in graduate school admissions in the last decade. The traditional complaint of professional leaders that higher education is too theoretical, too ivory tower in attitude, has been acknowledged by a majority of professional graduate programs. Many experienced applicants are swelling graduate applicant pools, and their accomplishments are being considered as strong evidence of their capability and willingness to undertake serious graduate work. The average age of enrolled students in all of the professional schools today is well above that of graduating college seniors.

MAUREEN: *taking the right steps to law school*

Maureen majored in English at Beloit College and graduated in the upper fourth of her class. Her extracurricular activities centered largely on music—glee club and the a capella group—and she spent the summer months teaching sailing on Lake Michigan. A record of comparable academic achievement and extracurricular involvement would be sufficient for admission to a good undergraduate college, but not to a top law school. Maureen applied in her senior year with an above average LSAT score to match her grades. She was rejected by the law schools of Northwestern, Michigan, Columbia, the University of Wisconsin, the University of Minnesota, and the University of Pennsylvania.

Maureen came to see us to discuss what she had done wrong and how she could make herself a more attractive candidate for a future round of applications. We recommended that she build a stronger record of life experiences that would single her out from the majority of qualified, but not brilliant, candidates. First, she enrolled in a community college paralegal program in her hometown, which qualified her to become a paralegal in a major Milwaukee law firm. After two years, her firm offered to help pay for her legal training because of her excellent performance on the job. Her undergraduate major in English, not so incidentally, enabled her to communicate well in her position. This time Maureen had no problem getting into the law schools of the Universities of Minnesota, Wisconsin, Washington, and Southern California. Because she liked the firm for which she was working, she decided to enroll in Wisconsin's excellent law school, since this would prepare her best for law practice in that state.

The Varieties of Life Experience

What about the student who is still in college and wants to go directly to graduate school? Obviously, such a student cannot have had full-time employment unless he or she had taken time off from college. This student, short of being an academic whiz, must demonstrate accomplishments that are evidence of talent, character, leadership, self-confidence, and an ability to handle responsibility well.

The outstanding student with a 4.0 GPA and high test scores will usually be admitted to the top graduate schools on academic merit alone, with MBA programs being the possible exception. Most applicants have a GPA of 3.2 or lower. When committees look at a number of comparable applicants, each deserving admission to a graduate program with a limited number of places, they must decide whom to accept. Then they must examine closely the nonacademic record to see how the candidates have functioned in settings unrelated to the classroom. This record can be separated into campus activities, including sports, and off-campus activities pursued during vacations. To have weight with graduate admissions committees, campus activities must be significant; mere membership in an organization is relatively unimpressive, but if you have been in the glee club for several years and served in a leadership position, be it president, treasurer, or organizer of its performance schedule, you can justifiably consider this an activity you took seriously.

A long list of organizations to which you managed to belong may give an unfavorable impression that you are an indiscriminate joiner, unless, like one successful law school applicant, you can show that your widespread activities were related to your interest in law. Volunteering in the college's local community, assisting in legal aid advising, and interning in a Washington, D.C., governmental program are prime examples of what this particular candidate and others have done. In athletics, you should be a letter winner, a captain, a record holder, even; in other activities you should be a responsible office holder or top performer; common examples are star of the dramatic club, editor of the campus newspaper or yearbook, manager of a varsity team, head of a fund drive, or head of a community service program.

What you have accomplished away from college on a job or internship can help secure your admission to a well-rated graduate school if you can show how it relates to your graduate plans, or describe the skills you have attained that predict you will be a success in graduate training and in your career. Being a counselor in a summer camp may have helped you to understand the behavior of youngsters and taught you how to handle difficult communal situations. Such experiences, as in the case of one young woman we counseled, led to a decision to do graduate work in psychology.

A junior of average achievement in a state university, wanting to study law at the University of Texas, managed to secure a job as a uniformed security guard in a bank for two of his summer breaks. He was able to relate this low-paying work to his conception of the legal issues involved in the surveillance of bank customers—photographing customers at an ATM, for example, or automatically looking askance at poorly dressed people, people of color, and teenagers entering the bank. He developed a discussion of these issues on his law school application. We believe this thoughtful reflection on the place of the law in everyday situations helped in his acceptance to the university's law school.

An urban affairs major at the University of Southern California wanted to get a master's degree in television journalism. She had no journalistic experience until the summer of her junior year, when she got a position as a copy girl on a Los Angeles suburban daily. This led to the occasional assignment during her senior year to help reporters run down information for stories on community affairs. She presented her case to several graduate communications schools, arguing for acceptance on the basis of the combination of her strong academic record and her journalism experience. She was accepted by several of her top choices and chose to enroll in the University of Missouri's elite School of Journalism.

In Seattle, a senior at the University of Washington joined a group of volunteers who drive cancer patients to hospitals for therapy. In applying to a number of graduate schools of social work, he reported that this experience had convinced him of the importance of the attitudes of those with whom such patients come in daily contact. "You must always give the sick a sense of hope," he said, and went on to describe the case of a patient who had broken down after a volunteer driver had spoken condescendingly and critically to her. As a result of his experiences, he had devised a questionnaire to screen out volunteers who might not empathize sufficiently with patients. He described this experience convincingly to admissions committees, which led to his enrollment in the School of Social Work at the University of Chicago.

If, before applying for admission to a graduate program, you still have time to get some summer experience as an intern, trainee, or volunteer in a position that relates to your field of interest, by all means arrange to do so.

Another option for liberal arts students is to work with a faculty member on a project, even as an unpaid volunteer if necessary. A college senior majoring in education at the University of New Mexico joined an Earthwatch expedition to San Miguel de Allende in Mexico, working with a professor of archeology to unearth precolonial ruins. In his application to Harvard's Graduate School of Education and Columbia Teachers College, he stated that this exhilarating experience would be useful to him as a grade school teacher. In his personal statement he articulated his philosophy of teaching children by a multidisciplinary approach, and described his plan to show his classes his slides of the work done in Mexico. He would explain how evidence of the earliest civilizations is found and used to create theories about them. He added that he planned to participate in another Earthwatch archeological expedition before enrolling in graduate school. He was admitted to both of these top schools of education.

An Impressive Résumé Can Make a Difference

In Step Four we described Samuel's background, personal statement, and ultimate acceptance to Harvard Law School. Now consider the portion of his résumé that presents his many leadership positions and work experiences that reveal his talents, initiative, and readiness for the study of law in a highly intense atmosphere. You can use his list of experiences as a model against which to measure your activities and initiatives.

SAMUEL'S RÉSUMÉ: LEADERSHIP AND WORK EXPERIENCES

EMORY UNIVERSITY, B.A., Political Science/Religion, May 2000

HONORS

Phi Beta Kappa

Goodrich C. White In-house Merit Scholar

Pi Sigma Alpha Political Science Honor Society

Theta Alpha Kappa Religion Honor Society

Order of Omega Greek Honor Society

ACTIVITIES

Fraternity, Founder and President

Election Chairman of Student Government Association

New Student Orientation Leader for Classes of 2001 and 2002

Study Abroad: Emory Summer in Israel, 1999

EXPERIENCE

Freshman Advisor and Mentor, Emory University, 1997–2000

Advised students regarding course and professor selection. Helped students to acquaint themselves with the City of Atlanta by organizing social outings and community service projects.

Founding President of College Programming Board (College Council
Vice-President of Programming), Emory University, 1998
  Led a large committee and supervised planning of college-wide
  events in order to promote school spirit and unity, including tailgate
  parties and dances.
Director of Tennis Program, Camp Harmony, Warren, NJ, Summer 1998
  and 2000
  Developed and engaged in eight-week program for teaching
  basic tennis skills to groups of 12 children ranging in age from
  5 to 13.
Intern in Office of Deputy Governor, Office of New Jersey Governor,
  Trenton, NJ, Summer 1997
  Performed daily activities, including setting up for press conferences
  and coordinating meetings with state and local political officials.

Making the Most of Your Summers

Working summers is the in thing these days for college students, not so much for earning money as for getting acquainted with a field they think they might like to enter, be it business, government, research, communications, medicine, architecture, or virtually any profession you can name. Most professional enterprises offer some internship or training program to encourage talented individuals to check out their field, and, in many cases, to have a look at these earnest learners for potential hiring in the future.

Undergraduates destined for law school can help their admissions chances by interning in a law firm or in a legislative office. Premed students often become summer interns or lab assistants in hospitals. The main usefulness of interning lies in the impact it can make on career choices. Graduate schools are impressed when an applicant can state career goals based on firsthand internship and work experience. A possible additional dividend is the academic credit you may receive from your college for your summer's work.

Review the case studies we have presented throughout this book and you will note that most of these successful graduate school candidates interned in positions that matched their intended profession during the summer or the school year, or on a year's break from their schooling. We advise you to begin your search for the right internship as early in the academic year as possible. You can be certain that the good learning opportunities will be snapped up early.

Once you have identified a number of opportunities that appeal to you and meet your needs, you need to follow an action plan that will give you the best chance of landing the internship. Be sure to check the exact requirements and the deadline for applying. If a formal application needs to be filled out, do this first. Check to see if you need to send your academic transcript or letters of recommendation. Update your résumé to send with a cover letter to the appropriate office. Most organizations today are happy to receive your materials over the Internet, but again be certain this is encouraged by those you have targeted.

WHERE ARE THE INTERNSHIPS?

Where to find information on summer or interim-year internship and job opportunities? The two best sources of information for undergraduates are your college's career counseling center and your faculty. The career center should have files and directories of worthy internships that have served past students successfully. Also, there should be a list of alumni who offer to act as mentors in their field or workplace for undergraduates of their alma mater. The faculty in your academic major often can recommend internship programs or people to contact. Be certain to consult with both of these resources to discover leads on opportunities that relate to your intended graduate and career goals.

The other excellent source of information both for undergraduates and graduates is the Internet. The Internet is an efficient and easily accessible source of information today. We offer several recommendations for your search:

SERVEnet.com works for nonprofit organizations who are looking for volunteers and interns. These organizations list information and opportunities on the SERVEnet web page, which you can easily access. You can link to numerous related nonprofit organizations from their website.

Rising Star Internships (www.rsinternships.com) is a private group that lists internships by college major, region, and professional fields. It links you to thousands of openings.

Internshipsforstudents.com is the largest website listing internships located around the world. Hundreds of internships from all fields are listed. This website can be browsed by major, industry, or region.

Action Without Borders (www.idealist.org) is another excellent source for nonprofit internships.

WetFeet.com offers advice on careers and internships.

Two weeks after you have sent out your packet of information, telephone or e-mail the organizations to ask politely if you can provide further information. This also gives you another opportunity to express your strong interest in the position you have applied for. This assertive behavior never fails to impress prospective employers and supervisors. Offer to come for an interview, if this is realistic for you to do. Many colleges have dedicated funds for interns to help support their experience. If you are a scholarship student, the odds are high that you can receive some assistance for a worthy nonpaying internship.

ABOUT INTERNSHIPS AT THE CORPORATION FOR NATIONAL SERVICE

The Corporation for National Service offers the following guidelines for interested applicants:

The Corporation for National Service is a federal government corporation whose mission is to engage Americans of all

(continued)

backgrounds in service that addresses the nation's education, public safety, environmental and other human needs to achieve direct and demonstrable results and to encourage all Americans to engage in such service. In doing so, the Corporation will foster civic responsibility, strengthen the ties that bind us together as a people, and provide educational opportunity for those who make a substantial commitment to service. In partnership with state and local organizations, we administer AmeriCorps, Learn and Serve America and the National Senior Service Corps.

Our internship program is designed to give students with differing education levels and backgrounds an opportunity to complete substantive projects from a wide range of fields within a federally funded corporation. Summer interns broaden their learning experience by participating in a weekly speaker's series featuring specialists in the community service field; in addition, interns may familiarize themselves with the Corporation's initiatives by partaking in a variety of service projects. Please note that the Corporation for National Service is unable to offer stipends, relocation or housing assistance.

Departments: Throughout departments, interns are engaged in substantive research projects and/or special event coordination. Internships are available in each of the following offices:

AmeriCorps Recruitment
Chief Financial Office
Learn & Serve America
AmeriCorps*NCCC
Chief Operating Office
Planning & Program Integration
AmeriCorps*State/National
Congressional Relations
Public Affairs

AmeriCorps*VISTA
  Evaluation & Effective Practices
  Public Liaison
Chief Executive Office
  General Counsel
  Senior Corps

Majors and Areas of Study
  Students of all majors are encouraged to apply. However, specific departments may be interested in students with related majors. For example, General Counsel may seek a law student; Public Affairs may seek a Communications or related major. The following majors are typically relevant: Accounting/Communications/English/Political Science/American Studies/Computer Science/Government/Public Policy/Business/Economics/Education/Marketing/Social Work

Application Procedure
  The summer program normally runs from early June to early August; fall, winter and spring sessions are also offered. Applicants are advised to apply at least two months prior to the session in which they wish to participate. Send a cover letter and resume to the attention of the Intern Coordinator, Corporation for National Service, 1201 New York Avenue, NW, Washington, DC 20525 or fax it to 202-565-2784. The cover letter should contain the department(s) in which the applicant is interested; otherwise, a selection official will refer the applicant to those departments which most closely match his or her skills, interests, and experience.
  Please send questions or comments to: internships@cns.gov.

CONSIDERING A BREAK BETWEEN
COLLEGE AND GRADUATE SCHOOL?

The Corporation for National Service oversees AmeriCorps, which is our country's domestic Peace Corps. At any time, there are 40,000 volunteers and interns working in specific projects to help individuals and communities in need of assistance. The Corporation for National Service describes the advantages of the program as follows:

As an AmeriCorps member, you'll receive a wealth of benefits, starting with the satisfaction of getting things done for and with people who need your help. Whether you're tutoring kids, building homes, clearing trails and streams, mobilizing resources to create a local health clinic, or doing any of the hundreds of other goal-oriented AmeriCorps projects, you'll be able to really see the results of your work—and the smiles on the faces of the people you work with.

But there's more. As an AmeriCorps member, you'll be eligible for a variety of benefits that make the dedication of a year of your life worthwhile:

Money for college—*After you successfully complete a year of AmeriCorps service, you will be eligible for an education award of $4,725. (If you serve part-time, you'll be eligible for a portion of that amount.)*

Living allowance—*If you serve full-time, you'll receive a modest living allowance. You won't get rich from it, but other AmeriCorps members have found that it covers their basic expenses.*

Help with student loans—*If you already have student loans, you can use your education award to help pay them off. And while you're an AmeriCorps member, you may be eligible for deferment and forbearance on your student loans. Your lender can tell you for sure. If you're eligible, AmeriCorps will pay for the interest that is accrued on student loans for members who complete their service.*

You'll also receive health insurance, may qualify for childcare assistance, and may get your relocation expenses covered (depending on your specific program).

In addition, you'll get a super career experience and job satisfaction. AmeriCorps members frequently talk about the difference the experience has made in their careers—from technical job skills to experience as a manager, team member, coordinator, facilitator, and developer. AmeriCorps members get things done, and that kind of results-oriented experience pays off when you're finished with your service and considering your next steps, whether in education or employment.

Here is a sampling of opportunities within the field of education to demonstrate the range of learning experiences available to volunteers:

AmeriCorps*NCCC teams tutored and/or mentored more than 7,500 children between kindergarten and high school in subjects ranging from reading, writing, arithmetic, and social studies to environmental studies and American Sign Language.

In Maryland, members worked within seven Harford County Public Schools to create a mentoring program and crisis prevention center. They assisted students, including at-risk and special needs students, with their social and academic development and tutored students to help increase their high school state proficiency test scores.

Applications for internships are accepted throughout the year. All internships at the Corporation for National Service are unpaid. To apply for an internship, send a detailed cover letter and resume to:

Corporation for National Service
Internship Coordinator
1201 New York, Ave., NW
Washington, DC 20525

Further Examples of Useful Experience

If you are wondering what constitutes good practical experience that confirms your career interest and enhances your candidacy, here are some recent examples from our files:

Stacey, from New York City: In two separate terms as an undergraduate at Dartmouth, Stacey participated in an alumni-sponsored program at A Better Chance (ABC), a national program that identifies and counsels outstanding students of disadvantaged backgrounds. Upon graduation, she was hired as a full-time employee by ABC in its national office. Used her computer and organizational skills to set up more efficient records and communication with the schools that admit ABC students. Career objective is to teach in an inner-city school first, and then become an administrator and education policy maker. Accepted into the master's program at Harvard's Graduate School of Education.

Eleanor, from Pennsylvania: Eleanor worked as a pie maker in a small-town bakery, an au pair in France, a clerk in a New York law firm reviewing hiring procedures for a corporation that had been charged with unfairness toward minorities and women, an interviewer of clients in a public interest law firm, and a teacher of dance/theater in a ghetto school in Cambridge. Her career objective was to become a partner in a small urban law firm. Placed on a waiting list by Harvard, she chose to enroll in Columbia's law school.

James, from suburban New York: He interned for his congressman, who wrote this recommendation when James applied to law schools: "a valuable and capable asset to my office. I recommend him highly for any professional or academic endeavor whatsoever." His career objective was to work for Assyrian independence (his family fled Iran after the revolution there). James was admitted to Columbia, Cornell, Chicago, and Georgetown law schools.

Olympia, from Athens, Greece: Olympia was a shareholder in the family shipping business, in which she had participated actively since she was in high school. She was also a summer trainee at E. F. Hutton's London office. Career objective is someday to manage family shipping business. Admitted to MBA programs of Vanderbilt, Georgetown, University of Michigan, and the University of Southern California, where she enrolled.

Writing Up Your Experience Persuasively

You might think that experience speaks for itself, but admissions committees have no time to spend inferring the worth of what you have done. They must be told in convincing statements what your experience has been, what you have made of it, and how it will relate to your graduate work and to your career.

We present another case study for you to reflect on. Compare the sketchy and not very readable preliminary profile of Frank, candidate for a graduate degree in industrial psychology, with what he wrote about himself on his applications. Frank turned the facts of his experience into a moving and convincing personal statement on his graduate applications.

PRELIMINARY PROFILE OF FRANK SMITH

University of North Carolina, B.S., Class of 1995.

Majored in psychology. Weak marks in math and science.

GRE verbal 480, quantitative 610, analytical 86 percent.

Research experience:

"Chronic Amphetamine Treatment: Effect on Behavior and Local Cerebral Glucose Utilization," a paper written with faculty under grant from a pharmaceutical company, later published in *Neuroscience Abstracts*. We conducted experiments to replicate an earlier study on the exhibition of paranoid schizophrenic behavior by rats. Significant results were found in activity and local cerebral glucose utilization. Also wrote a study of burnout in pre-hospital emergency medical care as it affects the volunteer EMT. Two burnout inventories were administered and correlated with the MMPID. Results to be submitted for publication.

(continued)

Experience:

Mt. Auburn Hospital, Cambridge, Mass., June 1996–September 1997
Medical Communicator. Relayed complicated medical instructions verbatim. Maintained radio and telephone contact with police and first aid. Served at central communication facility for part of city during disasters.
Local Chapel Hill Volunteer Ambulance, 1993–1996
Emergency Medical Technician.
JFK Medical Center, Edison, N.J., 1989–1993
Junior Volunteer Day Chairman. Won competition to supervise and schedule junior volunteers throughout the various departments of the hospital.

FRANK'S PERSONAL STATEMENT

Since the age of twelve I have been very interested in the field of medicine. During my high school years, I put in well over 1,500 hours volunteering at my local hospital. When I arrived at college, I simply maintained my high level of extracurricular involvement, volunteering for various ambulance services and different student government organizations.

My long hospital-based career enabled me to interact and communicate with many different people under many different conditions. The human mind began to fascinate me to such an extent that, although I was a premed student, I had no doubt that I would major in psychology. Throughout my first two years, although doing well in my psychology courses, I struggled with my premed sciences. Physiology was one of the few science courses in which I excelled. This was due to the knowledge I had gained from working in various departments of the hospital. I someday hoped to combine my two interests in psychology and medicine by working in such fields as psychotherapy and drug treatment of mental problems.

At the end of my sophomore year, I realized that I was having academic problems and that they could not continue if I planned to reach my professional goals. Over that summer, although I completed my last premed requirement of physics, I decided that medical school was not where I really wanted to be. Throughout my ongoing hospital work I had always been interested and involved in the management of the hospital and was able to experience first-hand many different kinds of management styles and techniques. I saw how stress and poor management can create poor morale and a work environment that is not conducive to productivity.

I began to realize that I could combine my interest and ability in psychology with my interest and broad experience in the health-care delivery system. This realization soon turned into a passion and my grades dramatically jumped to a 3.3 and climbed higher to a 3.7 at the end of my junior year.

Throughout the last semester of my junior year, and continuing into my senior year, I have been involved in research. During my physiological psychology course I was a researcher in a study that was published in *Neuroscience Abstracts*. I have been able to integrate my ambulance involvement into my research. A lot of research has been generated recently regarding burnout in the health-care professions. However, research subjects almost always have been nurses. The pre-hospital health-care system can be just as, if not more, stressful than in-hospital care. I decided to study burnout in one of the largest work forces in pre-hospital emergency care, that of the volunteer emergency medical technician, a group to which I have long belonged. This study gave me great experience and a point to expand upon in future studies. I plan to continue my research in my last semester as well as throughout my graduate education.

I feel that this experience will enable me to expand my knowledge in this area, as well as enable me to continue to enjoy the methodological aspects of the experimental method in psychology. Once I attain my ultimate goal of a Ph.D. in industrial/organizational psychology, I hope to continue my research while being a consultant, specializing in the area of health-care administration.

Frank was admitted to graduate programs in industrial and managerial psychology at Columbia, Rensselaer Polytechnic Institute, NYU, and the Stevens Institute of Technology.

Frank's statement does several things for an admissions committee: It tells them that his passion for helping people is undiminished by his failures in critical premed subjects, emphasizes that his study of burnout among volunteer emergency workers is original, and shows evidence of his ability to put to theoretical and abstract use things he does know well. It also shows commitment and a sense of direction derived from concrete practical experience.

Frank is an object lesson to anyone who despairs of achieving his or her graduate school goals. Learn from failure and from experience where your future lies. Don't fight city hall, as we have cautioned already. If you are not a science or math whiz, find out what you are good at. Be flexible; it is a sign of maturity. Stubbornly pursuing a direction in which you consistently stumble is a sign not of persistence but of unwillingness to stand back and admit that you have chosen the wrong path.

Summing Up the Experience Step

Nonacademic experience has become an increasingly important criterion in graduate schools' admissions decisions. Since your objective is not to be admitted to just any graduate school, but to aim for acceptance to the best possible program for your level of performance, you should do two things:

- During and after college, engage in nonacademic activities, whether jobs, trainee positions, internships, pro bono volunteer work, or extracurricular activities and athletics, that can directly or indirectly relate to your career objectives.
- Write about your experience in such a way as to convince a committee looking at your record that you are mature and focused in your career goals.

A dramatic indicator that experience means a good deal to admissions committees is their interest in admitting older applicants who may have slightly to very rusty academic skills. "We know they must struggle with the books at the beginning," one graduate dean said to us, "but their long habits of problem solving, meeting deadlines, and responsible decision making allow them to respond more quickly and surely than their more academically acclimated younger peers." Many young college graduates have exclaimed, "If I had worked as hard while in college as I am in my job, I would have been a Phi Bete!"

We close this step with an excerpt from the advice we presented in Step Three by Robert Swieringa, the dean of the Johnson School of Business at Cornell to reinforce the important factors necessary for success in any profession. Development of the characteristics articulated so well in this statement has to begin before entering any professional graduate school. These factors are learned and developed through all of the work, internship, volunteer, and leadership experiences we have described.

> The business world is looking for leaders. I believe that the most successful MBAs not only master the analytical foundations in key areas, they also are highly effective in working with and leading others. They exhibit a consistent pattern of taking initiative and engendering change—they size up situations to see how to make them better, wherever they are. They balance academic and professional achievements with activities outside of school or work. They are comfortable taking calculated risks. They have a genuine desire to leave a legacy that lasts beyond their involvement in an organization, often by actively engaging others. MBAs need to have it all—technical competence, interpersonal effectiveness, and long-term vision.

Step Seven Checklist

- Relate your work experience to your graduate aims. An admissions committee must perceive your jobs as fostering meaningful personal development.

- If you lack work experience, spend one or more years getting it. Develop an extracurricular record late in college if necessary.

- Your work experience can compensate for lackluster grades and test scores to a certain extent, so make your achievements on the job or as an intern clear to admissions committees.

- While in college, make the most of summer vacations with jobs or internships or volunteer projects. Even if you are not certain of your future direction, use the summer to test the waters in at least one of the major fields you are considering.

- In your application to a graduate school, write about your relevant experiences with enthusiasm; show how important they have been to you in setting career goals.

STEP EIGHT

Market Your Strengths

The Self-Marketing Concept in Admissions

In *Making It into a Top College* we wrote that self-marketing is the great neglected step in the college admissions process. We cannot emphasize this enough about applications to graduate school. Marketing brings together seller and buyer—applicant and graduate school. We use these commercial terms to underscore the fact that you need to sell yourself to the right graduate program, making the committee want you to enroll. This does not mean exaggerating or misrepresenting yourself in any way. It does mean putting your best foot forward and highlighting your strengths.

A fine example of self-marketing came to our attention recently. Linda persuaded Boston University Medical School to allow her to study for her degree part-time. Her winning argument was that she was engaged in vital work at a medical research center, and the study on cancer would not be completed for some time. She completed her studies in seven years, instead of the usual four, but she did graduate with excellent grades and was offered a good internship from a Boston-area hospital.

Linda talked directly to the university's administration about its policy of allowing special students to pursue "alternative pathways" to a medical degree. Her argument was persuasive, although she was strongly advised to take review courses in biology and chemistry since she had been out of college for 10 years.

"I found the BU Medical School faculty to be very sensitive to my personal requirements," she says. "I think what I have done creates something of a model for more women to manage medical careers on their own terms. I never felt that I was waiting to start my life. I lived my life fully as a medical student." While interning on a part-time basis, she has applied to another hospital for admission into a program in psychiatry.

Most medical schools only rarely accept part-time medical students, and some never do. Linda found the program that might admit her and convinced the admissions committee of her ability to complete the work.

You cannot accomplish what this ambitious woman has done without impressing the administration with your determination and capabilities. Yet there are hundreds and even thousands of openings in graduate programs for the right people. If you believe you are the right student for a particular program, let the administration know this; make them feel your enthusiasm and hunger for what it has to offer you.

Medical school deans will tell you that you must be a full-time resident to study at their medical schools, but a person who has strengths that appeal to a school can cause rules to be bent. Linda's is an exceptional case, to be sure, but we cite it to persuade you to set aside all preconceptions when it comes time to make your case as an applicant.

Don't Be Overly Modest

Market your strengths! In applying to graduate school, neither reticence nor unassuming modesty is appropriate. Soon after learning that Columbia University had started a master's program in real estate finance and development, Richard came to us for advice in getting accepted into this program. His academic record at the State University of New York was not exceptional and neither were his GMAT scores, but he was an outstanding student leader—president of his class, of the student council, and of his fraternity. He also demonstrated entrepreneurial talent by starting a laundry service that netted enough money to allow him to invest in local real estate opportunities. By graduation, this enterprising young man owned outright $500,000 worth of commercial buildings.

At the age of 28, Richard was now a successful salesman of commercial properties for a large Albany realty company. He also carried on civic activities in Junior Achievement, introducing high school students to business concepts and the principles of free enterprise, which are the two guiding goals of this national program. He viewed master's training as essential to his long-term goal of securing his own commercial real estate group.

In helping assess his strengths, we urged him to write about his sensitivity to the needs of local communities and their fear of the negative impact commercial real estate development can have on their neighborhoods. He could cite examples of provisions for playgrounds and affordable housing that had helped win approval of his projects. Richard was also able to document the number of new jobs that development projects had created in the community.

"You will be competing with a lot of New York City hotshots," he was told, "but Columbia does not want a monolithic group of students, all with the same background or work experience. What you lack in exceptional academic allure, you make up for in specialized knowledge few other candidates will probably have."

To make the point that Richard could add to Columbia's program by bringing to the classroom his experience in dealing with the boards of small communities, we suggested that he recapitulate his experience in six one-page summaries of real estate deals he had arranged, each requiring the solution of some special local problem. These summaries had the merits of brevity and readability. Furthermore, they are full of human interest and displayed Richard's concern for his community and its citizens.

Richard also requested an interview, saying he wished to find out whether he would make a suitable candidate for Columbia's program. During the interview, he probed assertively, without being aggressive. At the conclusion of the interview, he announced that he now knew that this special degree program could do remarkable things for his career and that he would send in his application immediately. He told the admissions interviewer that he also planned to apply for admission to real estate programs offered by MIT and the Wharton School to keep other opportunities open. In due course he was one of only 40 students admitted to the first-year class in Columbia's outstanding real estate management program.

Making a Class Pie Chart

What Richard did, in part, was to make use of the class pie chart concept, a model for looking at graduate schools and planning one's strategy that we introduced years ago in our counseling and continue to find highly successful. Put simply, every class in every graduate school is made up of a diverse student body. The better schools are national in character and wish their enrollments to reflect the nation's diversity. This means they seek as large a percentage as possible of women and minorities, some international students, a representation of diverse undergraduate institutions, good geographical distribution, and students with something special to offer.

Richard's strength was his experience in selling commercial real estate in a regional market. In this respect he faced little competition. As close as Albany is to New York City, there were no other candidates for this special program. Richard had the field all to himself. Also, his application and interview helped to make the case that his work experience was all in a regional real estate market, which meant he had unique opportunities and challenges unlike those of those who were in urban real estate markets. A pie chart of his chances would look like the following graphic.

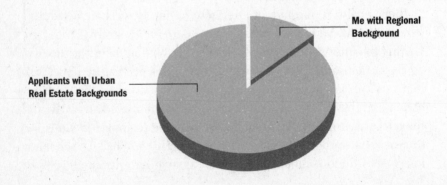

Finding Your Own Special Slice of the Pie

In slicing up a class pie, you may find a small specialty slice into which you can fit. For example, business schools are under pressure to admit more applicants who will go into manufacturing or nonprofit work rather than into general management or investment banking. By making your intention known about such careers, you may add to your chances of acceptance. Review the profiles of Matthew and Sven presented earlier to see how each fits one of these niches.

Applicants to medical school who express a keen desire to work in rural or blighted areas are often more attractive to admissions committees than others with similar qualifications who intend to stay in big cities or affluent suburbs. Remember how this sincere approach helped Doug get admitted to several top medical schools after he had worked in Spanish Harlem as a teacher for two years.

Candidates with foreign language fluency or an international background should conceive of this as a possible pie slice. This is especially true for business and law school applicants, but it also holds for those who want to do graduate studies in government, law, medicine, public policy, teaching, and other major disciplines. Recall that Carl's knowledge of French helped him gain work in international marketing; Doug's Spanish fluency was a boon to his future medical work with inner-city families; and Karen's language and international work experiences helped her get into an international law program. The multinational corporation is now so common that one large executive firm says that 40 percent of the requests it receives are for high-level executives who have lived and worked abroad at some point in their career. Business schools know to take this factor into account in reviewing candidates for their programs.

As you examine a graduate program, look for the specialties within it and evaluate them as possible niches for you—specialties like Berkeley's master's and doctoral programs in human ecology and environmental studies, appropriate for candidates concerned about urban planning and the issues of social impact due to development; Yale School of Management for those interested in nonprofit management of schools, foundations, and cultural institutions; Boston University's master's in arts management, which seeks candidates who will be managing every conceivable kind of entertainment enterprise. In today's complex society, the lines of demarcation between the various professions are blurred, and thus a majority of highly trained professionals will find themselves in need of more in-depth skills and knowledge across several specialties. This has resulted in the development of dual-degree programs in all of the major professional graduate schools and even in the academic degree programs. Consider whether any combination of disciplines appeals to you and for which you would legitimately qualify. Duke University's law school, for example, offers a combined program that leads to the traditional J.D. degree with an LL.M. (master of law) in comparative and international legal studies for those talented students who want to prepare for a career in international law. Students are required to study for one summer at one of Duke's Institutes of Transnational Law, in either Hong Kong or Geneva.

Note in your application if a specialty appeals to you; the fewer people in that specialty, the better your chances for acceptance in many cases. Be sure your academic and employment background is appropriate to this special area of the curriculum. Aiming for that special niche in which the competition is less intense is a sound strategy for many candidates, who recognize that their credentials otherwise make them look-alikes with all the other applicants.

You may learn of a specialty by talking to faculty at your college or at the graduate school. A professor may say to a prospective candidate for a master's in English literature, "Not much has been done here on Swift's poetry. Would you be interested in doing a thesis on it?" Of course this might not interest you, but your abiding interest in the translation of Camus's novels might be similarly attractive to a different graduate school.

When you have discovered one or more specialty slices in each of the programs to which you intend to apply, you can gather what your admissions prospects are. And this is where self-marketing comes in: When you deal with each admissions committee, enlarge on your own particular interest and competence in these specialties. You first find, by means of the pie charts, those graduate programs that might have room for such a specialist, and then you market yourself as someone who will bring a special concern and point of view to a graduate program. Let's say that your abiding interest is in returning to your native country in Southeast Asia after you attend graduate school to build a model elementary school based on the best practices in the United States and England. Your search reveals that Stanford's and Harvard's schools of education offer doctoral degrees in planning and curriculum that will give you the training you will need to achieve your goal. Your next step is to communicate with both of these outstanding schools regarding your special field of interest and your particular purpose in wanting to attain an advanced degree. This is exactly what a young woman from Thailand did during her senior year at Yale. She was admitted to both schools, thanks in part to the way she had delineated her unique interests and professional future.

Making pie charts for several graduate schools will help you see just where your chances of admission appear to be best. In Richard's case, his chances at Columbia were improved by the nature of his employment. What was true at Columbia did not appear to be so for MIT, because the average competing applicant there was so much stronger academically than Richard, and with more technical and engineering training, something he had not studied at all in college. He knew that his chances at MIT were marginal, and he was turned down by their admissions committee.

Sven had considered many of the top business schools in the country prior to meeting with us. Since his undergraduate major and work experience were not as strong for the pursuit of an MBA as the majority of his potential competitors, we suggested he concentrate on the Yale School of Management because of its emphasis on the nonprofit sector. He was accepted early in the admissions cycle by Yale but was turned down at the three other more traditional MBA programs where his profile did not match as well.

If you are a woman, a member of a minority group, or an international applicant, your chances for admission may be better than those of other candidates to the same school, but you must be sensible about where you apply. It is not advisable to apply to a program for which you are clearly not qualified. Being a female from Alaska may give you an edge at eastern universities where the stiffest competition is among eastern candidates, but you must be capable of meeting the particular academic standards of the institution. As noted before, there are no free passes handed out to women, minorities, and internationals applying to the highly selective graduate schools. They must meet all of the standard requirements at the upper end of the applicant pool. Then their special status may weigh in their favor.

What about reverse discrimination, favoring historically disadvantaged minorities at the expense of more qualified nonminority applicants? In the famous Bakke case in the 1970s, the University of California's rejection of a white medical school applicant, Alan Bakke, was challenged on the grounds that his qualifications exceeded those of black applicants who were admitted. The U.S. Supreme Court ruled in 1978 that Bakke must be admitted and that no quotas could be established to ensure a specific number of minority students in each class.

At the same time, the Supreme Court affirmed the institution's right to consider race, religion, ethnicity, gender, and a history of lack of opportunity as factors in admitting applicants. The result has been that some graduate programs pursue minority enrollment goals more vigorously than others do. Minority applicants should acquaint themselves with each program's records and admissions statement on this subject. Some will obviously be more encouraging than others will, but we can assure you that every nationally prominent graduate school strongly encourages qualified minority and female candidates to apply to its institution.

Stanford's law school makes it clear how it feels about diverse representation in its selective law school: "Because of its strong belief in the value of diversity, the school especially encourages applications from African Americans, Mexican Americans, American Indians, and Puerto Ricans, as well as others whose ethnic and social background provide additional dimensions that will enhance the school's program." Note the declaration of interest in individuals from a wide range of backgrounds. You will find that Stanford's peer institutions share the quest for a population that represents the nation as a whole.

Finding Your Combination of Slices

The more slices of a pie chart that you can find yourself in, the better your chance of admission to that particular graduate school. Take the following two charts as examples. You can develop your own chart for any kind of graduate program once you have an accurate picture of its admitted class and all the academic programs it offers.

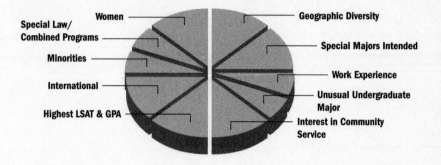

The University of Chicago Law School entering class, 2000:
Total enrollment: 183 (out of 2,972 applicants)

Male: 59%	Average GPA: 3.45 to 3.81 (25th to 75th %)
Female: 41%	Average LSAT: 165 to 171 (25th to 75th %)
Minorities: 18%	Undergraduate colleges: 180

Geography: 47 states and 24 foreign countries

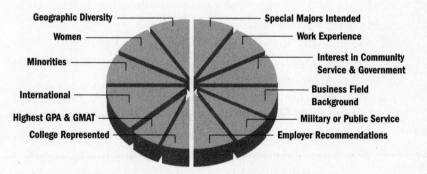

University of Pennsylvania, The Wharton School of Business
entering class, 2000:
Total enrollment: 784 (out of 7,358 applicants)

Male: 72%	Average GPA: 3.5
Female: 28%	Average GMAT: 700
Minorities: 15%	GMAT Range: 640 to 750 (mid 80%)
International: 39%	Average age: 28.6

Intended major:
  Finance 30%
  Entrepreneurship 20%
  Strategic management 13%
  Multinational management 8%
  Health care 6%
  Marketing 4%
  Real estate 3%
  Public policy 3%
  Operations 2%
  Other/undecided 11%

Here's what the statistics included in the full profile of the Wharton School indicate:

1. Northeastern candidates, especially those from the most competitive colleges, will have the most difficulty getting admitted. GPA, GMAT, and general application quality must be at the top end of Wharton's profile.
2. Racial minority candidates from any section of the United States have an excellent chance of admission if their GPA, GMAT, and course background are solid.
3. Women with strong credentials have a good chance of admission, because the school's goal is to increase their representation well beyond the present 28 percent.
4. Applicants from the South and Midwest are in the smallest geographic pool and thus stand a good chance of admission if their GPA and GMATs are strong.
5. The top-of-the-class student from a good but less renowned college or state university may offer special appeal.
6. A senior in college has virtually no chance of admission. Three to four years of work experience is a must.
7. Students interested in special programs may stand out. Examples: the Lauder Institute for International Studies and Management; the combined master's and MBA program offered in conjunction with the Johns Hopkins School for

Advanced International Studies; and less popular majors, such as health care, marketing, and operations.

8. Well-qualified international students are encouraged to apply and are accepted in good numbers.

9. Work experience at a highly advanced or responsible level will help greatly.

10. Unusual work experience of an entrepreneurial, social service, or governmental nature will be attractive.

As you complete your pie charts, bear in mind that they are not just pointing you in the direction of graduate programs that will most likely admit you; they provide you with a very sharp tool for marketing yourself. One student we counseled remarked that her pie chart revealed that she probably was the only applicant to several graduate schools who had traveled with Turkish relatives buying vegetable-dyed rugs from Anatolian peasants for resale in New York. In a personal statement on each application, she told how her observation of the rug-making process helped her as an apprentice saleswoman sell these products. She also wrote eloquently of the beauty of a traditional art form and her appreciation for the skills of the local villagers she had watched producing the rugs.

What Makes You Different?

In marketing yourself to any graduate program, it is also important to focus on one or two of your leading achievements or characteristics. Given the limited amount of time any committee member will be able to devote to a consideration of your application, you are doing him or her a service when you force attention only to one or two factors that make you different—say, competence in a foreign language plus experience abroad in museum work if you are applying for admission to a graduate program in art history, or advanced capability in computer programming if you are applying to a master's program in information technology.

You target these valuable qualities in your essay and in your interview. You ask those who are recommending you to stress these same qualities in their remarks. One young woman we counseled wrote all of her correspondence with graduate anthropology programs on the stationery of a Mexican farm cooperative where she was working as a volunteer. She wanted to make committees particularly aware of her qualifications to do field work under harsh conditions.

We directed Rita toward Union College when she was in search of a small undergraduate college that combined liberal arts with engineering. Her career plan was to practice engineering in the field for several years and then return to graduate school for business management training. Following graduation from Union with a major in civil engineering, Rita worked for one of the largest construction companies in the Northeast. She helped in the planning of a major project in upstate New York to rebuild a highway and bridge system. As she described her working environment to us when she began her search for the right MBA program, we imagined Rita with her hard hat on, supervising a crew of surveyors and work bosses. She described the challenges she faced daily in asserting herself in the face of the male chauvinism of the construction supervisors and crews. In addition to encouraging her to describe these circumstances on her applications to business schools, we suggested she submit a series of pictures of herself on the job. The vision of petite Rita in her hard hat on top of a massive earth mover with blueprints in her hands made a positive impression on the admissions committees of five of the top business schools to which she applied. Any young woman with the determination to cope in this environment was a sure bet to succeed in an intensive graduate school world. Determination was the particular strength that she articulated in her personal statement and in her interviews. Rita is now a student at Columbia Business School.

Here are some examples of how you can identify your strengths and target them for admissions committees:

- A champion tennis player applying to medical schools constantly played up his athletic ability in order to demonstrate his manual skill, his stamina, and his competitiveness. He even mentioned turning down an opportunity to go on the pro circuit because of his determination to enroll in medical school.
- A southerner with a modest academic record and LSAT scores made a big point of his lineage in applying to several prestigious

northern law schools. This included a U.S. senator, two governors, and a state supreme court justice, as well as some minor government officials and a law professor at the state university. His argument was that he was determined to make a name for himself and continue the family tradition of service to its state and nation. He was not saying that he could inherit success, but simply that a tradition of public leadership gave him reason to work hard. Consequently, he was admitted to several top law schools.

- A woman who had been a national squash champion in college fixed admissions committees' attention on her social experience as an athlete, which she expected to turn into an asset as a businesswoman. She was accepted into the Wharton School and, after several years in marketing and public relations for a professional baseball team, established her own sports agency for women athletes.

- A middle-aged journalist who had squeaked through college was admitted to a master's program in history at Columbia on the basis of a series of articles he had written on the history of his New England hometown. He took the trouble to photocopy and package the articles in loose-leaf binders for easy reading and submitted them to four graduate schools, all of which accepted him. His writing displayed the sharp eye for small but telling details that makes for a good historian.

In each of these cases, the applicant marketed a strength in such a way that he or she stood out sufficiently to warrant admission. They triumphed over other students who were just as smart, or smarter, and just as accomplished, but less appealing, because they were less imaginative in presenting their strengths.

Identifying Your Particular Strengths

There are many strengths you may be proud of that admissions committees take for granted in all candidates—your energy, your honesty, your forthrightness, sense of justice, mental stability, good health, and so on. Their assumption is that a college graduate who has demonstrated social and academic success, or someone who has held one or more responsible jobs, possesses these traits. You must always keep in mind that there are many, many applicants with such qualities. In regard to most of the qualities mentioned above, no graduate school would want anyone without them. What educators are looking for is evidence of the capacity for carrying out excellent graduate work in a demanding environment and the ability to relate well to their faculty and fellow students. Experience shows that a person who has been capable of performing well at something honorable and constructive is likely to do well in a graduate program, providing he or she has the necessary academic qualifications.

Admission choices at the top and bottom of an applicant pool are simple: The obviously brilliant are admitted, and the obviously unqualified are rejected outright. You should understand that top academic candidates for the very top graduate programs compete against one another for a limited number of places in the entering class. These star students must also be sure to present themselves well, and separate themselves from the pack by articulating their special skills and talents. They should not take it for granted that top grades and test scores will automatically result in acceptance to the most selective schools.

The applicants in the middle always concern the members of the admissions committees. This usually is the largest number of applicants, and making distinctions among them is not easy.

One faculty committee member at a top medical school concedes, "I hate to say it, but many of our decisions are purely arbitrary. We can take only so many candidates. Here is a group that by objective standards could be admitted and would complete the program satisfactorily. It then becomes a lottery as to who among these equals will be offered a place." Candidates who fall into this middle group but have a specialty that is relevant to the professional field may be the candidates who are admitted. This happens when they have managed to present something in their record that jumps off the page.

How do you, if you are not an A student with high test scores, identify other strengths that will impress a graduate admissions committee? Let's go through the possibilities, including some already mentioned in previous chapters:

Extracurricular accomplishments: As extracurricular activities, in college or thereafter, you might highlight athletic achievement; campus awards and nonscholastic honors; competitive achievement in such things as bridge, chess, debate, and public speaking; theater; writing for publications; managing athletic teams; and working as a research assistant or teacher.

Work experience: Make your work experience meaningful by describing what you have learned on the job, even though the job may not have been part of a training program or an internship for the field in which you wish to study. You must see your work as something unique to you, even when it may appear routine. What you did to earn money for college may reveal a special talent, and certainly a determination and independence.

Volunteer work and community activism: This can reveal talents for organization, getting along with people, and leadership. One woman played up a single episode of social work. This was a day when she helped handicapped skiers in a race in the White Mountains and found that her life's calling was to help others. She applied to and was accepted at several graduate schools of social work, after committing all her free time in her senior year to the Special Olympics.

Travel: In itself travel is not a rarity and will not make you stand out. But if you have traveled to some unusual place like a small village in India, this is out of the ordinary. If you can make something of that experience other than a mere travelogue, if it has changed you in some significant way that bears on your desire for further education, a committee may take a closer look at your application. This is the objective of the exercise we call marketing your strengths. Recall Amanda's story, presented earlier, and her description in her application of her experiences in a rural Indian village and its influence on her decision to apply to graduate school at the University of Chicago in anthropology.

Marriage and childraising: Like travel, such an experience usually signifies nothing very startling. In fact, committees may wonder if you can handle graduate studies and caring for a family at the same time. What you have learned from marriage and childcare may be unusual enough to point out. A woman in her late thirties, who studied medicine at Harvard, said that she thinks she was accepted because she told the committee that her experience with her own children and running a toddler's program in her house made her realize she would make an excellent pediatrician.

A COLLEGE GRADUATE BUILDS HER DREAM JOB

The Career and Counseling Services at Dartmouth College published Beth's story on its website. Note that her particular strength in art and design helped her to market herself at each stage of her journey from college to job to graduate school and career:

> Do you have a love of architecture and design? Are you curious about what steps to take while here at Dartmouth that could put you on the path to becoming an architect? Beth is one alumna who has pursued a career in architecture; she currently runs her own architecture business on Martha's Vineyard, though she has had a variety of experiences leading up to her present position.
>
> An art history major while here, Beth always harbored a desire to become an architect, but she did not enter the field until several years after graduating from Dartmouth. Initially, Beth worked in account management with an advertising firm in New York City. She remained in advertising for two years before returning to graduate school at Syracuse University to pursue a master's degree in architecture. Beth had taken the advertising position because she had been nervous about entering graduate school directly out of college; eventually, however, she decided that she would prefer a career in architecture.
>
> Beth enrolled in a summer architecture program at Columbia while still working in advertising in order to gain insight into the

field. Since Dartmouth does not offer a degree in architecture, Beth undertook three years of graduate school, followed by three years of work experience, before sitting for the certification exam. Beth strongly recommends a liberal arts background for aspiring architects, for it prepares students for the variety of responsibilities they will be faced with on the job. She emphasizes that students of virtually any major can go on to practice architecture.

Throughout her career Beth has worked in architecture offices of various sizes and in various locations, including Colorado and Florence. She worked for three years with a large firm based in Manhattan, focusing on retail projects. Since they were in New York City, most of the work centered around renovating interior spaces rather than altering the existing exterior structures. Beth was frustrated in a large firm because she sought more direct responsibility than they provided. For those looking for internships, however, she explains that larger firms tend to offer more opportunities to undergraduates. After her stint in New York, Beth took an opportunity to work with a small firm on Martha's Vineyard. Here her responsibilities were more varied and she had greater input into the process. From this experience, Beth went on to form her own business.

Beth is self-employed and works in the resort community of Martha's Vineyard. Her business focuses on residential architecture, which combines both practical and creative processes. Some clients choose to stick to more functional designs, such as renovating a kitchen, while others are more adventurous, tearing down existing houses to create their own unique homes. Beth finds trying new things to be the challenge of residential architecture—combining a cozy New England feel with new spaces and ideas. Dartmouth's liberal arts education has proven to be valuable in Beth's practice as she constantly juggles marketing her business, generating new sales, meeting with clients, writing proposals, designing homes, and monitoring construction. As in

(continued)

> *any small architecture firm, marketing and interpersonal skills*
> *are as essential as sculpting and designing abilities.*
>
> To those considering a career in architecture, Beth under-
> scores the need to attend graduate school, and she encourages
> work in an architecture office during a leave term to gain a bet-
> ter understanding of the field.

How to Market Your Strengths

Once you have identified the graduate programs for which you think
you are qualified, and the strengths to which you would like to call
attention, you have the following opportunities to market yourself:

- Your application as a whole
- Personal statements in particular
- Interviews
- Recommendations
- Meetings with faculty

RICHARD: *marketing his real estate and development experience*

Let's return to Richard and follow his steps as a candidate. There
are several key self-marketing aspects of his application, which he
brought out in his personal statement:

> I believe my average academic performance in college was due to
> a lack of motivation. I was already making money in real estate
> and could not relate my coursework to business. Then, as my
> experience in selling commercial property broadened, I found
> myself doing business with men and women who frequently chal-
> lenged my assertions. After a few deals fell through, I learned
> from a competitor that I was considered too cocky and not believ-
> able in the local real estate community. I was getting by in many
> cases on fast talk.

That is when I began reading something more than trade magazines. Because I was continually contacting various municipal
boards about variances, land use, and such things, I signed up for
a night course in municipal government at SUNY Albany and
achieved an A grade. I know that I would have no trouble in doing
MBA level work.

I truly believe that my experience in a mid-size real estate market is unusual for someone my age. I consider myself a professional now, but a professional limited to a niche that offers only so
many opportunities. The course content of Columbia's MBA program in real estate is a pathway to major real estate dealings. I
want the chance to move into an urban realty operation (not necessarily in New York City). At present, my ambitions are greater
than my qualifications. The training I would receive in an MBA program would help me move into a bigger arena and become a
leader in the profession.

Richard also wisely defined his strengths in specific terms:

Since my initial brash entrance into the world of real estate, I have
learned many important lessons. Today, I am a detail man. I have
to know everything about a property before I begin to market it. I
never exaggerate nor do I conceal anything from a potential buyer.
I always investigate a potential buyer's qualifications, financial
and professional. I have, on occasion, broken off a negotiation
after discovering something unfavorable about a buyer. I have
studied government regulations concerning land use, and made
myself knowledgeable about perc testing, building codes, bank
practices, tenant habits, and so on.

In his interview at Columbia, Richard continually referred to his
experience as a top salesman of commercial real estate and his volunteer activity in the communities in which he had led development
projects.

For recommendations, Richard enlisted two undergraduate professors and two professionals in real estate, telling them that he was

emphasizing his practical success, since his academic record and tests scores spoke for themselves. He encouraged the professors to speak to the academic promise he had shown in their courses and the professional realtors to describe his productive work. In sum, Richard presented himself as a candidate who was already a student of real estate and its many complexities and challenges and now wanted to expand his knowledge to move to the next level of his profession.

Marketing Your Passion

LUCILLE: *turning compassion and social concern into a career*

Lucille's passion as an undergraduate at Harvard was helping neglected children. She worked in a city program teaching fifth and sixth graders dance and theater. From this vantage point, she was so appalled when state funds for the program were eliminated that she became an intern in a public service law firm specializing in children's rights. Here is part of the personal statement she sent to law schools:

> More than once I have been called a "modern woman." If this means that I have seized every available opportunity, then I suppose the proverbial shoe fits. I have been co-founder and owner of my own business, a quarterly publication for Boston-area college and graduate students, and served as both business editor and special publications manager of the Harvard daily newspaper.
>
> While taking advantage of all (well, not quite all) that college has had to offer, I have continued to participate in programs centered around children, my primary field of interest. The stark contrast between the world of opportunity available to me and the universe of obstacles faced by children of low-income families has proven impossible for me to ignore. One response on my part has been to adopt a "little sister" named Keri, who lives in a Cambridge housing project with her unwed mother.
>
> One way I helped Keri was to introduce her to City Step, a community dance-theater activity. . . . But on returning to college in

September, I was outraged to discover that legislative budget cuts eliminated this program in the public schools.

As a result of these experiences, my new project was to intern at Lawyers for Children, an organization whose work includes helping foster children. I was able to help one child, Chris, who was for some time a bureaucratic victim, unable to return to his own home where he was truly wanted. This experience revealed to me how flawed the juvenile court system is. I am now seeking a legal education in the hopes of serving children like Keri and Chris. I hope to prove that I am no mere "modern woman," but a woman with a heart and mind and goals for many future decades.

Self-Marketing for Liberal Arts and Science Graduate Programs

If you seek admittance to a nonprofessional graduate program in the liberal arts and sciences, your self-marketing should begin in college. For acceptance at distinguished graduate programs in the top universities, almost everything depends on one or more faculty recommendations. An outstanding student will have no problem being admitted into some kind of a graduate academic department, but if you have your eye on the elite graduate departments in your discipline, your grades and test scores may not be enough. The great research universities are looking for students who are considered by their undergraduate professors to be intellectually remarkable. Remember our earlier discussion of how admission decisions are made at academic graduate schools: The faculty in each discipline are the final arbiters of who will study with them. Since academic master's and doctoral programs, in contrast to the professional schools, are not overly concerned about undergraduate extracurricular or leadership experiences, intellectual performance and test scores play an even stronger role in the selection of candidates.

What if you are shy and uncomfortable in interacting with your teachers and strangers? It is up to you, in many instances, to make your personal qualities and strengths known to key faculty. How do you do this without appearing aggressive on the one hand or obsequious on the other?

First, you make your objectives known. Good teachers like to train potential good teachers or good researchers. A student who talks of plans to carry out scholarly work in English literature at a major university will quickly find out if this ambition is reasonable. A teacher will point out what must be done to become eligible for such graduate work, or will begin to pay more attention to the student, ask for more work from her, suggest possible lines of research, help her get a paper published, and arrange for a fellowship for summer study. In the scientific field, the teacher might invite the student to participate in his own research project or set up an experiment on which to work.

You must pick your favorite faculty member, if someone does not first pick you, with an eye to the record: What has happened to his or her former students? The faculty member with whom you feel most comfortable may be less of a scholar than his or her colleagues, and the great star in the department may not have time for you, since she has her own research projects and outside consulting to contend with.

A virtue of early self-marketing is that you may be directed toward a particularly excellent graduate program that a faculty member knows well. Your undergraduate work can then be shaped to meet a specific need. If you learn early on of a new Latin American art history program at NYU and are interested in it, you can cover ground in undergraduate work that will be helpful to you later. Another opportunity to self-market yourself in advance is to apply for any summer fellowships that relate to your interests. Many successful doctoral students learned that the first fellowship leads to contacts in the discipline and opportunities for further fellowships, all of which will impress any graduate faculty.

Self-Marketing Can Only Help

Suppose you are a Phi Beta Kappa and have terrific test scores. Are you wise to think that self-marketing is unnecessary or beneath you? We doubt the wisdom of assuming this posture. The fact is that graduate schools like to be sold on candidates, and in the case of the top programs, need help in discerning the very best of the lot. They do not resist marketing efforts at all, for from them they learn more about the candidates. It is a mistake to think that graduate faculties and admissions committees are cold and impersonal, riveted to numbers, indifferent to the individual character and qualities they are considering.

It is very important to take Step Eight seriously, however qualified you are. In most cases, there are many others like you, and there are only so many places in each graduate class. To make sure that you will occupy one of them, market yourself.

Step Eight Checklist

- Work out a self-marketing strategy as part of your attempt to qualify for graduate studies. It is an essential element in the competition for admission to the selective universities.

- Try to avoid false modesty or exaggeration. Either extreme will affect your presentation negatively.

- Make use of class profiles and pie charts to find small slices where you can fit, in order to help you market yourself to programs to which you have the best chances of being admitted.

- Identify your strengths and call attention to them when appropriate in the admissions process.

- Even if you are a top candidate, market yourself. Admissions committees welcome the candidate who puts his or her best foot forward.

STEP NINE

Examine the Many Ways to Finance Graduate Education

Graduate School Is Costly but Feasible

We're not being unreasonable when we say that the high cost of graduate education should not stand in the way of your earning a postgraduate degree. Despite the heavy monetary burden, thousands of financially strapped graduate students successfully carry out their studies. However, for some, financing their education is less nerve-racking than it is for others. The difference lies in their willingness to take the time and make the effort to plan ahead, and to take advantage of the many opportunities they discover in their search for sources of funds.

No doubt you are aware that graduate school

1. Costs as much as or more than undergraduate education.
2. Costs more if you're in a professional program than if you're in an academic master's or doctoral program.
3. May necessitate the postponement, for a year or more, of studies in order to accumulate required money.
4. Has more limited available governmental grant aid than do undergraduate studies, and relies primarily on educational loan subsidies.
5. Often imposes a heavy debt burden.
6. Usually makes working your way through inadvisable, because the heavy academic load allows so little time for a part-time job, and because it is important that you do well in your courses. Remember, a B– is considered a failure in most graduate programs.

7. Professional schools provide far less financial aid than do academic master's and doctoral programs, because they receive less governmental and private research funding and they assume that graduates of their esteemed schools will have substantial earning power to repay educational loans.

FINANCIAL AID FOR GRADUATE STUDIES BY FUNDING SOURCE

Sources of Aid

Source	Proportion of Aid
Federal government	49.3%
State government	4.1%
Colleges	43.4%
Employers	9.6%
Other	22.7%

Type of Aid by Degree

Degree	Any Aid	Grants*	Loans	Assistantships
MBA	51%	37%	18%	5%
Education (M.A./M.ED.)	41%	23%	18%	4%
Arts and Sciences (M.A./M.S.)	58%	31%	24%	19%
Ph.D.	67%	40%	19%	41%
Medicine	81%	40%	71%	7%
Law	81%	36%	75%	3%

*Grants include scholarships, fellowships, tuition waivers, and employer aid.

Source: U.S. Department of Education, Federal Student Aid Information Center, "Student Financing of Graduate and First Professional Degree," www.ed.gov/prog_info/studentguide.

Our point is this: Earning a graduate degree will not be easy; nor will it be impossible. Graduate school means hard work academically, and financing it means making sacrifices, for all but the well-to-do. But because you are intelligent and energetic enough to do graduate work, you can meet the financing challenge with the same determination and drive that will land you a place in a top graduate school.

Average Cost of Annual Tuition and Fees and Living Costs for Graduate Schools, 2000-01

	Private Institution	Public Institution	
		Resident	Nonresident
Tuition and fees:	$21,000	$5,400	$12,000
Books and supplies:	$750	$1,800	$1,900
Living expenses:	$12,000	$10,000	$11,000
Total costs/year:	$33,750	$17,200	$24,900

Note: Averages never present the full picture. For example, medical school costs for a private university can run as high as $32,000 for tuition and fees alone. Cost of living can vary greatly by region of the country and locale (city or country campus). Private law school tuition and fees range from $19,000 to $27,000. We use the national averages here for the sake of simplicity; you should check with every institution you are considering to find out exactly what their full costs are. For public universities be sure to learn the difference in tuition for residents and nonresidents, since this can vary greatly from state to state.

Medical School Costs: Public versus Private

Public: University of North Carolina	Private: University of Pennsylvania Medical School
1999–2000 expenses	1999–2000 expenses
In-state tuition: $2,796	Tuition: $29,670
Out-of-state tuition: $23,688	

(continued)

Required fees: $831

Room and board: $18,791

Financial aid (1999–2000 academic year)

Students receiving any financial aid: 76%

Students receiving loans: 69%

Students receiving grants/scholarships: 76%

Students receiving work-study: 0%

Average indebtedness for graduates who incurred medical school debt: $53,634

Required fees: $1,680

Room and board: $15,505

Financial aid (1999–2000 academic year)

Students receiving any financial aid: 76%

Students receiving loans: 76%

Students receiving grants/scholarships: 46%

Students receiving work-study: 2%

Average indebtedness for graduates who incurred medical school debt: $84,000

The Graduate Financial Aid System

If you received financial aid in college, you will recall how you went about securing what was called a "financial aid package." This consisted typically of a grant or outright scholarship, a loan, and a part-time job. You filed the federal government's Free Application for Federal Student Aid form (FAFSA) and possibly the Financial Aid Form (FAF) of the College Scholarship Service (CSS), a program administered by the Educational Testing Service. Both of these forms, completed in collaboration with your parents (if you were a dependent), whose income and general financial situation (assets, outstanding debts, number of children in college, medical bills, etc.), created a needs analysis Financial Aid Form. This information was used to determine the amount of the aid package for which you qualified. This determination is based on an elaborate formula that includes federal criteria set by the U.S. Department of Education.

The main point is that the majority of colleges and universities base financial aid to undergraduates on need. While many institutions attract top candidates by awarding merit scholarships that do not require financial need, the bulk of aid comes from the federal and state governments, and family need is the defining criterion. Need is the amount of money necessary to close the gap between the full costs of a year of college and the amount the student and his family can put toward these costs.

In contrast, almost all scholarships in graduate school are awarded on the basis of academic excellence, or merit rather than need. This is especially true of academic as opposed to professional graduate programs. The applicant who excelled in undergraduate work is the most likely to receive a scholarship and/or a fellowship that is renewable for the length of his or her graduate studies. This is another reason to perform at the highest level possible in your undergraduate studies and to present yourself persuasively in your applications and interviews. Most of the need-based financial aid is in the form of student loans, which will have to be repaid upon completion of your degree.

All graduate students who are applying for need-based financial aid must complete the FAFSA materials. Again, the largest amounts of funding are in the form of subsidized loan and work-study programs. You should set a timetable for submitting all required applications to make acceptance to graduate school a reality, and plan to fill in the FAFSA information as early as possible. You can download the FAFSA from their website: www.fafsa.ed.gov. The application is made available by the Department of Education at the beginning of each new year. You then provide all the financial data requested for the year just ended. Most applicants find the task much easier if they have already completed their state and federal income tax forms for the same year. The sooner you return the FAFSA, the sooner you will know what your "Expected Family Contribution" is and thus how much you will be able to borrow on the subsidized loan program and whether you qualify for a work-study grant. This same information is used by the graduate schools to which you have applied to establish your financial need (the cost of attendance for one year minus your Expected Family Contribution) and determine whether you qualify for all the forms of financial awards.

Many universities require applicants to complete the CSS's Financial Aid PROFILE in addition to the FAFSA to be considered for aid from the universities' own resources. The basic information you will have to provide for CSS is the same as for the FAFSA. Many universities require the PROFILE because they can ask for additional information that helps them to decide on the allocation of their institutional scholarship funds. You can find out which graduate schools request that the PROFILE be completed by going to the College Board website. Be certain to check if this is a requirement for each university to which you plan to apply. Several hundred independent scholarship programs also require applicants to complete the PROFILE, and these, too, are listed on the College Board website. If you do not complete CSS's form, you will automatically be disqualified for financial assistance from all universities and scholarship programs that ask for it.

APPLYING ON-LINE

The College Board's College Scholarship Service makes it easy to apply for aid on-line. (www.Collegeboard.org/profile/index.html). All you need to do is register. You can either request that the form be sent to you by regular mail or complete the form on-line. Applying on-line saves you time and some extra mailing costs. It takes CSS only a day or two to process on-line applications and send out reports. Paper applications take longer because of the mail delivery time involved. It will cost you $6.00 whichever way you submit your application for processing, and an additional $16.00 for each report you have sent to universities or private organizations.

Financial aid directors are also receptive to personal information that is not explained on the application forms, but will affect directly your financial situation when you enroll. Typical examples are a recent illness of yourself or your spouse, or a dramatic change in your income because you no longer are working.

There is much work to be done in collecting all the data necessary to complete the two applications correctly. As one college wit said, in the case of receiving financial assistance from the government and the universities, it is the early bookworm who catches the prize.

For Financial Reasons, Apply to Two Tiers of Selectivity

We have already recommended that you apply to two levels of selective graduate schools to guarantee your chances for acceptance. But first we must state again that second-tier does not mean second-rate; this is simply a comparison of the richest and most selective institutions to others of excellence. Here we want to remind you of this strategy for still another reason: to increase the possibilities of garnering a large financial aid package. In general, the richer the universities, the more financial aid an applicant can expect. But institutions with limited funds may selectively distribute them with considerable generosity in order to attract applicants they want the most in their graduate programs. In this sense, there is a merit basis to aid distributed by the great research universities, and also by the so-called second-tier institutions that are outstanding in their own right.

So, if you think you can compete against the best applicants for admission to the more competitive schools, you should do so because of the educational advantages such programs provide. At the same time, you should not neglect the strong second-tier programs, because they are considered excellent training grounds and they may offer you more aid. This aid can be distributed in the form of teaching assistantships, fellowships, and internships that can advance your learning and experience faster than one of the more prestigious schools. There is something to be said for finding yourself in the position of choosing which graduate school to attend with all or most of your costs covered by a generous aid package.

The Many Ways to Finance Graduate Education

Over the years, private and public agencies have worked together to ease the graduate students' burdens. Before World War II, there was hardly any money available to assist these students to meet the expenses they incurred to realize their degree. To take advantage of the billions of dollars—yes, billions—available today from a combination of federal, state, institutional, and private funding, you should begin as early as possible to work out two key figures: what your graduate education will probably cost and what you can reasonably expect in aid from all sources.

There are three basic categories of money for a graduate student's education. The first includes grants, fellowships, and scholarships. These are outright contributions from government programs (including the GI Bill assistance), educational institutions, foundations, corporations, and other private sources. In the second category are education-related salaries, such as those paid for teaching assistantships, research assistantships, and college work-study programs, or salaries for jobs in the community, unrelated to the graduate school you attend. Third, there are loans from government, institutional, or private sources.

Close to 61 percent of all recent doctoral candidates received fellowships or teaching/research assistantships as their main source of financial support. Many university departments automatically review all candidates for funding from all available sources, while other universities require you to request consideration for aid. The simple rule to follow is this: Read all application instructions carefully! Typically, 50 percent of those who received their degree had to assume personal debt to complete their degree. The figures for professional degree recipients are even higher: 75 percent of recent graduating classes of all professional degree programs had to take out educational loans during the course of their studies. Debt has become an established reality for the majority of graduate students, and will continue to be a significant element of graduate education as we view the trends at the governmental and institutional levels.

Scholarships and Fellowships: Scholarships and fellowships really are one and the same thing because they are outright grants of money given by a university at large from their endowed funds or from the department to which a student is admitted, or by an outside organization such as a foundation or special interest group. Most of these cash awards are offered on the basis of merit and outstanding overall achievement, depending on the field of study, but some are dedicated to encouraging more minorities and women to apply and to enroll if they meet all of the standards of the graduate school program. The primary advantage of an awarded fellowship or scholarship is obvious: It is a gift of money (in the form of reduced or no tuition) that does not require hours of work while trying to concentrate on one's studies and does not result in the accumulation of debt that will need to be repaid in time. These awards also add distinction to your educational résumé and will rightly impress prospective employers when you apply for a job. It is up to you, as much as it is to any academic department, to learn about and pursue all potential fellowships that are relevant to your interests, background, and experience.

Teaching Assistantships: Teaching assistantships are offered by the graduate department or the university that has accepted you. Anyone awarded an assistantship is required to perform some kind of work on a regular basis in return for a salary or stipend and, usually, a partial or full waiver of the tuition. Of course you will want to compare the value of all assistantships you might receive to determine which one would give you not only the greatest freedom from debt but also the optimum professional experience. An assistantship can take the form of teaching a class or overseeing student laboratory work under the supervision of the professor who is responsible for the course. A teaching assistant, or TA, will lead small seminar discussions, read and grade papers and exams, and/or supervise laboratory work and review students' findings. Any of you planning for graduate school are aware, we are certain, of the tension in many research universities today between the administration and teaching assistants because of the low compensation for the many hours of work demanded by the faculty. The teaching assistants at a number of research universities, including Berkeley and New York University, have become highly activist in demanding better pay and working conditions, to the point of unionizing. This situation applies primarily to graduate students in the academic disciplines at very large institutions where they are needed to cover large undergraduate classes and labs while the tenured faculty go about their research, writing, and consulting. The primary advantage to taking on a teaching assistantship is the financial savings; the secondary advantage is the opportunity to teach and advise students, and to engage in research with senior mentors.

Research Assistantships: Research assistantships involve graduate students in the research of a faculty member in their discipline. Almost always the funding comes from research grants secured by the faculty from government or foundation sponsors. When a professor submits a proposal to fund a research project, he or she builds into the costs a budget for one or more research assistantships. Naturally, the professor in charge of the project chooses graduate students who have demonstrated their ability and interest in the research topic. Securing a research assistantship has the same advantages as securing a teaching assistantship: real income and reduced or no tuition. But there is the potential for additional benefits as well. A graduate student is more likely to bond with her professor and establish her talents for future recommendations. She may also carry out research that relates to her own special interests and thus lead to the degree sooner or at least on a smoother track. We advise any student who is offered a research assistantship to find out if the assignment is applicable to his or her specialty and is financially worth the time and commitment that will be required.

Administrative Assistantships: Administrative assistantships make up the smallest number of awards in most universities. They are just what the name implies, paid positions in administrative positions on campus. The ideal situation is one in which the job relates directly to the student's field of study; for example, working in the medical, business, or graduate school library or in the hospital overseeing operational needs. One of the authors had the good fortune to be offered an assistantship working in the undergraduate admissions office of his highly selective university. Not only was he paid enough to cover a good number of his expenses, but also he gained a knowledge of the admissions process and realized this was an area of serious future interest as he pursued his graduate degree. This administrative position came about by checking with the dean of the graduate school. Today many of these paid positions are listed on a university's website and are usually open to any graduate student; they are not necessarily administered by the specific school or department in which one is enrolled.

When a graduate program offers a student an aid package, it is likely to be a combination of the three categories above—outright contributions (this can include a tuition waiver), loans that must eventually be repaid, and a job, usually within the graduate school itself. Thus, the word *aid* has three meanings: funds that are a gift, funds that must be repaid with interest, and funds for which services are performed.

We should also mention the possibility of an employer's financing graduate training and the opportunities for graduate work at federal expense if you are a member of the armed services or certain government bureaus or agencies, such as the State Department. Some aid is available only to women and minority applicants. Further on we list a number of informational resources for you to search for any and all possible funding for which you might qualify. If you plan to continue working while pursuing your graduate degree, be sure to check with your company's human resources department to learn of any potential sources of funding. You may be pleasantly surprised.

Using Today's Smart Tool—The Internet

The Internet is your most efficient means for researching all possible sources for funding your graduate education. It will provide you with the most up-to-date information on the qualifications for all types of financial awards and loans. We include in the Bibliography a number of helpful websites, but here we call your attention to several comprehensive programs that will enable you to begin your search.

The first is the Financial Aid Information Page at www.finaid.org. This site presents a comprehensive overview of the many kinds of financial aid that are available. It also lets you complete a detailed personal data questionnaire that serves as the basis for researching all matching scholarships and loan programs. FinAid also helps you calculate your estimated expenses and the amount of money you will be expected to contribute to your education. It provides links to the FAFSA and CSS sites, where you can complete the applications and send them on electronically.

The second helpful website is FastWeb, at www.fastweb.com. Once you complete a questionnaire on your academic interests, background, and intended field of study, FastWeb searches its comprehensive database of over 200,000 scholarships and fellowships for those that match your qualifications and credentials. You can then contact the sponsoring organizations directly for detailed information and an application. The good news is that this is a free search service. Throughout your search process be certain to indicate that you are applying for graduate school degree programs, and be as specific as possible about your field of study to save yourself time in checking out scholarship leads.

Search for the Right Fellowship

Being the perennial optimists and cheerleaders that we are, we encourage you to launch an in-depth search for scholarships or fellowships, because new and generous programs are continually being created for which you may well qualify. Three examples of recently instituted programs illustrate our point:

1. *The Gates Cambridge Scholars* was recently established by the Bill and Melinda Gates Foundation with an endowment gift of $210 million to Cambridge University to create 225 Gates Cambridge Scholars. These merit-based scholarships will enable students from all over the world to study any subject of their choice for one to three years with all costs provided for. Although similar to the Rhodes Scholarship program at Oxford University, the Gates Scholars will be chosen from a field of candidates who demonstrate the potential to "take the lead in addressing global problems related to health, equity, technology, and learning."

2. *AT&T Labs Research Fellowships* provides funding for doctoral studies in computer and communications-related fields for women and minorities who are U.S. citizens. The fellowships cover all educational expenses during the school year (tuition, books, fees, and travel expenses) plus a stipend for living expenses (currently $1,400 per month, paid for 12 months the first two years and 10 months in the ensuing year). The fellowship is renewable for up to six years of study.

3. *The Park Leadership Fellows Program* provides a two-year, full-tuition-and-stipend MBA award for up to 30 Johnson School of Business students who have demonstrated outstanding academic and professional performance. The Park Leadership Program "seeks candidates who are driven to excel and will lead lives of professional achievement and personal contribution to the world."

FACTS IN BRIEF: THE NUMBER OF DOCTORAL DEGREES AWARDED BY U.S. INSTITUTIONS CONTINUES TO RISE

The number of doctoral degrees awarded by U.S. universities has increased steadily for the past 13 years and reached 42,683 in 1998, according to data from a report of the National Opinion Research Center. Other report findings include:

1. U.S. citizens earned 71 percent of doctorates awarded in 1998. Among non-U.S. citizens, students from China earned the most Ph.D.s (6 percent), followed by students from India and Taiwan (3 percent), Korea (2 percent), and citizens of Canada (1 percent).

2. Women earned 42 percent of all doctoral degrees awarded in 1998—the highest rate ever. In contrast, the percentage of degrees awarded to men declined for the second consecutive year. Nearly 15 percent of all doctorates earned by U.S. citizens were received by students of color. African Americans earned 1,467 doctorates;

(continued)

Hispanics, 1,190; Asian Americans, 1,168; and American/Alaskan Natives, 189 doctorates.

3. The average 1998 Ph.D. recipient was just under 34 years of age and had earned his or her doctorate 10.4 years after receiving a bachelor's degree. Among U.S. citizens, 50 percent planned to work in academe, while 8.2 percent planned to work in some level of government. The remaining graduates planned to work in other forms of employment or be self-employed.

4. The largest percentages of doctoral degrees awarded in 1998 were in the fields of life sciences (20 percent), followed by social sciences (17 percent), physical sciences (16 percent), education (15 percent), and engineering (14 percent).

Source: *Doctorate Recipients from United States Universities: Summary Report, 1998* (Chicago: National Opinion Research Center).

The Federal Work-Study Program

While most of the funds allocated by the federal government to the work-study program go to undergraduate students, a number of graduate schools also participate. As mentioned already, graduate students must demonstrate financial need to qualify for any subsidized federal funding. If you are interested in a work-study award, you must complete the FAFSA in a timely fashion. Like all the other opportunities to earn money while in graduate school, the work-study award will require you to put in 15 to 20 hours per week in a position with a nonprofit or public organization, most often the institution you attend. The government pays 75 percent of your salary and the institution or organization the remaining 25 percent. You can see why this is a popular program in many universities—they have to put out only one quarter of the money to subsidize a student.

Once again, we advise graduate students in need of funds to support themselves to check carefully with every institution to which they are admitted to learn about work-study opportunities. It is important to know if this program is in place and to understand the terms of the work. Is it in an area related to your degree interests? Will the place and time be convenient to your study and classroom schedule? Is the award renewable for each year you are a full-time student? Can you accept a job that you have located on your own and that you prefer?

Borrowing for Your Education

As we have mentioned, assuming debt over the course of your graduate studies is the most common means of paying for at least part of your expenses. For many students it is the largest source of money to cover living expenses and tuition. Before you make any commitment to educational or personal loans, ask yourself, Is the degree worth going into debt? Only you can be the final arbiter of this critical question. We believe it is, as do tens of thousands of fulfilled and successful professional people who borrowed against their future. We do caution you to work out all the financial figures carefully and conservatively before you sign on to a loan, so that you can project the amount of debt you will incur by the time you receive your degree and your ability to repay it as you build your career.

While there are many public and private organizations available to you for borrowing, the single largest source is the Federal Student Loan Programs, what are referred to as the Stafford and Perkins loan programs.

The Stafford Loan Program provides low-interest loans to graduate students through participating banks, savings and loan institutions, credit unions, and some universities that participate in the government's Direct Lending Program. There are two kinds of loans administered under the Stafford program: subsidized and unsubsidized. For the first, you need to demonstrate financial need; for the latter need is not a factor. Under the subsidized program, the government pays the interest that accrues while you are enrolled half- or full-time in graduate school, while under the unsubsidized program you must pay interest on the loan during your graduate studies. Under the terms of the Stafford program, repayment of the principal amount borrowed begins six months after you have finished your full- or part-time studies.

You may borrow up to $8,500 a year in subsidized loans. In combination with the subsidized loan, a student can borrow up to a total of $18,500 in subsidized and unsubsidized loans. The actual amount a student receives in the subsidized loan is deducted from the $18,500 in order to determine eligibility for the unsubsidized loan. Thus, a student who demonstrates significant amount of need will first receive the maximum amount for which he or she is eligible from the subsidized program, up to $8,500.

The Perkins Loan Program was created to subsidize the neediest category of students. Under the terms of this program a student who qualifies can borrow up to $6,000 per year, to a maximum over the course of his or her education of $45,000 (this includes undergraduate borrowing). The interest rate is purposely low, on average 5%, and no interest accrues while the student is in college or graduate school at least half-time. The loan must be repaid starting nine months after you complete your studies.

Schools of Education: Public versus Private	
Public: University of Michigan, Graduate School of Education	**Private: Harvard University, Graduate School of Education**
1999–2000 expenses	1999–2000 expenses
In-state tuition: $10,150	Tuition: $21,410
Out-of-state tuition: $20,974	Room and board: $10,800
Required fees: $555	Books and supplies: $1,500
Room and board: $10,800	Miscellaneous expenses: $4,240
Books and supplies: $800	
Graduate appointments	Graduate appointments
Total appointments: 923	Total appointments: 420
Fellowships: 464	Fellowships: 136
Teaching assistants: 90	Teaching assistants: 226
Research assistants: 169	Research assistants: 53
Other appointments: 200	Other appointments: 5

Coping with Loans

"Neither a borrower, nor a lender be," said Polonius, but this adage must be ignored by most graduate students today, for whom debt is a fact of life. Scholarships, fellowships, and governmental aid have not been able to keep pace with the acceleration in the costs of attaining a graduate degree. On average, every year 75 percent of all professional school students and 50 percent of all master's and doctoral candidates take out loans. The Law School Admissions Council reports that approximately 80 percent of law students rely on educational loans as the largest source of aid as a means to cover part of the $140,000 tab for a three-year law education. The number of students who borrow from all sources to pay for their education is continually rising. The debt burden is heaviest on those students with the least means. But even middle-class students feel the impact of money owed at graduation time. You, as a graduate student, must somehow manage your finances to prevent your indebtedness from forcing you to make a career decision that flies in the face of your original goals and dreams.

Anyone who is in graduate school today can borrow money from the many sources discussed throughout this step. We want you to pause before you make a commitment to assuming major debt. We are not financial consultants, so we must leave to you the personal decision about what is a reasonable amount of debt. Doctors may start out their career owing $75,000 or more, and thus decide to accept a position in a managed care group to make certain they will be able to liquidate the debt eventually. This may or may not be the professional direction they intended originally. A doctoral student who wants to devote his or her life to teaching and scholarship is less likely to have the level of income to pay off such large debt. So fellowships, grants, tuition waivers, assistantships, and outside awards become critical to avoid compromising one's future. Business or law students may need to recognize the importance of saving as much as possible from earned income before enrolling in law or business school so as to avoid accumulating more loans than they will want to pay off when they reenter the work place.

The counselor instinct in us simply cautions you to act like bird dogs when it comes to paying for your graduate education: track down potential funding wherever the scent leads. We can only warn that one easy scent is loan money, and this track should be the last one you choose to follow, and the least made use of. But we recognize that this is easier said than done.

SAMPLE FINANCIAL WORKSHEET			
	Graduate Schools		
	_____	_____	_____
COSTS			
Tuition	_____	_____	_____
Living expenses	_____	_____	_____
Fees	_____	_____	_____
Books and supplies	_____	_____	_____
Travel	_____	_____	_____
Medical insurance	_____	_____	_____
Child care	_____	_____	_____
Total one-year budget	_____	_____	_____
SOURCES OF FUNDS			
Savings	_____	_____	_____
Earnings, one year	_____	_____	_____
Parents' contribution	_____	_____	_____
Spouse's contribution	_____	_____	_____
Fellowships/scholarships	_____	_____	_____
Governmental aid (administered by the graduate school)	_____	_____	_____
Loans	_____	_____	_____
Any other sources	_____	_____	_____
Total available	_____	_____	_____

It Can Be Done

Without underestimating the financial burden many graduate programs will require, we encourage anyone seeking a quality graduate degree not to abandon such a wonderful project for purely financial reasons. It may be necessary to postpone graduate studies to save a sufficient sum for completing a degree program. It may be that you have to stretch out the number of years of actual study as you work to support yourself. But we say from a good deal of experience with thousands of graduate students of modest means that financing graduate work can be done.

The fact is, it *is* being done, as the number of new graduate students continues to grow. Another way of looking at your own situation is, if I do not move forward to secure my dream, someone else with similar dreams will, whatever the financial challenge.

We hope that you will follow Step Nine and it will help you surmount difficulties in financing your further education. Do not miss the opportunity of a lifetime because you cannot afford it. You can afford it if you really want it. What you cannot afford is to disappoint yourself. Apply to a good program and apply for an aid package, and plan to enroll in a financially workable institution. What happens after that depends on your ingenuity and determination. We are betting that you can do it. The rewards for achieving your graduate degree are well worth the effort you will make.

A Summary of the Steps to Take in Applying for Financial Aid

Let's pull together the sequence of steps you must take if you are applying for aid:

1. Begin the financial aid process during the month of December to be ahead of all university deadlines. You need to know at the time you are accepted what your costs will be and how much aid, in all the forms we've discussed in this step, you will receive.
2. Obtain the FAFSA from your undergraduate college's financial aid or career services office, from one of the graduate schools to

which you are applying, or from the FAFSA website (www.fafsa. ed.gov).

3. Complete the FAFSA and designate the names of the graduate schools you want to receive the information. You can get the institutional code numbers at the FAFSA website.

4. The FAFSA requests information about your income, assets, and any other financial resources. One caveat: Be certain to answer "yes" to the question "Will you be working on a degree beyond the bachelor's degree?" For the purposes of analyzing your financial need against income and assets, all graduate and professional school candidates are independent of their parents.

5. Check with each graduate school about completing the CSS PROFILE financial information. If this is a requirement, complete this form at the same time you are working on the FAFSA.

6. Each graduate school to which you apply will determine the amount of money or other awards it will offer you based on your need analysis and its degree of interest in you.

7. Once you determine which graduate school you will attend, you can begin the federal loan application process.

8. Determine realistically the total cost of each year of your graduate education and weigh how much money you might have to borrow. Be certain to add the costs of housing, food, books, travel, and personal expenses to tuition and fees. Then check all sources of education and personal loans available to you. Remember that federal, state, and university sponsored loans have the lowest rates of interest.

9. The financial aid offices of the universities are a significant source of information on all the potential sources of aid— federal, state, and private. They can alert you to special merit scholarships they might offer.

Step Nine Checklist

🎓 Study carefully the financial aid data of each institution to which you plan to apply.

File all of the requisite forms for financial aid: state, federal, private, and institutional.

Research other aid opportunities such as grants, fellowships, and corporate backing.

When borrowing, make sure you will be able to afford interest payments and reduction of principal as required by the terms of each loan.

Explore all alternate graduate programs in your intended field to see what the range of costs is.

Determine the maximum amount of money you can expect from your own and family resources. Make up a tentative financial worksheet for decision making and planning.

Take time off to save money rather than stealing study time to pursue part-time jobs while in graduate school.

If you're accepted to your first-choice school, meet with the financial aid director or chair of your program to review all possible sources of additional aid to make it possible for you to enroll. Do not be shy in requesting a teaching or research assistantship, work-study position, or any other income-producing position if you were not offered one of these initially.

When aid has been allotted by the graduate program you plan to enter, and you have all other support lined up, draw up your final financial plan and stick to it.

STEP TEN

Complete the Admissions Process Scrupulously

Having taken the first nine steps toward applying to a graduate school, you now must be careful not to stumble on Step Ten, which consists of actually completing a number of applications, some of which are quite different from others; considering the wisdom of interviews and visits to institutions; and, finally, choosing among programs that accept you. These activities are unusual and you are doing them for the first time. You may say that you went through this routine when you applied to college, but remember, that was several or more years ago and graduate school is not the same as college. The wise and successful candidates complete the admissions process with the greatest of care, because it is at the culminating point of a crucial personal presentation.

In the prior steps you have sought to construct a record of academic and nonacademic accomplishments that speaks for itself. You have sought to match your capabilities to some graduate programs you believe are right for you. Many other candidates have done the same thing. Admissions committees will therefore be looking for further evidence of your qualifications, and they will be sensitive to signs of immaturity, ambivalence, or poor communication skills, as evidenced in any carelessness or superficiality in your application materials.

The Application Is You

"Sad to say, but we reject a number of candidates every year simply because of sloppy applications," stated the former dean of admissions of the Wharton School of Business. "We have enough good candidates to choose from, and we think that anyone who won't take the time to prepare an application with scrupulous thoroughness will not do satisfactory graduate work."

It would be a shame to be denied admission to a fine graduate program just because you were too casual in completing your application. We encourage you to review some of the case studies we have presented in this book, not just for the content of the applicants' essays but also for the care taken to write well and thoughtfully. The other parts of their applications were treated with similar care so that their entire presentation impressed the decision makers in the graduate schools.

An application form of any sort looks dry, lifeless, and forbidding in its cold request for information or self-revelation. Initial reactions as applicants complete this critical admissions document may range from boredom and indifference to outright hostility. Beware, however. A sloppy application at the very least shows that the candidate does not take the process, and thus his or her interest in the university's program, as seriously as he or she should.

It seems so obvious that an application to any graduate program should be carefully drawn up. It should hardly be necessary to dwell on such things as the need to study application instructions; to read through the entire set of questions and then answer each question carefully; to proofread your answers for typos, spelling errors, and incorrect wording; to meet deadlines; to make sure your college transcript and entrance test results are sent to the proper office; and to check that recommendations have been sent in by faculty, employers, or other supporters of your candidacy. You must also be sure to sign each application and enclose the fee. Further, if you are applying for financial aid you must check the appropriate box on each application and understand the steps necessary to qualify for consideration.

Review every institution's catalogue or website to determine if you are encouraged or required to apply on-line rather than by printed application. Either way, you will want to follow the specific procedural steps laid out clearly.

Attention to detail is essential. Many candidates have woken in the cold light of morning to realize they left out information necessary to complete their application or failed to meet the deadline. It can happen easily when you are under the stress of meeting college studies or work deadlines while applying to graduate schools. We urge you to take the time to complete a perfect application, error free, easy to read, providing all the information required. You must keep in mind that this is the chief document in your file, one that may be reviewed several times by different committee members. It is the equivalent of a self-portrait, a text that says this is ME, this is the person you will have in your classroom and eventually in your profession.

This is why you should study application forms early in the admissions process, because the graduate application is far more complex in most cases than an undergraduate application. You are now assumed to be a mature adult with a determination to undertake intensive professional studies. Therefore, few allowances are made for missing information or making errors.

As a fairly typical example of mistakes to be avoided, a number of careless applicants every year have their transcripts sent directly to one or more law schools instead of to the Law School Data Assembly service of the Law School Admission Council/Law School Admission Services. This is not fatal, but it delays processing the application and can make a bad impression if an admissions committee learns about it from a person in the office who had to return your transcript to you for resubmission. The same is true for submitting medical school applications through the American Medical College Application Service.

A typical slip, believe it or not, is to forget to include the application fee, without which the application file sits unprocessed until a check arrives. Some candidates forget to sign their applications. Others ignore the deadlines, or they fail to tell those sending in letters of recommendation to write their names across the envelope seal, as some admissions committees require, or they fail to include all required documents in one envelope to be returned to the admissions office. The possibilities for error are almost endless.

To keep the application process orderly, you should maintain a few files:

- File the names, addresses, telephone numbers, and e-mail addresses of key people at each graduate school to which you apply—such people as deans, admissions personnel, financial aid officers, faculty members you have been in contact with, alumni, or anyone else who can possibly be helpful to you.

- File copies of your written requests for your transcripts to be sent to graduate schools, and record confirmation that the transcripts have been received.
- File your correspondence with faculty members or employers or others who are writing recommendations for you, noting the dates of your requests and evidence that the admissions committees have received recommendations.

WORDS TO THE WISE THAT APPEAR
IN APPLICATION INSTRUCTIONS

Most application instructions underscore the importance of completing the application correctly:

MBA school: "The Admissions Committee urges you to exercise care in completing application forms. The information and statements that you submit to the committee are important factors in the admission decisions."

MA/Ph.D. program: "Incomplete applications cannot be considered. Make sure that you have submitted all required items and completed all forms. You are responsible for ensuring that your application is complete."

Law school: "No application to this school will be processed unless accompanied by a Law School Application Matching Form, which is found in the applicant's LSAT/LSDS registration packet. Since an LSAT and/or LSDS report cannot be produced by the Educational Testing Service without this matching form, it will be necessary to return to the applicant any application received without it."

How Application Forms May Differ

You will probably be applying to at least several graduate schools, in which case you must take care to notice when there are differences in applications, despite their common characteristics. Some applications have their own distinct components, so you must be thoughtful in your responses, and not become inattentive from the boredom or time pressure of completing a number of them. Increasing numbers of graduate school programs, particularly the business schools, encourage candidates to apply on-line. A random survey of three or four comparable business schools' instructions for completing electronic applications will make clear the importance of following each school's detailed instructions for completing and submitting your application. Some require you to submit supplemental paper information, without which your application will be considered incomplete.

Some professional graduate schools require you to use a common application service to process your information, so that you can apply to a number of programs by filing one application. A majority of medical schools instruct candidates to file their applications with the American Medical College Application Service (AMCAS). The names of medical schools that subscribe to the service are listed in those schools' application materials. Failure to follow this procedure can result in failure to gain admission to a medical school.

If you remember the need to tailor each application to its specific requirements, you will then be prepared to spend the necessary time it will take to complete each one. Treat the application process as you would an academic course requirement or a report you have to prepare for your boss. Familiarize yourself with each application before starting to fill it out. This will give you an idea of how much time it is going to take to complete a particular application. Knowing that you may have to spend several hours just responding to one essay question, you will then budget your time accordingly. As you read through an application, pay particular attention to the wording of each request.

Below are a few areas in which applications differ.

Length of Essay Questions

Some graduate schools put no limit on the length of responses to essay questions, but others ask you to limit the number of words you write.

Duke's Fuqua School of Business asks this question and tells you to limit your writing:

> Tell us about your personal history and family background and how they have influenced your intellectual and personal development. What unique personal qualities or life experiences might distinguish you from other applicants? How will your background, values and non-work-related experiences enhance the experience of other FSB students and add to the diverse culture we strive for at Fuqua? Note: The goal of this essay is to get a sense of who you are, rather that what you have accomplished. (Limit—3 pages)

Dartmouth's Tuck School of Business requires applicants to write three essays, none of which has a stated length. It is up to the writer to determine in each case what is important to present: "Discuss your career progression to date. Elaborating on your short- and long-term goals, how do you see your career progressing after you receive an MBA? Why do you want an MBA from Tuck?"

Harvard's School of Public Health asks you to confine your two personal statements to a single page of the application, but Johns Hopkins's School of Hygiene and Public Health does not limit the personal statement to the single page provided with the application.

Yale Law School explains the purpose of their required essay this way:

> Faculty readers look to the required short essay to evaluate your writing, thinking, and editing skills, as well as to learn more about such qualities as your intellectual concerns or passions, your humor, or your ability to think across disciplines. The subject is not limited; the choice of topic itself may be informative to the readers. A separate opportunity to discuss your personal background is available in Question 10, where you may add any additional information necessary for a full representation of your candidacy.

Northwestern University's Medill School of Journalism asks that you "tell us within 500 words what factors and influences have moved you toward a career in newspaper, magazine or television journalism. How have you pursued this career so far and what are your goals?"

In writing about yourself, it is usually harder to be succinct than to be expansive, so plan accordingly when asked for a limited number of words. Do not exceed the word limit by any substantial amount. Imagine yourself in the seat of an admissions committee member who has to read hundreds to thousands of personal applications, and you will understand why a clearly written, well-organized, and to-the-point statement is appreciated and respected.

The Number of Application Items

Typical of all graduate schools to one extent or another, Stanford's Medical School issues a full page of instructions to explain the many steps that must be taken to be considered for admission. We cite it verbatim here to emphasize again the importance of following all application instructions carefully. Remember that your application should reflect your maturity, your willingness to make that extra effort to double-check everything and to avoid careless omissions and mistakes. Make each application as easy to read as possible. With the ability to complete and submit your application electronically to a majority of graduate schools today, you have no excuse for not completing the application thoroughly, checking it with a critical eye, editing any mistakes, and only then sending it to the admissions committees. Be aware that there are several additional procedural requirements you must fulfill when you apply electronically.

> Initial application to Stanford University School of Medicine must be made through the American Medical Colleges Application Service (AMCAS). (See Association of American Medical Colleges Handbook: Medical School Admission Requirements for further information.)
>
> Requests for AMCAS applications are available from advising offices and AMCAS after March 1. AMCAS applications can be filed with AMCAS beginning June 1st. In order to apply to Stanford, all AMCAS materials MUST be filed with AMCAS no later

than November 1st. We do not give extensions to this date. It is in the applicant's interest to file early so that completed AMCAS materials will reach Stanford during the summer. (AMCAS, 2450 N Street, NW, Suite 201, Washington, DC, 20037-1131 Tel. 202-828-0600.)

When the Office of Admissions receives an AMCAS application, it is carefully evaluated, and the information and forms necessary for completion of our supplementary application are sent to students for whom a possibility of acceptance is considered.

Evaluation and selection are based upon standards of merit, and no quotas of any kind play a role in the admission process. No preference is given to California residents. (See Statement of Non-Discriminatory Policy.)

Supplementary application and recommendations. The supplementary application requests additional information about the candidate's significant extracurricular experience, personal background, career goals, etc. We request three complete letters of evaluation from persons who know the candidate well enough to evaluate his/her scholarly potential and promise as a physician. These letters may be accompanied by an undergraduate school's premed committee evaluation, but a committee evaluation alone is not advisable.

The final deadline for a completed application is December 15, 2001. However, it is strongly recommended that applications be complete as early as possible since acceptances are offered on a rolling basis. It is the applicant's responsibility to see that all materials are sent in time.

An application fee must be paid at the time the supplementary application is submitted. The application fee will be waived for applicants who have obtained a fee waiver from AMCAS. Otherwise, fee waiver requests must be accompanied by a supporting statement from the undergraduate dean or financial aid officer.

Interviews. Upon evaluation of the supplementary application, candidates are notified as to whether they will be interviewed. In recent years, about one in five applicants who complete the supplementary application has received an invitation to interview.

Most interviews are held between September and March. Applicants receive two approximately hour-long interviews, one with a Stanford Medical School faculty member and one with a current medical student. The interview is an opportunity for a two-way exchange in which the candidate can learn more about the school in addition to responding to questions intended to help the Committee on Admissions reach a decision as to the appropriateness of Stanford's program for the candidate's particular needs and goals.

Acceptance. Acceptances are offered on a "rolling" basis between November and May. Candidates who are not offered immediate acceptance are ranked in a "hold" list for possible later acceptance. Since the exact positions in the hold category change significantly over time, numerical ranking information is not made known. However, every effort is made to inform such candidates in general terms about their prospects of eventual acceptance in light of past years' experience.

MEDICAL SCHOOLS LOOK FOR CLEAR WRITING, NOT CREATIVE WRITING

Medical school applicants often worry needlessly about their limited writing abilities. Most of them have concentrated in one science or another, and such courses as lab work do not require the refined writing expected in advanced liberal arts courses. Medical school admissions committees recognize this and therefore, unlike the admissions committees in nonscience disciplines, do not necessarily look for creativity or soaring imagination in candidates' personal statements. What is expected is an ability to write clearly. We know that most applicants with a strong science background are used to writing clear, logical, coherent descriptions, analyses, and solutions to scientific problems.

If you believe you qualify for medical school, your admission will depend on your academic record, your MCAT scores, and the

(continued)

recommendations of your science professors and supervisors. Where the application calls for a personal statement, you need only write what you have to say in a straightforward style, without trying to be literary or verbose or clever for its own sake. Pay attention to grammar and spelling, of course, by proofreading. This will show that you are a careful and thoughtful writer who takes pains to express his or her ideas correctly. The personal statements of the two medical school cases we have presented are fine models of the essential elements of good writing for medical admissions committees.

How Many Applications Should You File?

When we hear of a good student applying to 20 medical schools, we shudder. Even though the American Medical College Application Service (AMCAS), through its centralized application-processing service for applicants to the first-year entering classes at participating U.S. medical schools, has made it relatively easier to apply to a large number of medical schools, the cost can become prohibitive. AMCAS charges $150 to register your application with the first designated school and $30 for each additional school to which you apply. For the 2002 entering class, 115 medical schools and 2 programs are participating in AMCAS. Applicants to medical schools that do not participate in AMCAS must contact their admissions offices directly for application instructions. The application fees can be as high as $75 to $100, which will be in addition to the AMCAS school fees for the other medical schools.

This kind of overkill not only wastes money, but is impractical. The student we have in mind was admitted quickly to seven of the best medical schools in the country and eventually was offered admission to six others. It is true that no one can guarantee anyone admission to a medical school or any other excellent graduate program, because the competition is so great today, but those who are likely to be admitted will not improve their chances by application overkill. If certain students feel that they are marginal candidates, a few applications to the next tier of graduate programs should be adequate. Rejection by such schools should indicate that medicine, or law, or business, or any other professional school is not for them, at least not at this point in their development. They can, and should, regroup and consider either other careers or interim steps that will build a more impressive profile for a second round of applications in the future. Every individual we have ever counseled to graduate school has commented on how much exacting work is required to complete all the necessary steps in the application process. This cannot be seen as throwing a large number of seeds into the wind and hoping that at least one will take root. Too much focus on completing the applications, gathering references from the appropriate people, visiting institutions, and interviewing is necessary to make it possible to take this approach.

In applying to graduate programs, the formula followed in applying to college still holds: Select schools that seem to be appropriate to your profile and to your capacity.

Here is a representative case. Hans, a Dutch student, was seeking an American business education. He had a slightly above average college record, and was now working for a Dutch international bank. Despite his profile, he applied to the graduate business schools at Dartmouth, Cornell, Duke, Vanderbilt, and Virginia, all of which turned him down. He simply did not have impressive enough grades, GMAT scores, or work experience to convince any of the admissions committees to accept him. When Hans turned to us for counsel regarding his professional future, we learned in several interviews with him that he had volunteered throughout his undergraduate university years in a large hospital in Amsterdam. He had at one point considered medicine as a career but found that he enjoyed administration and finance more than the required sciences. Hans seemed to us to be a natural candidate for professional hospital administration schools, since this training would allow him to bring together the several key interests he possessed.

We encouraged Hans to apply to eight hospital management programs: Cornell, George Washington, New York, Tulane, and Northwestern Universities, and the Universities of Miami, Michigan, and North Carolina. He was admitted to Tulane, George Washington, and NYU.

This is not to say that nine is either the limit on the number of places to apply or the average. You apply to the best graduate schools among those where you believe you have a chance of acceptance. Hans had a chance at the five programs that rejected him, but he did not make it. These were not simply wasted applications; they were necessary to bolster his general chance of admission.

Remember to Budget Both Money and Time

Graduate school application fees run from $50 to $100 each, but there are other costs attached to applying: postage, long-distance telephone calls to the various people you need to support your candidacy, fees for college transcripts, visits to campuses for interviews. Budgeting a minimum of $500 to pay for the entire application process makes sense. If you anticipate this necessary layout of funds, you will not be unpleasantly and inconveniently surprised in the middle of the admissions process by finding yourself short of money. For those candidates who know early on that the costs of applying will be truly prohibitive, there will be ample time to request application fee waivers. We know of no graduate program that will not honor a bona fide waiver request. You can also request a travel stipend if you are invited by the admissions committees to interview on campus.

How much time has to be devoted to the application process? More than you probably imagine. You should allow yourself ample time to:

- Search the Internet and graduate directories for relevant programs, and request literature.
- Peruse university catalogues and program brochures.
- Study each application form and its detailed instructions.
- Craft excellent personal statements and essays, and complete all parts of the applications.
- Line up your references so they will be prepared to respond in a timely fashion.
- Visit the most appealing institutions for in-depth looks and to meet with program representatives.

- Arrange for an interview if it is required or recommended.
- Prepare for entrance tests by self-study or a professional tutoring course that will ready you for the appropriate test date.

All this must be done with an eye to the time limit imposed by the application deadlines and by the constant drumbeat from admissions committees to apply as early as possible. And of course while you are doing all of this intensive work, you must also be carrying on your academic or professional responsibilities. Many a graduate school candidate we have counseled has said with a sigh that the application process leaves little to no time for a personal life. We would not disagree with this for one moment, but like all steep hills that have to be climbed, you eventually reach the peak and then the descent is a rewarding experience.

The Question of Interviews

There are several important points to make about interviews. Not all graduate programs require them, but some, like medical schools, will invite highly promising candidates to campus for an interview. Those that do rarely reject a candidate on the basis of an interview. Some programs do not grant interviews even if requested. Some candidates eagerly seek the opportunity to meet with an admissions committee representative, while other candidates are uneasy or even gun-shy about interviewing.

Our advice is this: If interviews are optional and you dread them, exercise your option and avoid them. On the other hand, if you approach interviews with a good deal of self-confidence, take the initiative to request a personal meeting with a department head or admissions committee member to make your case. We do warn some individuals who believe they can talk their way into a graduate school despite a weak or shaky background that they are unlikely to convince intelligent, experienced educators to give them a precious place in a competitive class. Such candidates often have some weakness in their college academic performance or in their job history that they seek to overcome through persuasiveness and charm. We have found that this rarely succeeds.

We do, however, strongly encourage candidates who have miti-gating circumstances in their academic or professional life that explain a less than stellar performance, to do all in their power to secure an interview. The sincerity and emotions that can be conveyed only in a personal interaction can go far to help the committee inter-pret your credentials in a more sympathetic light. We think of stu-dents whom we advised to discuss with admissions committees a serious illness they or a family member suffered. One young woman was determined to train for a career in law, but was convinced that she could not qualify for a top law school due to her undergraduate record. We knew about her family circumstances which we recom-mended she write about briefly in her applications, as well as request-ing personal interviews to explain her situation. When the committees of several highly selective law schools learned first-hand of the death of her father and her need to look after her ailing mother and earn extra income to help support herself and her brother, they offered her a place in their class. Suddenly her good, but not brilliant, academic performance in college took on a whole new interpretation. Who would not want a young woman with such a sense of responsibility and determination?

We can offer several pieces of advice for those who are uneasy about interviewing under stressful circumstances but have been asked to schedule a meeting with a graduate school representative. It is quite natural to feel a little anxious, since an interview comes down to a per-sonal evaluation of you by a stranger. It is a mistake, however, to try to quell your anxiety through a deliberate effort to make a favorable impression. It really is best to be your natural self. Reveal as much about yourself as an interviewer seeks to find out. If you are the quiet type by nature, let that be your manner in a meeting with a stranger. If you are naturally ebullient, do not try to suppress your style.

You should always avoid flattering the interviewer, since this will be perceived as false flattery. Personal remarks that are not directly rele-vant to the topic at hand can be risky. "I see you are a Phi Beta from the certificate on your wall. So am I," is not just idle chatter; it can be seen as effort to put yourself on the same level as the interviewer, who may be a potential Pulitzer Prize writer or Nobel Laureate—or thinks of him- or herself in those terms. Furthermore, the record of your academic prowess is already known to the admissions committee, so there is no need to boast about it. There are other important purposes to accomplish during the interview for both parties.

Remember that the interviewer has met with many, many candidates and will certainly be a shrewd judge of character, and on to all the tricks that have been tried. The self-assurance, and occasionally the self-importance, of an interviewer can sometimes be unsettling and tempt you into aggressive responses, even hostility if the questions are highly provocative. Avoid the temptation to counter. You are the guest; you are being tested for your maturity, your sense of propriety, and your ability to remain cool under stress. Remember that you are being judged in comparison with many very confident applicants who do not let anything get under their skins.

There is this distinction between undergraduate and graduate school interviews: For a graduate school interview you should arrive with an agenda. As experienced counselors, we advise applicants to graduate school to be fully prepared to answer the most fundamental of questions: "Why are you here?" Agenda items can run from questions about the program, to questions about the faculty or the resources for learning in your particular area of interest, to a discussion about the future of the profession you seek to enter, to governmental decisions that will affect the nature of your studies and professional future. Most of all, the meeting is about your capacity to persist in meeting all the intellectual and emotional demands graduate training will place on you. Take all interviews seriously, and keep your commentary relevant and well thought out by preparing ahead of time.

Some graduate programs do not have adequate staff to conduct as many interviews as are requested. Much as you might like to personalize your application and possibly influence a decision in your favor by what you convey in a personal meeting, you may have to forego it and, like most of the other candidates, rely on your record and what you have said about yourself on your application. While most professional schools do not request that you interview, they do schedule them when they feel it will be useful in their deliberations. Many candidates to business, law, education and other programs have been helped because of a positive meeting with an admissions officer or faculty representative. This is not to say that you should give up too easily if you are initially put off by your first contact with the admissions office at the schools that matter greatly to you. We are increasingly convinced that the harder you work at the admissions process on all fronts, the luckier you are likely to be!

Medical school interviews are a special case in the galaxy of professional graduate programs. When a medical school invites a candidate for an interview, it means that his or her transcript, test scores, recommendations, and application reveal a potential successful medical student and future physician. The interview will be highly evaluative, rather than primarily informational. You will be one of a number of qualified candidates who have been selected for final consideration from a much larger pool of applicants. Many medical schools will, on average, admit as many as one half of all the candidates whom they meet with personally. Such an interview can make the difference between acceptance and rejection. This is certainly enough to make anyone nervous, but the advice we have already given you applies in this situation. You should remind yourself that the committee member has reviewed all of the information you were required to supply, so he or she is not going to go over the same terrain. The interviewer's goal is to learn more about your personal strengths, your emotional maturity and stability to cope with the intensity of medical training, your degree of passion for the medical profession, your sense of ethics, compassion for others, your ability to communicate with patients and their families in the future, your awareness of the world around you and level of interest in important social issues. Often, the interviewer will pick out something you raised in your application to develop further as an indication of the depth and clarity of your thinking.

How does one prepare for such an encounter with so much potentially at stake? There are several basic elements to preparing for an interview. Review your personal application to remind yourself what you wrote, so you are not surprised by a question that relates to your own statements. You will also find yourself more articulate in responding to any questions that feed off of your application;. Do your homework on the graduate school and its programs thoroughly, so that you are prepared to demonstrate your considerable interest in the program and can ask your own questions to fill in information you need to have. You should dress well for any interview; jeans or casual dress is inappropriate. Women should wear skirts or dress suits, and men should wear a suit or sports jacket and slacks with a tie. Sneakers or sandals definitely do not cut it. We counsel present college students especially to be sensitive to their dress and appearance since they rarely need to dress formally, and their immediate role models, their teachers, dress as casually as they do. How you are dressed and groomed (this means hair length and style mostly) is interpreted by admissions committees as an indication of your maturity and seriousness.

Again, the cardinal sin in interviewing is artificiality. The most serious mistake you can make is to worry too much about the impression you are making. It is natural to be a bit tense and cautious with a stranger, especially one who has the ability to help determine your fate. But remember that in most cases the chance that you will affect negatively the admissions committee decision based on an interview is small. You do, conversely, have the opportunity to influence their decision positively by preparing well for your meeting and remembering our cardinal rules.

BE YOURSELF AT YOUR BEST:
A PRIMER ON INTERVIEWING

A graduate school official uses the interview as an opportunity to:

- Flesh out the data the admissions committee has in hand, to discover if your written presentation, background, and recommendations are supported by a personal meeting.
- Get more detailed information on a particular facet of your experiences and performance in college or in your job.
- Ascertain how mature, comfortable, flexible, and sociable you are and your potential compatibility with students and faculty in the program.

(continued)

- Assess your verbal skills, logical and coherent thinking, thoughtfulness, and self-confidence in your intellectual skills and knowledge of the subject field.
- Weigh the extent of your enthusiasm for the studies you wish to undertake and your excitement for the institution.

You can prepare for interviews by

- Reviewing your application, especially your personal statement(s), and the curriculum and major features of the graduate program.
- Preparing responses to questions you are most likely to be asked, such as, Why do you want to pursue our particular degree program? Why do you think this is the right field for you? What are your career goals? How prepared for the demands of our curriculum are you? What do you consider to be your major strengths? your weaknesses? What have you accomplished that you are the most proud of? What will you contribute to our community of learners and teachers?

Remember:

- First impressions really do matter, so dress appropriately and be on time for your appointment.
- Sincerity, warmth, cheerfulness, and humor will always win an interviewer to your side.
- Positive interaction occurs when you make eye contact with your interviewer. Sit forward in your seat as if you are ready to begin your studies this minute. Speak slowly and clearly, and keep your responses to questions brief and on the subject.
- Nervous habits such as drumming your fingers on a desk or chair, twirling your hair, clicking the top of your pen, chewing your nails, or pumping your leg up and down can easily irritate and distract the interviewer.
- The golden rule holds true at all times: You should not speak critically or harshly of your college or your boss or peers; you will only demean yourself.

- Avoid such sensitive topics as religion, politics, race, abortion, euthanasia, and so on unless asked to respond directly to such a question by your interviewer.

You should be prepared to

- Convey your special interests by asking pertinent questions, e.g., "As I indicated in my personal statement, I am especially keen on emphasizing my studies within this certain specialty, and so I would appreciate whatever you can tell me about the opportunities to study in this area."
- Participate actively in the meeting rather than passively, which would force the interviewer to carry the entire discussion.
- Fill in the interviewer with important pieces of your background if he or she has not had the time to review your full application file.
- Enjoy your opportunity to let a representative of the school you hope to attend know what you really are like and what you truly care about; the more you view the interview as a window of opportunity, the better interplay you will have with your host.

Visits to Graduate Schools Are Optional

Other things being equal, it would be useful to visit the graduate schools to which you are applying. However, it may not be practical to plan a number of trips to institutions, as it was when you were in high school and applying to seven or eight colleges. If you are completing your undergraduate studies, you will not have much time, and if you are working full-time, you will not in all likelihood have the freedom to take time to visit many campuses.

Still, graduate schools do welcome potential applicants to visit their campuses, and will show you around and answer your questions, without necessarily granting an evaluative interview. You can arrange to meet one or two faculty members on request, and you can sit in on a few classes, chat with students, and make your observations about whether you want to apply to the university.

The campus visit may be particularly useful to minorities and women. For them it is very important that the institution where they do their graduate studies responds positively to their needs and interests. Talking to students, faculty, career advisors, and deans will bring out the positive and negative aspects of pursuing a degree at that university. Naturally, it is essential to succeeding in one's studies over two to six years of study to feel welcomed and recognized for one's culture and concerns. A visit may also be useful if you have a spouse who needs work and wonders what jobs will be available at the school or in the immediate community. In these cases, a campus visit or two may be worth the extra effort and cost. It is better to avoid the wrong school than to enroll and then feel you have made a mistake and need to transfer. In a recent conversation with a very successful young business executive, we learned that his sense of loyalty and appreciation to the business school at Vanderbilt was based in part on the staff's enthusiastic effort to welcome his new wife to the community and their assistance in securing her an interesting administrative job at the university.

What is certain is that visiting graduate schools is not required in most instances (except when interviews are required or recommended) and usually does not have significant bearing on admissions decisions. It can affect your choice of institutions, and, providing you are admitted, the visit will have proved worthwhile. Later we will take up the importance of visiting a campus once you have been accepted.

The Nuts and Bolts of the Application Process

Assuming that you have submitted perfect applications to a number of graduate schools, now what do you? Do you just wait for responses and worry, or do you have a rational plan that tells you, for example, when to expect to hear from each institution? It will make a difference to your peace of mind if you keep track of certain things like the probable response date, and also whether the university has received your transcript, test scores, and recommendations.

It is easy enough to keep a file of photocopies or computer discs of all your applications. To each copy or disk, attach the following checklist, on which you can write the dates you complete the steps of the process.

Application mailed   _____

Response expected   _____

Financial aid forms sent   _____

Transcript acknowledged   _____

Test scores acknowledged   _____

Recommendations acknowledged   _____

Financial need analysis received   _____

Requested interview   _____

Letter of acceptance sent   _____

Letter of rejection sent   _____

Financial aid award received   _____

Action taken if admitted   _____

Deposit sent in   _____

Faculty contacts made, if necessary   _____

How do you get the necessary information? When in doubt, call or e-mail the admissions office and ask to have your file checked for all of the essential items. You generally know when to expect a response from instructions in the university's application information. Should something happen to your transcripts, test scores, recommendations, or financial application, the committee will inform you and ask for a resubmission. For your peace of mind, you may want to check with all of the admissions offices where you have applied, understanding that you will not be bothering them. You will only gain respect for your serious interest in the university and executing the full admissions process correctly.

Acceptance Means Choices

If you have followed these Ten Steps to graduate school admissions, the chances are good that you will be admitted to two or more of the programs to which you have applied. This will be both a euphoric and a critical moment: you have reached your penultimate objective, acceptance to a quality graduate school. Now you must choose which program is best for you. This choice should be made with the same exacting care that you have taken during the entire admission process. To help you reach a decision in an orderly, rational way, go back to Step One and look at the Graduate School Questionnaire that you filled out. Review the first six questions:

1. Why are you considering graduate school at this time, and what are your eventual goals?
2. What are the key characteristics you hope to find in a graduate program?
3. What degree or program are you considering pursuing? Are there any universities or programs you have an interest in at this time?
4. How important to you are location and size in selecting an institution?
5. Will you need financial aid?
6. Do you wish to work and study part-time?

Given that time has passed since you completed your answers, consider whether you would still answer each question in the same way, or if you have encountered circumstances that might change your mind. We suggest that you make any corrections that you feel are called for, and then create a short table as follows:

PROGRAMS THAT OFFERED ADMISSION

	Program 1	Program 2	Program 3	(Others)
1. Goals	_____	_____	_____	_____
2. Desired characteristics	_____	_____	_____	_____
3. Prior interest	_____	_____	_____	_____
4. Size and location	_____	_____	_____	_____
5. Financial aid	_____	_____	_____	_____
6. Work	_____	_____	_____	_____

Rate each graduate program in terms of your responses to each question, on a scale of 1 to 10, with 10 being the highest score. Adding up the scores will show you how far each graduate school goes in satisfying your interests and needs. Often, this tabulating surprises an individual by the heavier weighting of one school over another that was of strong interest. You may instinctively disagree with this finding, because you have given the same weight to each criterion, which may not accurately reflect your mind set.

To take a common example, let's say a key characteristic you are looking for in a graduate program is the prestige factor. You would like to enroll in what you believe is considered one of the top departments or schools of its kind. This answer, reported in Question 2, may outweigh in importance your answer to Question 4. The latter may suggest that you want to enroll in a small, intimate program in a smaller community, such as Hanover, New Hampshire. Now, you have been admitted also to the medical schools of Johns Hopkins, Boston University, New York University, the University of Chicago, and Dartmouth.

According to your table, you narrow your choice to Johns Hopkins, New York University, and Dartmouth. The other key factors are roughly equal in your making a decision, especially the financial aid one. Hopkins's medical school, you feel, has slightly more prestige than Dartmouth's, but it is located in Baltimore. How do you determine the relative importance of the two questions? This is a matter of your own choice, of course. Dartmouth may represent the perfect size school for you in the ideal small town. But Hopkins may possess some special academic allure and, being in a city, may offer more clinical opportunities in a specialized area of medicine to which you want exposure. In the end, you decide to give a greater weight to Question 2, feeling that the key characteristic you have chosen to pursue in a program, prestige, outweighs location and size of the institution. Allowing for this weight in your evaluation of all four programs will change the scores and give you another picture to contemplate.

You can do this sort of comparison with any kind of graduate program, professional or academic. Of course you can extend the list of factors you want to weigh into your formulation. For example, you may have a stronger interest in a particular area within your intended field of study than when you began the admissions process. One or several of the professors that attracted you to a graduate program may have left the university since you applied. Perhaps you have gotten engaged or married and your partner's career and interests need to be taken into account.

Once you have completed this rational, numerical calculation, you may still hesitate to make your final choice until you have talked to a number of people: faculty members at your college or the graduate school in question; your significant other; your accountant or financial advisor, if borrowing money or selling equities to pay for your studies is a consideration; your present employer, if the company is helping to subsidize your education; professional friends who have an opinion on the people trained in the various graduate schools. You will also want to consider the quality of life in the community and on the campus where you would be living, and recent graduates' record of success in job placement at the completion of the degree program.

Visiting Graduate Programs after You've Been Accepted

An option at decision time is to plan a visit to the graduate schools you are most seriously considering, even if you have made an earlier visit. Make formal plans well ahead of your scheduled visit dates so that you will be certain to meet the people with whom you will be engaged when you enroll. This includes faculty in your department or concentration, advisors, and financial aid officers. What happens during this time can tip the scales toward a decision for or against a particular school. In the case of the potential medical student, a visit to Dartmouth's medical school to meet with faculty and students and check out the community can have a strong impact for or against its particular brand of uniqueness. A similar visit to Johns Hopkins can also lead to a major reaction that says this is the right or the wrong place for me to study and live.

A visit can reveal new factors of importance, such as the departure of a professor you expected to work with, a university-wide or departmental budget cut that affects the quality of your department, or the loss from the community of a large corporation to which your spouse planned on applying for a job. Conversely, a visit can offer such pleasant surprises as an offer to increase your fellowship or provide a new teaching assistantship; an invitation to join a group of graduate students working on a special project that just received generous funding; an improvement in housing facilities you would occupy; or the inauguration of a new series of professional internships that will give you important access to exposure in your specialty.

Negotiating Your Financial Aid Offer

Many successful candidates find themselves caught on the horns of the financial dilemma. They have the opportunity to attend their first-choice university but have not been granted an adequate financial aid package, or another university has given them a more generous package. If you are fully convinced that there are enough sound reasons to enroll in your first-choice program, you should not hesitate to make an appointment with the director of financial aid of the graduate school or the head of the department that admitted you to discuss your situation. Now that both the university aid office and the academic department or professional school know how much money they actually have to distribute, because other aid recipients have decided to enroll in other graduate schools, they may well be able to offer you a more generous financial package. There may be an opening as a paid research or teaching assistant that was promised to another candidate but is now free to award to you. The rule of thumb is as plain as that bottom number on the financial worksheet you filled out when planning for graduate school: If you need more help to attend, you should ask for more help. You will be met only with respect for your desire to pursue your degree and to be realistic before making such a major commitment. Keep in mind that you do not have to commit to any one university prematurely. You should have in hand all your offers of aid and have the opportunity to discuss your package before you have to make a final decision. Normally, by common agreement among graduate schools, the decision date is not until April 15 prior to the following fall enrollment.

If all your efforts fail to increase the amount of aid your first-choice school offers you, you must rework your budget of expenses and sources of income to decide if you will be better served in the long run by opting to attend the other school, which will make the financial load more manageable for you. As we have said, it is not always wise to have to work too many hours at a job that steals time away from your studies or to take on a debt load that is plainly too debilitating to carry after graduation.

Deciding among Offers of Admission

There are two things in particular to observe about this final process of accepting one of several offers of admission:

1. Reason and emotion play roles that are different for each graduate candidate.
2. Your decision should, in the end, be yours and yours alone. Do not make your decision immediately after listening to a persuasive, powerful personality, for nobody can know you, or what is right for you, as well as you can. This assumes you have done the thorough and honest search we have recommended across the Ten Steps.

When you have made your decision, you have three final actions to take. First, let all the graduate schools that have been good enough to accept you know where you plan to enroll. This is simply a matter of politeness to the institutions and to unknown fellow applicants who may then be offered the place you have opened for them. Second, follow to the letter the instructions about deposits you are obligated to make before you enroll formally. This is your earnest money, evidence that you are making a commitment to a new and exciting opportunity in your life. Third, inform all those individuals who served as advisors and references for you over the course of your admissions process. They deserve your appreciation, and surely will be pleased that their efforts on your behalf had such positive results.

About Rejection and a Second Chance

We have mentioned the Harvard-or-nowhere syndrome, the emotional attitude that says, "If I can't go to Harvard Law School, I won't go to any law school." If you are tempted to adopt this attitude, certainly your peers will not object. Someone else will gladly take your place at any of the law schools you could get accepted to but to which you did not apply. We feel an obligation to point out that you may regret such a decision someday, and that you ought to keep your options open by applying elsewhere to create a number of choices. Attachment to a particular institution is admirable—sometimes—but it should not be based solely on the name factor. We say it again, at the risk of sounding like we really do protest too much: There are so many outstanding graduate schools in all the professions that to cut yourself off from almost all of them because you believe only one will suffice for you is a pity. So get a second opinion. This is one instance when absolute self-reliance is not the better part of wisdom. Ask those who are experienced and knowledgeable in your intended field for their insights and recommendations.

Of course, you can always reapply to that graduate school you had your heart set on. Many graduate students have, in fact, been successful in doing so. Remember we mentioned in an earlier step that transferring from one graduate school to another is not openly encouraged but is welcomed for those students who have performed at a high level of competency for at least one full year. You will need to show this kind of evidence of your potential if you have any hope of being accepted as a transfer applicant. This is the only way to convince the dean and the admissions committee that you have earned a place in their program. If you choose not to enroll in another graduate school but to work for another year or take additional courses to build a stronger academic foundation or improve your admissions test scores, you may well be admitted in your second attempt. Note that throughout this book we have never said, "You will never be successful in meeting your ambitions, so don't try." We would not be true to ourselves and our calling as counselor-advocates if we did so.

Step Ten Checklist

- Study application instructions for each graduate program to which you are applying, taking particular note of deadlines and requirements. Make sure you understand their preference of a print application or electronic application.

- Read the application thoroughly before filling it in.

- Be careful to limit essay responses to the specific lengths requested and stay to the point of the questions.

- Proofread everything you have written. Do not turn in a messy or incorrect application.

- Be sure to sign applications and enclose required fees.

- Keep a file that records dates of submissions of transcripts, test scores, financial aid applications, and recommendations to each institution to which you apply. Be sure to keep the name, address, telephone number, and e-mail address of the admissions officer, dean of the graduate school, and program director on your application list.

- Keep a file of correspondence with faculty who are writing recommendations, noting each program to which recommendations are sent, and evidence that they have been received.

APPENDIX
Graduate School Organizations and Website Addresses

Centralized Data Processing Groups

American Association of Dental Schools Application Service (AADSAS)
1625 Massachusetts Avenue, NW
Washington, DC 20036
(800) 253-2237

American Medical College Application Service (AMCAS)
American Association of Medical Colleges
2450 N Street, NW
Washington, DC 20037-1131
(202) 828-6000
www.aamc.org/stuapps/start/html

Law School Admissions Service (LSAS)
Law School Data Assembly Service (LSDAS)
Box 2400, 661 Penn Street
Newtown, PA 18940-0977
(215) 968-1001
www.lsac.org

Testing Organizations

Allied Health Professions Admission Test
c/o The Psychological Corporation
555 Academic Court
San Antonio, TX 78204
(800) 622-3231

Graduate Management Admission Test (GMAT)
Educational Testing Service
P.O. Box 6103
Princeton, NJ 08541-6103
(609) 771-7670
www. gmat.org

Graduate Record Examinations
Educational Testing Service
P.O. Box 6000
Princeton, NJ 08541-6000
(609) 771-7670
www.gre.org

Medical College Admissions Test
MCAT Program Office
P.O. Box 4056
Iowa City, IA 52243-4056
(319) 337-1357
www.aamc.org

Miller Analogies Test (MAT)
The Psychological Corporation
555 Academic Court
San Antonio, TX 78204
(800) 622-3231
www.tpcweb.com.mat

Test of English as a Foreign Language (TOEFL)
P.O. Box 6151
Princeton, NJ 08541-6151
(609) 771-7100
www.toefl.org

Professional Associations

American Association of Colleges for Teacher Education
1307 New York Avenue, NW
Suite 300
Washington, DC 20005

(202) 293-2450
www.aacte.org

American Association of School Administrators
1801 North Moore Street
Arlington, VA 22209
(703) 528-0700
www.aasa.org

American Bar Association
Section on Legal Education & Admissions to the Bar
(800) 285-2221
www.abanet.org/legaled

American Chemical Society
1155 Sixteenth Street, NW
Washington, DC 20036
(202) 872-4414

American Historical Association
400 A Street, SE
Washington, DC 20003
(202) 544-2422

American Institute of Biological Sciences
1444 Eye Street, NW
Suite 200
Washington, DC 20005
(202) 628-1500

American Institute of Physics
1 Physics Ellipse
College Park, MD 20740

American Nurses Association
600 Maryland Avenue SW
Suite 100 West
Washington, DC 20024
(800) 274-4262
www.nursingworld.org

American Political Science Association
1527 New Hampshire Avenue, NW
Washington, DC 20036
(202) 483-2512

American Psychological Association
750 First Street, NE
Washington, DC 20002
(202) 336-5500
www.apa.org

American School Counselor Association
5999 Stevenson Avenue
Alexandria, VA 22304
(800) 347-6647
www.counseling.org

American Society for Engineering Education
1818 N Street, NW
Suite 600
Washington, DC 20036
(202) 331-3500
www.asee.org

Association of University Programs in Health Administration
1110 Vermont Avenue, NW
Suite 220
Washington, DC 20005
(202) 822-8550

Computing Research Association
1100 17th Street, NW
Suite 507
Washington, DC 20036
(202) 234-2111
www.cra.org

Council of Graduate Schools
1 Dupont Circle
Suite 430
Washington, DC 20036
(202) 223-3791
www.cgsnet.org

Council on Social Work Education
1600 Duke Street
Alexandria, VA 22314
(703) 683-8080
www.cswe.org

Modern Language Association
26 Broadway, 3rd Floor
New York, NY 10004
(646) 576-5000
www.mla.org

National Association of Social Workers
750 First Street, NE
Suite 700
Washington, DC 20002
(800) 638-8799
www.naswdc.org

National Science Foundation
Oak Ridge Associated Universities
P.O. Box 3010
Oak Ridge, TN 37831
(423) 241-430
www.nsf.gov

The Woodrow Wilson National
    Fellowship Foundation
CN 5281
Princeton, NJ 08543
(609) 452-7007
www.woodrow.org

Students with Disabilities

Heath Resource Center
1 Dupont Circle
Suite 800
Washington, DC 20036
(800) 544-3284

Internet Sites

General Information

The College Board
www.collegeboard.org

Graduate School Guide
www.gradschools.com

Peterson's Education and Career Center
www.petersons.com

U.S. News Colleges and Career Center
www.usnews.com/usnews/education

American Medical Student Association
www.amsa.org

National Consortium for Graduate Degrees for Minorities in Engineering & Science, Inc.
www.nd.education/-gem/

Financial Aid

FastWeb
www.studentservices.com/fastweb

Federal Student Aid Information Center (Stafford Loan Program)
P.O. Box 84
Washington, DC 20044
www.ed.gov/prog-info/SFA/Student Guide

Free Application for Federal Student Aid (FAFSA)
P.O. Box 84
Washington, DC 20044
(800) 433-3243
www.fafsa.ed.gov

Minority On-Line Information Service
(Links to FAFSA and College Scholarship Service)
www.finaid.org/finaid/focus/minority.html

National Association of Student Financial Aid Administrators
www.finaid.org

Bibliography

Writing Correctly

Cook, Claire K. *Line By Line: How to Edit Your Own Writing.* Boston: Houghton Mifflin Company, 1985.

Follett, Wilson. *Modern American Usage, A Guide.* Revised by Erik Wensberg. New York: Hill and Wang, 1998.

Hayakawa, S.I. *Choose the Right Word: A Contemporary Guide to Selecting the Precise Word for Every Situation.* New York: HarperCollins, 1994.

Roget's International Thesaurus. 5th ed. New York: HarperCollins, 1992.

Strunk, William, Jr. and E.B. White. *The Elements of Style.* 4th ed. New York: Prentice-Hall, 1999.

Webster, Agnes, Sparks, eds. *Webster's New World College Dictionary.* 4th ed. New York: Hungry Minds, 1999.

White, E. B. *Essays of E.B. White.* New York: Harper and Row, 1977.

Writer's Digest Books. *Grammatically Correct: The Writer's Essential Guide to Punctuation, Spelling, Style, Usage, and Grammar.* Cincinnati, Ohio: Writers Digest Books, 1997.

Zinsser, William K. *On Writing Well: An Informal Guide to Writing Non-Fiction.* 6th ed. New York: HarperCollins, 1998.

Graduate Guidebooks

American Association of Dental Schools. *Admission Requirements of US and Canadian Dental Schools.* Washington, DC: American Association of Dental Schools, 2001.

American Psychological Association. *Graduate Study in Psychology and Associated Fields.* Hyattsville, MD: American Psychological Association, 2001.

American Society for Engineering Education. *Directory of Engineering Graduate Studies and Research.* Washington, DC: American Society for Engineering Education, 2001.

Association of American Medical Colleges. *Medical School Admission Requirements, 2001–2002.* Washington, DC: Association of American Medical Colleges, 2001.

College Bluebook. 5 vols. New York: Macmillan, 2001.

Doughty, Harold. *Guide to American Graduate Schools.* 8th ed. New York: Penguin USA, 1997.

Graduate Management Admission Council. *The Official Guide to MBA Programs 2001.* Princeton, NJ: Graduate Management Admission Council, 2001.

Guide to Distance Learning Programs. 5th ed. Princeton, NJ: Peterson's Guides, 2001.

International Student Handbook of U.S. Colleges. 11th ed. New York: College Board, 1998.

Jerrard, Richard and Margot Jerrard. *The Graduate School Handbook.* New York: Perigree, 1998.

Law School Admission Council. *The Official Guide to U.S. Law Schools, 2001 Edition.* Newtown, PA: Law School Admissions Council, 2001.

National Council for Accreditation of Teacher Education. *Teacher Preparation: A Guide to Colleges and Universities.* Washington, DC: National Council for Accreditation of Teacher Education, 2001.

Peters, Robert. *Getting What You Came For: The Smart Student's Guide to Earning a Master's or Ph.D.* New York: Noonday Press, 1997.

Peterson's Guides to Graduate and Professional Programs. vols. 1–6. Princeton, NJ: Peterson's, published annually.

United States Department of Labor. *Occupational Outlook Handbook.* Washington, DC: United States Department of Labor, published annually.

Veterinary Medical School Admission Requirements in the United States and Canada. Rockville, MD: Betz Publishing Company, 2000.

Volunteer: The Comprehensive Guide to Voluntary Service in the U.S. and Abroad. 5th ed. New York: Council on International Education, 1995.

Financial Aid Information

Council on International Education Exchange. *Student Travel Catalogue.* New York: Council on International Education Exchange, published annually.

Institute of International Education. *Funding for U.S. Study: A Guide for International Students and Professionals and Financial Resources for International Students.* New York: Institute of International Education, 1996.

McWade, Patricia. *Financing Graduate School: How to Get the Money for Your Master's or Ph.D.* Princeton, NJ: Peterson's Guides, 1996.

Making It into a Top College

ISBN 0-06-095363-2

This definitive step-by-step plan for organizing the admission campaign reveals an inside look at how the admissions process works at the most competitive colleges, what the top colleges are looking for, how to choose the best college for you and much more.

Making It into a Top Graduate School

ISBN 0-06-093458-1 (Available December 2001)

A ten-step strategy for finding and getting into the right graduate schools, complete with time-tested worksheets, executive task checklists, sample essays and résumés, inspirational case histories, interviewing techniques, and program categories and rankings.

Presenting Yourself Successfully to Colleges

ISBN 0-06-093460-3 (Available October 2001)

A step-by-step guide to help students market their strengths and uniqueness in outstanding college applications, including essays that will be noticed, targeted interest résumés, portfolios, and letters to coaches and instructors. Complete with actual samples from the files of thousands of Greenes' clients.

The Hidden Ivies

ISBN 0-06-095362-4

An in-depth survey of thirty colleges and universities of exceptional merit that will not only challenge gifted students but also provide them with the competitive edge needed upon graduation. This book distinguishes each college's personality as described by students and campus educational leaders, as well as its unique academic strengths.

The Public Ivies

ISBN 0-06-093459-X (Available August 2001)

An excellent resource providing a better understanding of the differences between various public universities, the contrasts between public and private higher education, the admissions process for public schools, and what it takes to succeed in the larger public university environment.

Inside the Top Colleges

ISBN 0-06-092994-4

The quality of education and quality of life at the country's 20 most elite universities are explored, based on a survey of 4,000 undergraduates using advanced polling techniques, extensive focus groups, and one-on-one in-depth interviews with students.

Available wherever books are sold, or call 1-800-331-3761 to order.